Fire AND Irises

A journey through therapy

Also by Margaret Nicol
Loss of a Baby:
Understanding Maternal Grief

Fire AND Irises

A journey through therapy

MARGARET NICOL

HarperCollins*Publishers*

HarperCollins*Publishers*

First published in Australia in 1996
by HarperCollins*Publishers* Pty Limited
ACN 009 913 517
A member of the HarperCollins*Publishers* (Australia) Pty Limited Group

HarperCollins*Publishers*
25 Ryde Road, Pymble, Sydney, NSW 2073, Australia
31 View Road, Glenfield, Auckland 10, New Zealand
77 – 85 Fulham Palace Road, London W6 8JB, United Kingdom
Hazelton Lanes, 55 Avenue Road, Suite 2900, Toronto, Ontario M5R 3L2
and 1995 Markham Road, Scarborough, Ontario M1B 5M8, Canada
10 East 53rd Street, New York NY 10032, USA

National Library of Australia Cataloguing-in-Publication data:

Nicol, Margaret
    Fire and irises : a journey through therapy
    ISBN 07322 56607
    1. Nicol, Margaret. 2. Psychotherapy. 3.Psychotherapy
    patients – Family relationships. 4. Psychological abuse.
    5. Adult child abuse victims. I. Title

616.8914092

Cover illustration by Russell Jeffery
Printed in Australia by Griffin Press

9 8 7 6 5 4 3 2 1
99 98 97 96

Our thanks go to those who have given us permission to reproduce copyright
material in this book. Particular sources of print material are acknowledged in
the text. Every effort has been made to contact the copyright holders of print
material, and the publisher welcomes communication from any copyright
holder from whom permission was inadvertently not gained.

Contents

This book is dedicated to

'my Auntie', who showed me it only takes one person to
make all the difference.

And to the therapists who walked beside me and who
showed me you always have a second chance.

———⇒⦾⦿⦾⇐———

Introduction

This is a story about a lost child. It is also a story about the hopes and dreams of that child. Every child is dependent on their parents for the essential ingredients of love, trust, respect and honesty in order to grow and become their unique selves. The bond with the mother is the most powerful of all human bonds. The template of loving set in this primary relationship affects all aspects of the future life of the child. When a child is embraced in this love, they will naturally develop self-love, self-respect and a sense of self-worth. These foundation stones pave the way for an adulthood rich with a sense of connectedness to self, to others and to life. The person is attuned to their inner voice, which enables an unfolding of their true potential. Creativity, peace of mind and loving relationships will be the hallmarks of their life.

What happens when that bond is broken or is absent? What happens when the one person who is their connection to life turns away? What happens when the child looks into the mother's eyes seeking love and attention, but sees instead hatred and rejection? How does a child grow without the warmth of a mother's love? How do they begin to perceive themselves and the world around them?

The house in which I grew up was built on fear, mistrust, abuse and neglect. Love was painfully absent. Hiding my feelings, thoughts and talents became my tool for survival. However, I was able to keep my hopes and dreams and the essence of myself securely contained deep within because of the love of a great-aunt.

Throughout my life I had been enshrouded by a nameless, empty depression that left me deadened, often immobilised with fear and lacking in self-confidence and self-motivation. A sense of worthlessness was always present. My lifelong search was to find a way to put the pieces of my shattered self and the hopes and dreams of my childhood back together. This led me on two convergent main roads. The first was to study psychology and eventually become a therapist. I specialised in the area of women's grief following the death of a baby. I later wrote a book about this, unaware that its pages contained my own story. I was trying to fathom my own grief. At that stage, I was unable to face the pain of not having had a mother who loved me. I was trying unconsciously to find ways to tell my story of a death within my own self at birth. *I* was the dead baby I so often spoke of in my lectures and seminars on grief.

The second road I took was to seek the answers through personal therapy. For thirteen years I continued my search in therapy after therapy. None of them really touched the core issues or alleviated the depression or led to a deeper understanding of myself. Most of them led to dead-end streets and the blur of drugs. Therapists wanted to make me happy, to fix me up, to help me fit in more, to function and to cope better; none allowed my story to unfold. They turned away from the enormity of the pain. By my late thirties I held out very little hope for myself or for my profession. It was then that I entered a training program in self psychology, which later led me into this form of therapy. Because I had tried so many other paths, I knew this was the right one.

Through self psychology I gradually gained access to my previously secret childhood and to the hidden parts of myself. I also came to understand my depression, which subsequently lifted. I learnt that you always have a second chance. This new therapeutic space gave me the strength to claim the life I never had and the courage to follow my own dreams.

CHAPTER 1

White coats and emptiness

I can never remember a time when it wasn't there. Yet I've never found words for it. The closest I came was to call it 'blackness' or sometimes 'the black hole'; a horrible sense that there is nothing in life, or rather that there is nothing in *me*. But to even produce these meagre descriptions seems to have taken forever. I think I've spent most of my life running from it, trying to escape or trying to find diversions so I wouldn't think about it or feel it. I pretended life was interesting. I filled my time with people, work, and study. But it never filled the space inside. I would observe how other people lived and I'd try to imitate them. I was like a chameleon, and a particularly adept chameleon when it came to relationships with men. It began right from my very first boyfriend. I really didn't have any interests of my own so I took on the interests of those closest to me.

Baseball. I wonder how many baseball games I sat through as a teenager. I met Jim at camp in my first year at high school. I thought he was absolutely wonderful. And he played baseball. So every weekend I watched baseball games. The relationship lasted the summer. I can't recall how it ended, but it did. Then in the fall his older brother began to ask me out. He didn't like baseball at all. But he was a great basketball player. So basketball became my forte. Well, *watching* basketball, that is, until that relationship ended. Then at the age of sixteen I started to go out with Ian, my first real love. We went together until I was twenty-one. Ian's passion was ice hockey and, in summer, baseball. So there I was back on the bench every weekend, watching games. I wasn't really involved. Just watching. But you'd never know it.

Looking back, threads of understanding form a pattern, which allows me a deeper insight into the nature of the black hole. I left home when I was about eighteen and moved to Ottawa where I studied medical technology. After three years, a friend and I travelled across the country to Vancouver where I got a job as a research assistant in the department of medicine at the university. That was where I met Mark, who was interested in books. It was a refreshing change, for I don't think I could have sat in one more freezing icerink and remained enthusiastic.

I began to read avidly, which wasn't a totally foreign experience as I had read a great deal as a child. I found out what books Mark liked and who were his favourite authors, and I immersed myself in them. During the short time we lived together I read all of Hemingway's books and all of F. Scott Fitzgerald's. I also read the letters between them. I found it all so intriguing. Although the writings of both really held me, what held me more were the letters: trying to see, to understand how two seemingly diverse people had had such a deep friendship. True to form I had adopted Mark's interest in literature. But for the first time my passion was genuine.

There was also a deeper intrigue at that time for me. Mark was writing a book. Each day I'd come home from work as a medical technologist (which I hated), and I'd read what he had written (which I loved). I was amazed to see someone write. I don't know how I thought books were written, but I certainly never imagined I'd be with anybody who wrote one. Those were sweet and warm days for me. After I read what he had written we would go for long walks by the ocean and talk about the story. And have fun: we actually had a lot of fun on our walks. There was a lightness, a soft bubble that surrounded us in those early days.

Not too many months later, the bubble burst. Mark was going to England, but I knew that was only a story: he had tired of me. He had also started a relationship with someone else, I guess because there was so little of me inside and I was so dependent on him. I was totally devastated, so not long after I decided to go to California.

Initially it was exhilarating to be in the sunshine. I always hated the hostile, barren Canadian winters. As a child I used to despair looking out my window at the unending grey sky. Winter seemed to last forever. California was almost the reverse of Canada. The summer days refused to disappear, even in winter. I had never seen such extravagant, vibrant beauty. Yet, while the sunny skies and the inviting colours did persist outside, they couldn't hold me longer than a Canadian summer. After five months the colours faded again. This time it felt even worse, for I could find no external cause.

Although I had landed on my feet, the inner ground was not yet firm enough for me to stand. I was back again on tenuous, shifting sands. I can say the words 'I was depressed' and they seem meaningless, almost trite. Then again, words are all we have to give our inner feelings and experiences some form, some shape. I felt so empty, so *nothing* – just like a void. Everything began to lose its meaning – I forgot about the beauty and the warmth. I went to bed. The only way I had ever coped with the blackness was to go away and pretend that like winter it would eventually end, and that one morning spring would surprise me. But no, it wasn't going to go; it refused and I couldn't figure out what was wrong with me. I spoke to a friend who was doing her final year of medicine. Maybe she would know what was wrong. Before I could say much more than the word 'depression', I had a referral slip in my hand to see the professor of psychiatry.

So there I was sitting on one of a long line of neat chairs with neat patients in a despairingly white hospital corridor, waiting to see my first psychiatrist. My mind was going at a rate of knots – 'Well you really must be sick, how can he do anything? Maybe I could just run out. What if he says I'm crazy? What if he locks me up in a mental hospital? Oh God, what am I doing here? Why can't I just get things right? Why am I so hopeless?' And then my name was called and I walked neatly behind a big man in a white coat into the biggest office I had ever seen in my life. I suppose he introduced himself, but I couldn't hear anything except the thundering of my heart.

I could hardly take a breath between answers to this man's seemingly unending list of questions. I certainly had no idea of what it all meant. What I do remember of those early sessions was the feeling I got when he raised his eyebrows: you know that feeling you get when you think you've said something quite ordinary and then there's a hushed silence that makes you think you've really said the wrong thing at exactly the wrong time. It's a strange feeling because you don't know what it is you've said that has drawn such attention, and you wish you knew what is going on in the other person's mind. That threw me a lot. He'd ask simple questions like 'How many brothers and sisters do you have?,' and when I answered 'I'm an only child', his eyebrows would come together and his glasses would slip down his nose.

So we went on with his glasses going up and down and his cigar burning red at discrete intervals. I can't remember how long this interrogation lasted; perhaps a number of weeks.

Then one day he leaned back in his big leather chair and smoked his cigar with more ease than when he was pursuing the pages on his desk. He actually stopped writing, and presented me with my diagnosis. His first words were etched forever in my mind. 'There is actually nothing wrong with you,' he said. What a relief! I wasn't crazy. I wasn't going to be locked up. There was such a joy, too, somewhere inside: his words reverberated at a depth that had no words of their own. It was like a child flying a kite.

He went on to say that he had done every assessment he could think of and had finally decided I was suffering from exogenous depression. Needless to say I didn't have a clue what that might be, but luckily this time he responded to the confused look on my face. He explained that the cause of my depression was a series of major separations in my recent past: the leaving of my home, family and friends, as well as the relationship break-up I'd experienced before I left Canada, which was still painful. So that was that. I was not only cleared of insanity, I was given a reason as to why I felt like this. It all seemed very neat and reasonable. I continued to visit him every week and we would talk. The room was still pretty overwhelming and I felt like a kid sitting in this low chair with him behind his enormous desk. But hope brought me to each session.

The weeks came and went and the depression continued. I could tell that after a while the professor began to regard me as quite an enigma. Why wasn't something shifting? Why wasn't I feeling better? I certainly didn't know. In most of our time together he seemed to be trying to push me forward, to push me into the sunlight. I remember he kept pointing out all the positive things in my life. In fact, he mainly used himself as a yardstick. He used to say 'Look at me. I'm in my sixties, my marriage is not happy, we've stayed together just for our children. Now they are grown up and have left. I'll retire soon. Now look at you – you're young, you're attractive, you've got a great job, you have no responsibilities. Go out and enjoy life'. He was insistent that I see the joy of life and youth. He was certainly enthusiastic about the idea of my breaking out of this prison and being fully alive. But I knew that wasn't how I felt. I didn't feel young or pretty or enthralled by my work or study. I didn't feel much of anything.

Eventually, we reached a stalemate. In one of the last sessions I had with him he said that he was concerned that I could remember virtually nothing of my childhood prior to the age of twelve. He couldn't understand why, but maybe that was the problem. He couldn't make me remember, either. The only thing he could think of was for me to be admitted to hospital for a few days and he would give me sodium pentothal, which would allow him to find out more about me while I was asleep. As soon as he said that, my anxiety hit the roof. Maybe it was the idea of being drugged, or of his finding out something terrible about me, or maybe even of just being admitted to a psychiatric ward – to me a sure sign of insanity. He let me think about it, but not for the life of me could I agree. That's where we parted. I said I didn't want to do it and he conveyed that he really couldn't help me any further.

I often wonder what would have happened if I had gone in for treatment. What would he have done if he had found out what has taken me over twenty years to discover? There is no way I could have handled the reality then, so I think it was a wise decision. But then there were many times when I was in the middle of the blackness when I wished that he could have helped me somehow. There were many psychiatrists and psychologists I went to for help after that day. The pain of those years seems unbearable to look back on; they were such a waste. Did it have to be this way?

In my remaining years in California, the same patterns persisted in my relationships with men. I went out with a fast-moving stockbroker and became interested in the stock market. Then I met an art critic and found myself frequently at art galleries. But there was one man with whom things were different.

He was a doctor who worked in the same department as I did at the university. He had many interests, but I never cultivated any of them. It was quite remarkable. There was something special between us. When we were together we were just ourselves. He had an outrageous sense of humour, a deep compassion for people, and an enthusiasm for life. Somehow, he got me to talk about *me*: what I thought and what I liked. It was a very peaceful relationship. I ran away. There was something happening inside me. I had actually let someone in again. I guess that was more scary than keeping the focus on the external Me. The irony was that I felt he must have been mistaken, that if he actually knew the *real* Me he wouldn't like her. I was so frightened of his future disappointment that I managed to end the relationship. I felt so inadequate, so worthless in comparison to him. It was as if I had devised an outer, false Me that was based on what I felt the other person liked, wanted, needed. Yet if they liked her it was a sham, for they really only saw a mirror of themselves. If I didn't build my shiny shell, there was an even greater sense of shame: how could they like the Me that I felt was a 'nothing'? Not having an awareness of my inability to maintain a relationship, I just convinced myself it was time to travel.

During these two years Mark had been in London writing his book and teaching. We had kept in contact and I felt there was still a link between us, so I entered into a relationship with him. The first year we lived in a condemned house in Camden Town. Looking back, I see how it was the relationship that was condemned. It was exciting to be there initially – the house and street were filled with amazing characters: out-of-work actors, disillusioned hippies, artists and other writers. There was no lack of colour, except inside me. My life was like putting together a puzzle, working out what pieces were needed for this new space and putting them together in the shape required. Eventually I got a job as a research assistant at the children's hospital. I don't know why I had ever chosen medical technology, because I found it both boring and draining. Test tubes, microscopes and viruses really were not me. It was such solitary, isolating work – just like everything else in my life. It was a sterile environment, inside and out.

London seemed full of everything you could ever want, but I would sit and wonder how people could be so interested in anything. I read drafts of Mark's chapters, and watched while he played grass hockey in Dulwich and tennis in Regent's Park. But like all charades, I couldn't keep it up for long. Soon Mark suggested it would be best if I lived somewhere else. The relationship continued on different grounds. I must have had some idea as to why it was dying, for I remember trying desperately to conjure up some interests of my own. I couldn't think of one thing to be involved in; nothing attracted me. So I got another job working all day in a lab, and at nights and weekends I worked as a barmaid. The rest of the time I mainly spent by the phone, waiting and empty.

One day while on my way to work, I caught a glimpse of my inner thoughts: death. Why, I asked, am I always thinking of death? Surely this can't be normal? Surely most twenty-five-year-olds aren't consumed with thoughts of death? I decided to return to California. I needed to leave Mark.

Marriage, birth and memories

When I got back to California, I was feeling pretty insecure and wasn't sure what had drawn me back. A few weeks later I enrolled at teachers' college. That year was probably one of the most exciting years of my life. I loved studying education. I was fascinated by the psychology of how children learn. There were many new ideas; a real revolution in educational thinking was occurring. I had three very progressive lecturers and a course booklist containing titles such as *Teaching as a Subversive Activity*, *Deschooling Society* and *The Pedagogy of the Oppressed*. Our debates in classes were hot and alive. I really began to think for myself. I obtained my teacher's certificate, and after the summer holidays set off on my first teaching job some distance away.

In the spring of 1974, I was married. How amazing! For some reason I didn't believe that anyone would want to marry me. However, I gradually became quite depressed shortly after my marriage. We were soon to be travelling to Europe and England for my husband's study tour. But even that didn't lift me. I was deep in blackness. Despairing.

My doctor referred me to a therapist. I had some sessions with him but I seemed to feel heavier and heavier as he handed out a variety of interpretations. I recall one session where he mentioned that I always slouched and never sat up straight. I thought 'Yes, I know, my parents told me that'. He asked me why I thought I did. I said I didn't know. But he had an answer. 'You're ashamed of your breasts . . . your sexuality is frightening to you.' He waited for my response. There was none. I felt awful. I couldn't seem to say that that wasn't how it was for me. I just put my head lower and cried, not because I was ashamed of my breasts or my sexuality, but because I had given up. I had hoped he would help me. I looked at all his degrees on the wall and realised I had believed he knew how to cure people. I felt I was one of those incurables.

So I left for my holidays with a six months' supply of antidepressants in one hand, and a label of 'Anxiety neurosis' in the other. My husband and I arrived in Greece and I felt drugged out of my mind. A lot of the trip was a blur, yet I went through the motions. We saw all the museums and art galleries that could be fitted into one day. There were some things that lifted my spirits: the blue of the Aegean Sea, the Greek cafés along the water, the city of Florence, the statue of David, the paintings of Van Gogh, the tulip fields in Amsterdam. At those times the black cape dropped and I soared, but those moments were fleeting and I kept religiously taking the drugs. It wasn't until our flight home that I decided I'd had enough, and threw out the remainder of the tablets when we arrived.

Within weeks I was pregnant. Another surprise. There was no concrete reason for me to think that I couldn't have a baby, but deep inside I felt as though I weren't good enough to be a mother. Most of my friends were surprised as well. I had created an impression of being the busy, professional woman.

I began 1976 teaching in a very progressive high school. I also started studying first-year psychology. I felt wonderful.

Pregnancy agreed with me and I loved psychology. Life became colourful. I enjoyed my teaching and the students so much. I was finally in a truly egalitarian school with a principal who supported innovation and lateral thinking. It was a joy to be at work. Maybe life was opening up for me, or rather *I* was opening up to life.

When my son Michael was born, I held him in my arms with immense joy and trepidation. He was wondrously beautiful. I'll never forget the ride home from the hospital. It was one of those exquisite moments in time when everything seemed right with the world. I had a sense of completeness, of family, with my husband beside me and Michael in my arms. Everything seemed vibrant: the grass was so green, the flowers so bright, the air so light, the sun so warm. It felt magical. I was happy to be home and away from the hospital.

For a month or so everything went well, but then the blackness arrived almost overnight. I didn't know (and never knew) what triggered it, but everything became dull and meaningless. Sometimes I'd just sit in the kitchen and stare at the walls. It was almost as if I didn't deserve all this happiness, or that deep down I didn't know how to be a mother. Why had both my marriage and the birth of my son thrown me back into darkness?

I spoke to a friend who was a careers officer. I said I didn't want to see a psychiatrist, but I needed to talk to someone. She suggested a psychologist. Before long I began my next journey through therapy. I saw her for about two years and I recall that time with warmth and fondness, even though it was also painful. Anne was a kind, soft, gentle woman. Her room reflected her sensitivity; it was cosy. There were plants and paintings and little objects that fascinated me. No degrees on the walls and two identical chairs. During the sessions she never took notes. The only time she ever wrote anything was when I told her of one of my dreams; she would write it down so we could both look at it. We mainly followed my dreams, for it seemed I would inevitably have one just before each session. We also talked about my childhood, but more in the context of either the dream or what was happening in my life at the time.

She wasn't full of endless questions, nor did she push things further than I wanted to go.

After a few sessions with her she mentioned to me that I might like to paint my dreams. I thought that was outrageous. I couldn't paint; I couldn't even draw. She assured me that it had nothing to do with drawing ability and that whatever I did would be just fine. So after each session I'd go into a room at the back of the clinic that had an easel and paints of every imaginable colour and I'd paint an image from my dream. Sometimes I'd get so immersed in painting I'd lose touch with time and find I'd been there for two hours. I loved it. In the next session she would have my painting in her room with my name and date on it and we'd explore it together. That was often distressing for although I loved the experience of painting, it was very confronting to look at what I had painted.

I could feel the hurt and emptiness inside, but it was another thing to give it form and colour. I recall two of my paintings, vividly. The first was of me as a little girl. In the centre of this big piece of butcher's paper was a tiny, almost invisible child with blonde hair and a blue dress. Until Anne brought it to my attention I never noticed that I hadn't drawn any hands, legs or feet. I felt very sad to see this painting; the child was like a waif and clearly there was no sense of her having any strength, power or vitality in her world.

The other painting I shall never forget was one I drew from a dream of my mother's face. It was horrific to look at. It was like a person cut in two. On one side was a soft, gentle face and the other was like that of a mad woman. It reminded me of the painting called *The Scream*. It was of tortured rage. It was also like a witch: bizarre, wild and out of control. We would often go back and look at it at times when I was trying to fathom my mother's behaviour. I really did feel sick every time we looked at it. I was relieved that Anne never used jargon or went into interpretations. We just looked at it together. That was hard enough.

In the time I spent with Anne, we explored my relationship with my mother and my father, but the time span we looked at was mainly from ages twelve to eighteen, when I left home. However, a few earlier memories did seep through …

I spoke of what it was like for me to live in that house. I had never really told anyone before. It was like living in a pigsty. I would hate to come home from school. Usually my mother would be out or lying on the porch reading. Inside there was only chaos, with things scattered everywhere. The kitchen was full of dishes that hadn't been cleaned for weeks. You'd have to step over frying pans and plates on the floor just to get to the sink. The bedrooms were just as filthy. The beds were usually heaped with books and clothes. When my father got home, the fights would start. He'd yell and complain, and I'd feel awful. Often I would try to clean the place up. I think I really wanted some clean space myself and I also wanted my father to stop yelling. My father would congratulate me, but my mother would become enraged and the mess would return almost immediately. Sometimes I'd try to make things different, and sometimes I'd just pretend and play in my own world or with my dog.

I certainly never invited any friends over to my house; I was ashamed of it. Luckily I made friends with kids who were happy to have me over at their house. There was one particular friend who I remember. I was twelve years old and in my last year of primary school when a new girl came into the class. As soon as I saw her I knew we would be friends. We hit it off just like that. Every day I'd walk home to Judy's house and spend time there and not leave until their dinner time. We also spent most weekends together. Her home was beautiful.

Judy had a big room of her own with an enormous white and gold bed, a dressing table to match, and beautiful dolls all reflected in the mirrors. Her parents were lovely to me. Her father was Scottish with a dry sense of humour, and as they would often have to prise me out of the door as darkness fell, he would kid me about whether I had a home at all. I could tell they were very fond of me and I always felt welcome. Little did they know how much of a life raft they really were to me. For it was only when I began to see, with Anne's help, how destructive it was for me at home that I realised how much I needed a sense of belonging. Judy and I were inseparable throughout the five years of high school and even today our friendship is untouched by the physical distance between us.

I was able to talk to Anne about some of the really hurtful things my mother did to me. I told her how I had had a close relationship with my great-aunt. She was very special to me. She lived with my mother's parents and I always felt loved when I was there. Even though Auntie was seventy when I was born, I had so much fun with her and I remember her largely for her youthfulness.

When I was about fourteen or fifteen, Auntie died. On one occasion my mother had gone to see her because she was sick, but I wasn't allowed to go. No one ever mentioned she might die. The next thing I knew, my mother rang to say she had died. I was devastated; I was beside myself with grief.

My father and I drove down for the funeral. At the funeral parlour I saw Auntie in the coffin. I sobbed. It just couldn't be true. My mother came up to me and told me not to be silly, that she was only my great-aunt. I remember saying 'No, she is my Auntie and she loved me!' My mother responded by saying 'No, Auntie loved everyone – you weren't special to her!' I ran out as though I could escape her words. I found a park and sat there for a long time trying to recall my Auntie, trying to remember her love. I didn't know how to express my love, I didn't know how to say goodbye. Eventually I went to a florist and asked them to make a corsage of two baby white roses with a blue ribbon around them. It was lovely. I took it back to the funeral parlour, pinned it on my Auntie's dress, and kissed her.

When the funeral service was about to begin, I became fearful of someone removing the corsage before they closed the coffin. I really wanted my gift to stay with her. So foolishly I went to my mother and told her what I had done, and that I didn't want the corsage taken off Auntie's dress. I begged her to make sure it stayed on. She nodded. When we got home from the cemetery, my mother came to my room and dropped the corsage on my bed. She turned and left without a word.

Her need to control me increased as I grew in independence. When I was sixteen I took driving lessons at school and really enjoyed them. I had a terrific teacher. On the day I was to go for my test, I had to return to my house with the driving instructor and two other students because I needed the signature of a parent beforehand. I went racing into the house and asked her to sign the form. She refused. I was overwhelmed and ashamed. My friends and the teacher were outside, waiting for our initiation into the adult world, and here I was inside arguing with a mother who wouldn't let me grow up. I kept asking Why? Eventually she said 'I'll sign it only if you promise never to drive your father's car'. She made me sign a piece of paper saying just that.

I signed it.

I went to the police station. I did the written test and got all the answers right. I was so happy. Then came the road test. It was a very cold, snowy day and the road conditions were pretty terrible, but everything went fine. I passed 'with flying colours', the sergeant told me. What ecstasy: I had a driver's licence! When I got home I told my father and he was very proud of me. He handed me his keys and said 'Take the car out for a drive!' What was I to do? My mother was looking at me angrily. I suddenly remembered that anyone under twenty-one isn't legally allowed to sign a document. So I told my father what my mother had made me sign, and went over to the drawer in which she had put it. I took it out, ripped it to shreds, then took my dad's keys and went for one of the best rides of my life. Anne helped me see that it was one of the first times I was actually able to stand up to my mother. That felt good.

Yet there were other times when I felt totally powerless. When I was halfway through my final year, I had to fill in university application forms. I had known for a long time that since I was born, my father had put part of his pay each week into a bank account so that I would be able to go on to university. I went to the bank to find out how much was in the account in order to know which university I could afford to go to. After explaining in detail to the person at the bank my reason for enquiring, he returned to tell me that the account recently had been closed and all the money withdrawn. I stood there in shock. I couldn't believe my ears. He said my mother had taken it out. I was frozen to the spot. Eventually a woman I knew who worked at the bank took me into an office, got me a glass of water, and sat with me. I explained what the man had said. She just shook her head and said she knew my mother had withdrawn the money and that she was sorry, but there was nothing she could do. I somehow made my way back home. I asked my mother what it all meant. She said she had run into financial difficulties and needed the money. She told me I'd just have to forget about university. 'You must never tell your father,' she said. 'If you do, he'll have a heart attack and it will kill him!' I went to bed.

The rest of my final year was hopeless. My dreams were gone. I didn't care anymore. As the time for exams drew closer, I became more and more depressed; I became sick and began having horrific nightmares. I remembered I was away from school for several weeks. I simply pulled the blanket over my head, and went into the darkness and slept. Doctor MacDonald, our family doctor who I liked very much, came to visit me a few times. I don't recall saying anything to him about what had happened, but he knew me very well so maybe he could see more than I realised.

One day he visited and this time he closed my bedroom door. He pulled up a chair beside my bed and sat there and held my hand. He said very quietly, but very firmly, 'There is nothing really wrong with you, but you must leave this house'. My heart heard him. I wasn't quite sure what he meant, but I felt his caring. It was as if there was a tiny light at the end of this black tunnel and the light was the voice of Dr MacDonald. I sat my exams and passed everything except maths, which I failed by two marks.

I had always felt ashamed of failing high school, so it was painful to tell Anne this story. But she was understanding. She helped me see that it was a most creative solution to an impossible position. If I had passed, my father would have expected me to go on to university. I couldn't have come up with a believable reason for not going and I was frightened that if I did tell him the truth it might cause him to have a heart attack. I found another way out. I failed successfully.

Gradually, Anne and I began to piece together some parts of my childhood. It was through my dreams that we entered all these memories. She helped me learn to listen to my dreams. It was my first experience with a therapy that showed me that the answers were inside of me. I began to trust myself a bit. There were two dreams that I recall during that time, which had a powerful impact on me. One was a dream I had when I was doing third-year honours in psychology. It was a very brief dream. I dreamt I was sitting on top of the psychology department, just sitting there on the roof in the sunshine.

It felt like a light-hearted dream and I thought it was a bit silly, but Anne took all my dreams seriously. Usually we explored them together, but her response to this one was different. I hardly got it out of my mouth when she sat up in her chair and said 'You're going to graduate at the top of your class'. I laughed. I was surprised both by the immediacy of her response, and also by the idea of getting top marks. I mean I was quite a good student and had got into honours, but there were a lot of very bright students in my group. She ended the session there, with me chuckling to myself at the audacity of my dreaming. I thought no more about the dream until a year later, as I stood at the university looking for my name. There it was: first-class honours. I remembered Anne and rang her. The dream came true!

There was another dream in that year that didn't lead to such an auspicious outcome. I told Anne about a nightmare that terrified me. I dreamt I was in a big swimming pool by myself when suddenly the water in the pool all rushed to one end, causing a huge tidal wave that was about to smash down on me. Anne's face looked grim. We didn't explore much of the dream, only my sense of being overwhelmed. She conveyed her concern and felt that perhaps it would be best if I went to see a psychiatrist. She suggested a private psychiatrist she knew. I agreed.

Once again I was looking over yet another enormous desk, answering endless questions. How I hated being there. Within days I was on antidepressants. I don't know even now why Anne felt she had to refer me to a psychiatrist or whether it was necessary. I have a sense it wasn't, at least I've never experienced anything positive by being drugged. I did continue to see her off and on, but my dreams stopped as the drugs increased, or rather my memory of my dreams stopped. So my therapy with her tapered off.

I was on these antidepressants for about eight or ten months. I can't really recall. I do remember the psychiatrist giving me yet another diagnosis. This time it was endogenous depression. Christ! I was fed up. I felt I was working my way through the *Diagnostic and Statistical Manual* – the textbook of psychiatric illnesses. What did all these labels about me really mean? None of them ever helped me, or helped me understand myself. I'd also bet they didn't do anything for the psychiatrists either, except perhaps make them feel as if they knew what they were doing. Eventually I began to see that regardless of the label, I got virtually the same drug, which did much the same thing: turn me into a zombie. As the months passed I began to wonder which was worse, the disease or the cure. Most of the time I felt I was living in slow motion behind ten layers of cloud. I didn't feel much of anything. God knows why they're called antidepressants; they should be called anti-expressants. I never became happy or light, I just became more moderate, functional and deadened.

CHAPTER 3

Learning and exploring

The completion of my honours year was a highlight. I think that failing high school had shaken my confidence in my abilities so much that I had wondered if I could possibly be successful in psychology. I was looking forward to the party the honours students had organised and was dressed and ready to go when my father phoned to say that my mother had just died. I still look back at that moment and wonder what really happened inside me. All I recall is taking in the information and saying some brief platitudes to my father. I went to the party, had a great time and did not even mention my mother's death to anyone. In fact, at no time in the years that followed did her death move me in any way. Her death was totally griefless for me. It was as if nothing had actually changed. I guess in a sense it hadn't.

The following year I gained a scholarship from the Department of Health to enter the Master's course in clinical psychology, so I abandoned teaching and continued studying. It was like a dream come true. The dream actually began in the first term of my first year in psychology, listening to the newly appointed professor of clinical psychology in the big lecture theatre. He was so different from our other lecturers: relaxed, light, interesting and funny. It was his warmth and openness that reached me. He spoke of clinical work with such enthusiasm and passion. It was then that I knew what my goal was. The years of left-brain knowledge, the statistics, the rigour of research design, the cramming of information – it all seemed worthwhile to discover I was accepted into this course. Yet it was not without trepidation.

Over those four years, I had walked past the clinical unit hundreds of times, each time sparking off such a push–pull feeling inside of me. It was like viewing a foreign country from across the street. The unit itself was very unimposing – just a wooden house constructed temporarily many years previously, like the poor cousin of the outstanding smart new psychology building in the centre of the main campus. It wasn't so much the building I found unusual but rather the Master's students I often saw sitting on the lawn with the professor and the other staff. It seemed that whenever I looked they were touching each other. I always felt like a voyeur as I walked by. What was the foreignness of this new land? What happens when you get to the Master's course? Why do people sit with their arms around each other? Why do they walk on campus arm-in-arm? Being supervised by the clinical professor for my honours degree gave me a two-year visitor's pass to this strange territory, but I still did not understand this touching. I think at times I wondered if it was a prerequisite and if I could handle it. In a sense it seemed that this conflict between the head and the heart was to be the theme of my future journey.

It is so difficult to capture the essence of those two years of the Master's course. When I look at the overall painting it seems like a huge canvas, incorporating every imaginable colour. It had breadth, depth and sharpness – contrasts I had never known before. 'Dynamic' probably best describes it. A rich, painful, joyful, demanding, difficult, fun, exhilarating two years. We were twelve students unknown to each other, thrown together one Monday morning, eager to hear the opening words of welcome and wisdom. But we were told that there were only two important things we must remember: never be late for a lecture and always wash your coffee cups. These words came from Dr Foster, the acting head of the clinical unit while the professor was overseas that year. What seemed like a potential disaster in having Dr Foster coordinate our course, we rapidly turned to great advantage. Since Dr Foster was extremely withdrawn and depressed and rarely available, we were able to organise a number of workshops by practitioners in the community. It was clear we all wanted to know about real clinical work. I was hungry to know more, to begin to understand how therapy really worked and how to help people. My unspoken question was, is there hope for me?

Some moments come back to me as vividly as if they happened yesterday. We had a series of training sessions with a very experienced child psychologist. I was listening intently as she described the real importance of the mother–child relationship. I could feel the depth of sadness inside me. Then she said that if the child doesn't have an adequate mother it only takes one person to make all the difference. I could feel the first bubbles of hope arise. She then went on to say that therapy always provides a second chance. Those two statements, for me, have remained like precious jewels; I could never count the number of times I've repeated them to myself when the darkness encompassed me. They gave me continual hope.

The other important moment occurred in an experiential workshop. A therapist worked with me for about two hours, trying to get me in touch with positive memories of my childhood. I was overwhelmed by feelings of being with my Auntie – her love, her gentleness, her laughter. I think that until that moment I hadn't really any idea of just how important she was to me. As my memories emerged, many of them were connected to flowers. When we came to the completion of the session the therapist took me to the door and opened it. I stepped out and saw hundreds of nasturtiums that I and the other Masters students had planted months earlier. It was like a waterfall of red and orange and yellow and green, and the colours merged with my tears of joy at remembering such a special woman.

Not surprisingly, the topic I chose for my Master's thesis was the mother–infant bond. I spent quite a lot of time at the maternity hospital talking with the paediatricians about recent research developments. What came out of our discussions was their concern for mothers whose baby had died. I began my research on maternal grief, thinking it was simply a thesis topic, never guessing it would be the foundation of my future career and contain the clues to the search for my own self.

The two years encompassed not only course work, workshops and thesis but also clinical placements for three-month periods with five different practitioners. I began my clinical supervision in psychodrama, which was like jumping into the deep end. Because I was so unconscious of my childhood it really shook me up to enter such a confronting form of therapy. The one memory that surfaced for me was of being locked in a closet by my mother.

Enacting this memory and fighting my way out was very distressing. It opened doors but left me without the support I needed to withstand the pain. Over the following months I could feel the depression rising – the 'nothing' seeping in – as if it were safer to be numb than to face what that closet really meant to me as a child.

My next placements were in fairly traditional psycho-therapeutic settings and models in the health department and at the university clinic. The main models I was trained in over that time were cognitive behavioural therapy, rational emotive therapy and transactional analysis and family therapy. Overall I saw improvements with my clients, but inside I felt uneasy; something wasn't right. While the models we used made perfect sense and the steps were clear and definable, it seemed superficial. I don't think our work touched the real issues. But it was a compulsory part of our training and we were all led to believe this provided what people needed, so we became fluent with the new clinical language.

It was with a great deal of excitement that I got my last placement with a woman who was regarded as the top therapist in the city. I had seen Ruth run groups and was attracted to her way of working; it was so different from our prescribed university models. She worked at a large psychiatric hospital mainly treating outpatients, as well as running groups for in-patients. This was my introduction to psychodynamic psychotherapy. I felt as though someone really reached into the depths and spoke a language that bypassed the logical mind. My heart rejoiced. I began to see the beauty of the inner world, to listen with new ears and see with new eyes. I was taken away from the surface and saw people grow and develop and blossom from the inside out.

I was on placement with Ruth for four months. Most of the time I spent sitting in on her therapy sessions with clients. She wouldn't let me take any notes, so I sat there taking in the experiences at a different level. Over that time, I began to see that her therapy space was an oasis in a vast wasteland. To venture outside her room and into the psychiatric wards was to really enter madness – not in the patients, but in the environment. I'm sure if you weren't severely depressed or psychotic before you arrived you would be within days. The deprivation and the absence of humanity were profound. The wards were clinical and barren, much like those in a prison. I recall the case conference presentations each week, where about fifty to sixty staff would sit in rows of straight-backed chairs facing the centre of the room where a patient sat staring blankly.

A psychiatrist from each of the six teams would present a 'case'. If you didn't know it wasn't the Middle Ages or the time of witch-hunts, you'd wonder how doctors could treat other human beings in such a degrading manner. Patients sat there as a psychiatrist divulged all the pertinent details of their lives which led to their present state of dysfunction. A label was then handed down like a death sentence. The types of medication were written on a blackboard along with the presenting symptoms and diagnosis. Then the other psychiatrists would throw questions at the patients as though they were on trial: 'When did you become depressed?' 'Was this your first attempt at suicide?' 'Why haven't you worked for the past three years?'

Usually my supervisor would come in at some point with the only human voice I heard in that psychological gas chamber. She spoke to the person by name and her voice had a warmth and a caring tone to it. She didn't ask futile questions, but made contact with a question or a statement connected with the person. You could see that there was often a response in the patient's eyes.

When I visited the wards I was astounded by the abuse of these people. Often drugged into a state of inertia, they were expected to attend workshops throughout the day. I went to all of these and I was about as bored as the patients looked as they made stuffed animals or placemats, or sat in groups where they were to talk about re-entry into the real world. They had to comply with the rules, which meant attending these meaningless workshops. If they didn't attend, they were considered non-compliant and their chances of hospital discharge dwindled proportionally. Then there was electroconvulsive therapy: if I thought the case presentations were disturbing, it was nothing compared to ECT. I learnt that mental hospitals depict inhumanity in a sanctioned, legal way behind closed doors and closed minds.

I completed my training with Ruth. I had learned so much from her – it was the beginning of my becoming a therapist. On my last day I left the hospital carrying a big lion which I had made alongside one of the patients in the workshops. I went to say goodbye and saw his lion on top of his dresser. I tried to convey that I hoped he'd find his lion's courage to get out.

Just as the placement came to completion so did my thesis and the Master's course. What a journey it had been. I'll never forget the day I took my thesis into the university. It had been an enormous undertaking to interview over a hundred women and analyse the effects of the death of their babies on their mental and physical health. As I handed it to the university receptionist, I knew that whatever mark I got didn't really matter: I was proud of my work. I felt I'd done something very worthwhile that would make a difference to the future care of bereaved women.

When I left the university campus I went to a jeweller to have a silver bracelet made. It was a gift to myself for completing my Master's degree. The jewellery shop I entered was tiny and even the jeweller seemed elf-like. There were no big display cabinets, no choices to be made; he designed jewellery from your own ideas. I told him what it symbolised for me. I said the bracelet needed to contain polar opposites – it needed light and dark, shiny and dull, smooth and rough. I also wanted it to have a sense of movement and to show both the inner and the outer aspects of a circle. That was really how I felt about these past two years. It had been both demanding and exhilarating, affecting me internally and externally. The jeweller seemed to understand the symbols I spoke of and drew me a picture of how he imagined this creation. We talked for quite a while about the importance of symbols in life. We agreed they were like a rite of passage onto a new stage, while honouring what had gone before.

This memory returned when I picked up my new bracelet a few weeks later. As I slipped it on my wrist I knew that it symbolised all I'd gained. It was to become my talisman. Somehow, I knew then that my search to find myself had become paramount. I wore it as a constant reminder of that wordless commitment. Would I or could I have made it if I'd known then what this agreement with myself would entail?

CHAPTER 4

Divorce, depression and disability

At the beginning of the new year I made an appointment to see Ruth. I knew I really needed to sort something out about my marriage. I sat in the chair that I had seen so many clients sit in when I watched therapy sessions. It felt good to be there for myself and not as an observer. I began directly by saying that the reason I'd come was that I was unhappy in my marriage and that I didn't know whether I should leave my husband or not. But just as my words entered the space, everything became crystal-clear: I knew there was nothing left in my marriage. That day was to mark both an end and a new beginning. It would be several months before I summoned enough courage to act on my decision, but I did leave.

Leaving a dead marriage sounds like a straightforward, simple action, but I could never have known, from hearing or from reading about it, just how painful it would be. What finally gave me the strength to leave was a voice inside saying 'I'll die if I stay here any longer'. The years of trying to work out what was amiss, what could be done, how it might be fixed or made different – all the pros and cons, and combinations and permutations – had ceased. I didn't know if it was right or wrong or good or bad anymore, but my heart felt like it was breaking.

It was wrenching to leave even though there was now so little between us; the pain was for all the hopes and dreams of what might have been. Everyone begins a marriage with delicate and delightful dreams of growth and blossoming. What did blossom was our home and our garden. All the energy we shared was placed outside but not between us. We had indeed transformed our house into a lovely home. I had looked at over one hundred houses in the search for this one. I'm not sure which I loved more – the inside of this house with its comfortable rooms, or the gardens and swimming pool. It was hard to leave.

What I missed most about our house was a huge tree in the backyard. I so often thought about it. It became the symbol of all the good memories over those years. That tree with its wide encompassing canopy somehow gathered the sweetness and joy under its arms. It was the tree outside my son Michael's bedroom. When he was a baby I would sit in his room in a rocking chair, nursing him and looking out onto the courtyard, feeling an undreamed of love and peace in being together. There was a sand-pit at the base of the tree where we had played many games with trucks and cars speeding around sandy hills, and where we had built and rebuilt castles with love and patience. It certainly was our favourite place, particularly in summer. When work stopped we would have lunch outside – the food always tasted better there. Maybe we were less formal, and less organised, outdoors.

As Michael grew he found the tree more intriguing, more of an adventure. At some point one of the branches also held a swing. I don't know who used it most – Michael or I. The tree was like a playground, a sanctuary; a retreat from a busy, demanding world. The tree also heard a lot of laughter and singing. Throughout the years we had many parties in the garden. I often had psychology students over and also my friends from teaching. The evenings were filled with excitement, lively discussions and music. I particularly remember the music. I had two friends who played guitar and we would usually end the nights with folk songs. Everyone would join in. It was a garden well suited for being together. Maybe that is where my real grief over leaving centred. More than anything I had wanted this marriage to be one of warmth and relatedness, but it simply never happened. The communication and relationships were with friends. My husband cultivated the practical, physical garden and I cultivated the emotional one, but both were outside of us; we never found a true, common inner ground.

My insides were screaming not to sign the divorce papers, but overriding this was my desperate need for peace – peace at all costs. I just wanted the emotional battles finished, so I settled for a price for our house that was far less than its value, and for a minimal maintenance from my ex-husband. From that point onwards life became hard.

To even attempt to describe the plain hard work and the struggle and loneliness of trying to work full time and be a single parent, is impossible. I wanted desperately to be a good parent and also to establish myself in a new career. There was never enough time for anything else, so my emotional needs were shelved and the time available to be with friends diminished more and more as time went by. I bought a house, but because I didn't have enough money to begin with, I was struggling to keep up with the mortgage repayments. I eventually sold that house and bought a cheaper one, but again I was always behind.

Nevertheless the decision I made that day in Ruth's office stands as a landmark in my life. Even though it signalled the end of a marriage, it was actually a day of commitment. Externally that commitment was to do personal therapy and clinical supervision with Ruth. But the real commitment was to an inner journey, although I still wasn't at all conscious of what that journey might involve or where it would lead. At the end of the session Ruth looked me straight in the eye and said 'You know, once you've bought the ticket, you can't get off the train'. There was something about the power with which she said it that totally anchored it in my subconscious. I could never go back, no matter how comfortable it seemed. Something kept pushing me forward and inward. Each experience of getting to know myself, even though painful, gave me hope that I would one day find my way home.

The ecstasy of successfully completing the Master's course was followed swiftly by the opposite swing of the emotional pendulum when I was notified of my posting. My scholarship committed me to work for the health department for two years after the completion of the course. I had hoped to work in a clinical setting, but was given a job working for the division for the intellectually handicapped.

I began my new job two weeks before Christmas, working with severely multi-handicapped adults and children. I was responsible for four hostels. My first visit to one of these hostels was unforgettable. It was like a nursing home; in fact all of them had at one time been old hospitals. It wasn't just seeing forty people in wheelchairs looking blankly at blank walls, nor was it being hit by the inexplicable pain I felt in realising that all these people were trapped inside totally unworkable bodies and minds. It wasn't even the hopelessness I sensed in the mechanical motions of staff. It was something more profound, sinister and elusive: the horrific deprivation echoing throughout the environment. It was akin to entering a leper colony: the unloved, unwanted, unseen rejects of our society. I wandered through the hostel for about an hour, almost oblivious to the verbal tour I was being given by the matron.

With my whole body overwhelmed by emotion and my senses swirling in a desert, I realised I was no longer at the matron's side nodding my head professionally, but running down the corridor to my car. Leaning against my car sobbing, I felt shaken to the core.

So this was my new career. I'm sure the matron wondered what kind of psychologist they'd sent her. My hopes and dreams of being a therapist, of exploring people's inner lives, were gone. It was months before I could tolerate more than an hour in these meaningless environments. The greatest dilemma was my prescribed role as a psychologist: to write behaviour management programs. My announcement that I wasn't a behaviourist and therefore didn't design behaviour programs brought a stunned look to all the matrons' faces. Their expression reflected my own confusion as to what I would actually do. From top to bottom, the system was a behaviourist's dream. Although normalisation was the philosophy of the organisation, it seemed like normalisation gone mad. All the clients in the hostels underwent about eight training programs a day. The staff ceaselessly recorded the achievements of each client's skill area, whether it was grasping a spoon or sipping from a cup. Due to the severity of the physical handicaps, hours and hours of patience went into these minimal gains. Each day was regimented from the time the residents awoke until evening. When they weren't doing programs the clients sat in the hallway waiting for the next training session or were put in front of the television.

A major part of my role was to keep up with these programs and to ensure that staff were technically sound in their tasks. My other task was to change unwanted behaviours: and the requests for these were endless. In reviewing client files and in listening to staff requests, I couldn't believe how punishing the programs were. It was not unusual to see children put in a 'time out' closet for extended periods of time just because they'd been aggressive or noncompliant. But it didn't stop there. They'd also deprive the clients of their favourite foods or take away personal belongings for poor behaviour. I thought I'd go mad. Not only did it contradict my educational beliefs and psychological understandings, but it sickened me. How could anyone think they had a right to inflict such pain on another human being? I had many disagreements with staff members who were as institutionalised as the clients and did just what they were told. Normalisation had come to mean a desperate attempt to make these people as normal as possible by totally focusing on their motor skills. I guess someone decided that if they were more skilled, they'd fit in better. The craziness was that there was no acknowledgment of how terribly handicapped these people were. The head of the department conveyed the belief that if we all worked hard enough, and the clients worked hard enough, they could go to university!

The monthly psychology meetings, attended by about twenty behavioural psychologists and myself, were torture. I felt more like a black sheep, listening to all the 'Rah-rah' about more programs and bigger, better computers to assess the clients. The unrealistic positiveness made the child in me want to scream about the total lack of acknowledgment of feelings. As if things would be so much better once the clients could hold a spoon! There was no sensitivity to the psychological pain these people must have endured. Trapped, totally trapped, that's what I saw. Inside, these people were like anyone, but their bodies wouldn't move and their voices couldn't speak; they couldn't convey their needs, their feelings, their desires, their pain. All they could do was just sit and look through the prison window. Only later did I come to realise that my empathy for these clients was based on my own imprisonment, my own deprivation of needs. At the time I felt only pain and depression.

The most bizarre aspect of this organisation was that while the focus was on making these clients 'normal', no one was actually treating them normally. My decision as to how I'd work in the system came through my supervision with Ruth. Once a week I'd travel across the city to her office and she'd help me analyse the system and look at it from a group process perspective. That really shifted my vision and I began to formulate a new way of working. I needed to work with the staff and explore what they felt the clients really needed. Essentially, all decisions about the care of clients came down from the top of the hierarchy. Since behaviour programs were fashionable, that's what the staff were required to do most of the day. The direct-care staff were never asked what they felt the clients needed, even though they spent all their time with them.

I introduced a new approach by conducting staff meetings that focused on Maslow's hierarchy of human needs: survival, safety, security, love and belonging. It took over a year before the effects were seen in the hostel, but the changes were real and delightful. One of the major things that had emerged in our sessions was the barrenness of the hostel and how unlike anyone's home it was. I explained the situation to the art department at a local university and asked what they thought of sending out some of their art students to see if they could come up with any ideas for improvement.

This was a most serendipitous call, for the lecturer I contacted became very enthusiastic and assigned a final-year student for each client. Suddenly the hostel was awash with young colourful students, paints, brushes and lively noises. While the art students initially found it difficult to handle the severity of the clients' handicaps, the lecturer and I talked with them and discussed their feelings. It wasn't long before each student had been linked to a client and they were off in corners getting to know them. The hostel was unrecognisable after a few months.

The students painted full murals on the walls in the sitting-rooms and hallways. They also painted the ceilings in the bathrooms, since clients spent endless hours being bathed, lying down in bathtubs looking up at nothing. But the best thing that happened was the formation of relationships. The lecturer asked the students to do a painting for the client they were linked to. The students spent weeks getting to know the individual backgrounds, likes and dislikes and unique personal qualities; they really began to see the clients in a new light. They'd been so caught up in the mechanics of programming they'd lost sight of the person. The individual paintings were incredible, almost matching the joy I could see in the clients' faces. It was probably the first time they had been acknowledged beyond their handicap – as people.

The one client I'll never forget was Stephen. He was eighteen years old and had no verbal communication skills. He could move only his left hand, which he used with extreme dexterity, particularly when he could pinch the nurses' bottoms. Everyone loved Stephen, his bright sparkling blue eyes and his sense of humour. He was always smiling even if his lips couldn't do it perfectly. His eyes lit up indescribably when he was presented with a painting of a nude woman, which was designed to fit on the tray of his wheelchair. That one moment was worth every second of the pain and despair I'd felt over the two years of working there.

There were to be many more changes in the hostel, but they came easily and mainly through the ideas of the nurses. They realised that nurturing, caring, fun and laughter were far more important than the ability to hold a spoon, and that such things were indeed crucial for someone even to want to learn anything.

Ironically, I received a fellowship for my work with handicapped children. Somehow, life seems to have a way of turning things upside down. I had developed an interest and a commitment in an area not of my choosing. The award was also because of my involvement with community groups in the area of maternal grief. The fellowship allowed me to travel for six months to study innovations in health services in both these areas. My son Michael and I set off for the tour the following year.

During my study tour I visited my father in Canada for three weeks. I hadn't seen him for four years and I was quite looking forward to the visit. He really grounded me when we arrived at the airport. I rushed up to him and he put out his hand to shake hands. In that instant I realised why the clinical unit at the university had seemed like a foreign country: I'd been brought up in a family where touching was not acceptable. I managed to break through that greeting, and gave him a hug and a kiss. The ice melted and he laughed, we both laughed. That visit didn't contain much additional joy. I really tried to get my father to talk to me about my childhood and about himself and my mother and their relationship. He gave some perfunctory information, but it didn't lead to any real dialogue. We also had a few predictable arguments.

Within days of being in the house I sank into depression. It wasn't clear to me until I returned home. I felt I was carrying an enormously heavy weight. I had such a strong sensation that I was covered in black from the waist down. It was so real – as though someone had poured black paint over me and I kept trying to get it off. I sat in my lounge room on a white couch just seeing this blackness and brushing my legs. I knew something powerful had happened in relation to my father and to being home, but I couldn't fathom it. I did know I needed help and made an appointment to see Ruth the following week. The result of the session wasn't what I'd hoped for. Although she listened carefully and acknowledged my distress, she finally said she felt I'd done enough therapy and should be starting to focus on my role as a therapist.

For a while I tried to take her advice and be positive about my life, but the blackness was there every morning and every evening.

I had completed training in psychodrama that year. In the new year I began training in Gestalt therapy, a form of therapy that does not recall past memories but that focuses on what is happening to the client within the present moment. We had weekly education sessions plus workshops every two to three months. The first workshop was a residential three-day retreat. The visiting therapist began the Friday morning session by asking us to go into pairs and sit on the floor opposite each other and just look into our partner's eyes. This was such a powerful experience for me – after about ten minutes I began to cry and that was it for the three days. Although this exercise lasted about two hours, it opened a floodgate that seemed unable to close. I just kept crying. The distressing thing was I couldn't tap into what it was about. The therapist tried to help me discover the experiences that were triggering the sadness, but no memories emerged. I felt I could have cried forever. The one image I had was of an inner well: I'd send down a bucket and bring up whatever emotions were there but all that emerged were buckets of tears and sorrow. I looked to the people in the group and they seemed to have joy, happiness, enthusiasm and excitement coming up in theirs. Why, oh why couldn't I have those feelings? Why was it only tears? The workshop ended and I was exhausted but no more insightful about the blackness.

When I got home I rang Ruth and told her I couldn't cope any longer. She was booked up and suggested I go to see a new therapist in town, a psychiatrist. Oh no, not another psychiatrist, I thought. How could I be back in that space? But the pain wouldn't leave and I had heard he was good, so I made an appointment. In the first session James asked if I had done any previous therapy. I felt ashamed as I listed the therapists I'd seen. It seemed like such an indictment of my self. I felt damaged, as though I was a failure at therapy for not being better by now. I had no idea what was wrong with me, no idea why I couldn't be like other people.

The months came and went. I was back in the antidepressant blur. I can't recall how many different drugs he tried, but it became meaningless after a while. I had adverse side effects to each one and so he kept trying to find the right formula, as if there was one. I trusted it was the right thing to do. I couldn't see through the fog; I only knew I felt I was being engulfed by the blackness. He told me I had 'chronic anxiety depression', but the labels had lost interest for me. I didn't care what I had anymore, I just wanted to get rid of it.

One memory does surface about a session early on in my therapy. I'd been talking about death, and I asked him 'Do you think there's life after death?' He gave me a bewildered look and said that no one had ever asked him that before, and also it was not a question for a person in their thirties to be asking. He said 'Wait till you're seventy'. He just didn't understand how dead I felt inside and I couldn't find the reasons or the words to explain the emptiness and fear inside me. I felt I must have been an enigma to those trying to help me. From the outside I suppose I looked as though I was fairly 'together'. I was a psychologist and held a full-time job, which I did adequately. But that was the cover story. I despaired that I would never be normal and wake up feeling happy like other people. I was also despairing about my own profession. If *I* couldn't find a 'cure', how could I believe that therapy actually worked?

CHAPTER 5

Hope

y closest friends over the past four years were Sophie and Mathew who had been in the Master's course. We seemed to speak the same language. I couldn't even begin to guess how many coffees we sat over talking about psychotherapy, politics, life, relationships, books, films and our own personal journeys. But whenever we did come together there was a depth we reached that was like striking gold.

Mathew later worked in another city for a couple of years and during his absence Sophie and I maintained the 'cappuccino institute', as we fondly called our weekly meeting place. Looking back, I realise those times were priceless for me. There was a sense of being known by Sophie, even if I didn't know who I was myself. With her, I was able to talk of the black hole and the emptiness, and although I would never find the words to make it any more clear or concrete she seemed to understand. She gave me a sense of hope; whenever I felt empty and worthless she saw a Me that I couldn't. Her friendship gave me strength. We both grappled with words, ideas and images, but mainly we shared an understanding of the inner pain.

We had also come to share our disillusionment with psychotherapy. We had both been searching for a long time and had not found any answers. So I was quite shocked one day, as we sat in the sun at the sidewalk café having a cappuccino, when she began talking enthusiastically about a study group that had recently been set up. She told me of this new form of therapy called self psychology and how she believed it contained something remarkable, something that made it different from every other form of therapy. I really was taken aback by her unfettered enthusiasm. She said they had organised some supervisors from other cities to conduct seminars and to train therapists. She insisted I join the group, saying 'Listen, it's really hard to explain, but I believe if you come along you'll be hooked. Something happens inside, you'll feel it. I'm sure this is the answer'. She also gave me a bundle of papers to read as I thought it over. To join meant leaving my Gestalt training and that had become a very important support for me. But although the friends I'd made in this group were a valuable part of my life, when I thought about it I realised this form of therapy was really for those who had a fairly secure sense of themselves and who wished to enhance their personal development and relationship skills. The focus was always on what was happening in the present, whereas for me I knew it was my past that was dragging me into the blackness.

So after a few more talks and seeing the light in Sophie's eyes, I took the all-important step that was to transform my entire life. Initially, belonging to this self psychology group was fairly academic. We discussed prescribed papers or books and about every two or three months there'd be a three-day training seminar. It would have remained quite low-key for me except for these seminars, to which we took along tapes of our therapy sessions with clients. For the three days we listened to each other's therapy cases and received comments from the visiting supervisors. This in itself was a big step forward for me, for I began to see a few clients for therapy in order to develop my skills in this area. It was such a boost for me to do some clinical work which was so different from my work with the handicapped, and I loved it.

The visiting supervisors varied a lot over the following four years, but one in particular had a profound impact on me. What really hit me was the depth of understanding in his voice. The closest I can get to describing it adequately is to say that when

Neil listened to a tape he seemed to hear the voice beneath the voice, the words behind the words, the feelings beneath the surface. It was as if he listened to the child within the adult. The child, who had been crying out to be listened to and understood, seemed to have a real presence in that space. To say I was blown apart, or to say I was touched to the depth of my being, still doesn't convey how moved I was by his compassion and insights.

There were many times when I'd sit there in our groups, crying. I didn't know why; I didn't understand what was happening and I felt ashamed about falling apart. When the pain rising up in me was too enormous to contain I'd leave the session. Sometimes I'd go down to the basement car park and curl up in the back seat of my car and simply hold myself. Other times I'd go to a park nearby and sit under a tree or just walk aimlessly, trying to soothe myself. Yet Neil never turned the focus onto me, although I had a sense he was acutely attuned to my feelings. He conveyed that this was a space where all feelings were acceptable and so if I was sad and felt like crying, that is what was inside and that was fine. At those times when I'd leave the room, he didn't question me. He'd simply come up to me at coffee time or lunch time and make some contact, saying that if I wanted to have a talk with him anytime that was also fine.

I never really knew if it was simply the sound of his voice or what he was saying in these sessions that brought up such overwhelming feelings. Whenever one of the group presented a client on tape, Neil would understand exquisitely the depth of their pain. It was, I'm sure, his understanding of the inner child or the childhood trauma of these adults that touched me so deeply. There were times he would get frustrated and even angry with the therapist for not truly listening. I recall him saying to a woman in our group 'You're not really listening to your client, she's floundering, lost and in danger. Her dreams are telling you that, but you're only hearing her outer story. You've got to tap into the feelings beneath the words, the story underneath what she's telling you'. I wept and wept at that point. I was hearing a man who not only listened to the depth, but one who stood up for the child, who was like a protector. Neil conveyed the delicacy and danger of the journey and that therapists need to know what they're doing, which meant listening with empathy. My pain and my tears were for the little girl inside of me who, for once in her life, heard someone who could understand that deep, wordless sea; someone who was adamant that the child should be honoured and protected.

Although I wasn't conscious of it then, it was like a breath of fresh air to hear someone speak of an inner and an outer self. Somehow I knew that all the therapists in my past had been listening to, looking at and addressing questions to my outer self. It was as if they'd been following red herrings because the Me I presented wasn't the real one. None of my feelings had any form or words at the time. But as I watched Neil work, I saw he went beyond the outer self – straight past it, no questions asked. So even though the 'nothing' was still my inner experience, I could feel small bubbles of joy arise. Maybe there was a Me inside. To listen to feelings – not words; how that gave me hope!

In my search, previous therapists asked 'how'-'what'-'why'-'when'-'where' questions. They all seemed to want to ask the questions that got clear, reasonable answers. But I didn't know. I couldn't answer questions about my own life. I couldn't tell them about a childhood I couldn't remember. I couldn't articulate the reason, the cause, the triggers of my pain and depression. I couldn't even tell them much of what I felt because the closest I seemed to get was 'empty'. Yet here was someone who was understanding and who never asked questions or made judgments or complex interpretations. This therapy was deeper, richer; it was a space for children who'd lost their way.

Sophie was right – I was hooked. The supervision weekends seemed to be my mainstay. I'd go on automatic pilot in between, but as the time came closer for workshops I'd start to come alive. I'd often buy new clothes, clothes that were bright, more vivid, more visible. Life would seem so different: colours seemed brighter, people friendlier and laughter easier to come by. But at the end of the workshops I'd feel bereft. I was right back in the centre of nothing. I'm sure I even looked like a different person. I'd even revert to wearing faded pastel clothes.

It is only now that I see the subtle changes that began to occur. Significantly, I began to keep a journal. It was so difficult to write anything at first, for it all seemed like a diffuse blank space inside. I also remember how hard I made it for myself even to begin to write a few sentences. I'd tell myself I had to write neatly and I'd have to draw a straight margin and put the date at the top. All these rules – where did they come from? It felt like a mammoth accomplishment to have made one small entry over a two-week period.

When I look at those earliest journals I feel the despair of someone so totally and utterly lost. I started writing in my journal about three months after I began self psychology. By this time, I had been doing psychotherapy with James for about a year and a half. What I wrote during that year seemed the same, over and over. My journal entries (made largely on weekends) contained such comments:

❖ I got up at 10 a.m. – can't believe how much I can sleep. I felt anxious all weekend, and so lonely. I keep going over and over in my head all the things I need to do and then I feel more anxious and hopeless.

❖ This evening I felt like crying and crying; I feel I just can't go on.

❖ I feel so down. Everything seems so black, like there's nothing I feel interested in or involved in; nothing to get excited about.

❖ I feel I'm frozen: I just sit and stare out the window for hours.

❖ I feel as though I'm falling apart, my anxiety level is so high. I feel as though I'm losing control and I don't have the strength to keep coping.

❖ I can't think at work. I just want to run away and escape. Everything seems to cause me anxiety.

❖ I wonder if the antidepressants are helping at all; I just feel so awful. It seems there is nothing in life that is really of interest; it all seems false. Other people seem to have a passion for things, but nothing grabs me. I feel just like an empty shell.

❖ My drugs were increased today. Shit, I feel awful.

❖ I feel so empty – I don't know who I am, I don't know what I want, I don't know what I believe in.

❖ That empty feeling was with me again today. I feel so saturated with loneliness and so desperately sad. I just can't continue like this.

❖ I feel so helpless. I don't know how to be happy. I don't believe the medication is working. My only escape is to sleep.

❖ I feel so physically awful. I just sit and sit; I don't want to do anything. I don't know if I should go off the antidepressants. I just feel so lonely, so withdrawn. Can't anybody help me?

Just reading those entries takes me back to the blackness. I realise how relentless it seemed: day in, day out; week in, week out; year in, year out – just nothing. I know, although I don't visit that space much anymore, it is important I don't forget where I came from, for it is my history.

I remember another very interesting therapist who influenced me at this time. This man had written a number of academic books on psychotherapy and everyone was excited about his coming. I wasn't particularly enthusiastic, perhaps because the theoretical aspects didn't interest me as much as the practical experiences. We had organised for him to speak to us one afternoon and then to have dinner together that evening. Although the title of his talk didn't attract me, I was simply mesmerised by his words. He said that after years of being a therapist he began to realise how frequently his clients talked about 'blackness' or 'the black hole'. I was riveted. I couldn't believe it; someone was telling me that there were others out there who had similar experiences to my own. I wasn't alone. It was just such a relief to know I had a shared language and that this therapist listened to and respected that unfathomable space. Why hadn't the therapists I'd seen been able to understand anything about this black hole? Why had they all tried to turn away from it, ignore it, dress it up or give me drugs when I started talking about it too much? Why had they tried to turn the 'nothing' into something? Why couldn't they have just sat in it with me to get a feel for what I had no words for? Not only did this therapist seem to have a true sense of the experience, he also added, for me, a new dimension, new words. He talked about autism. He spoke of the black hole as a deadened space where there is such unthinkable fear that there is no thinking; such unfeelable feelings that there are no feelings. He explained that for children who have been traumatised, this space is their escape, their safety.

I began to get a glimpse of understanding as he described the vital importance of the therapeutic space. He said it needed to be a safe, nurturing constant space, one where the patient could experience trust and acceptance. He conveyed that it was through the acceptance of the black hole that they were able to find memories that had been previously intolerable. The space needed to contain these previously uncontainable experiences, for if the inner space had been unable to hold the intensity of the trauma, there needed to be an outer holding – a place to explore these feelings. That's what I'd been crying out for. I knew then why I held my teddy bear so strongly when swamped by the blackness – it was I who was longing to feel held and contained.

At dinner that night I sat soaking in his conversations with everyone. I was a bit shocked, though, when I found myself speaking up and asking questions. I usually said little and found it difficult to be at all visible. Most of the group were surprised to hear me address him. It seemed very important to ask him more about the black hole. I recall saying 'Do you think there are many who suffer this autistic experience?' He seemed to mull this over for a long time and I became worried he'd begin to ask me questions, as though I'd somehow exposed my 'pathology'. Following this pregnant silence he looked at me with what seemed to be a deep intensity and respect, and said 'I think there are probably many, but only a few have the courage to speak of it'. I will never forget his eyes, his empathy and his answer.

That experience gave me the courage to try again to explain to James about my emptiness and to talk about the autistic space.

But it really was hopeless – we just weren't on the same wavelength. He was interested academically and said he'd read this man's book, but there was no shared understanding. Although there was no real breakthrough in my therapy, I guess there was something of a breakthrough inside me. I felt that for once it wasn't *me* that was hopeless. I was just in a space that had little hope of understanding. I decided I wanted to begin to come off the antidepressants. I could see that the drugs did the same thing as the black hole: they heightened the nothingness.

I wanted to begin to feel the unfeelable and think the unthinkable, whatever it was.

CHAPTER 6

Unfeelable feelings

*S*oon after I returned from my study tour I was transferred from the multi-handicapped area and for the next three years I worked with school-aged handicapped children. It wasn't long before I began to understand the grief parents suffered in having a handicapped child. Although the focus in this division was still on extreme positiveness, I could see that the parents mainly kept up a brave controlled face for our professional visits. In spending time with them and simply listening, their pain surfaced. In response to this I began the challenging task of conducting counselling groups that enabled parents to address their feelings.

I was also getting close to acknowledging my own feelings of grief and loss related to my damaged inner child. I had countless dreams about handicapped babies or babies who had died. In one, I dreamt I gave birth to a baby girl who died. The paediatrician tried to save her, but he didn't have the right instruments. In another dream, I had a handicapped baby and took her to many different doctors. They all shook their heads and said nothing could be done.

I also had dreams of attack. Either there were robbers trying to break into my home or I was being attacked outside. I'd wake up terrified. Looking back at my journals, I see that it was around this time that I began to write down my dreams. I hadn't recorded any dreams since my work with Anne, almost ten years previously. I must have lost confidence in my dreams after my tidal wave dream had resulted in a referral to a psychiatrist and yet more drugs.

It wasn't just my dreams telling me that something needed urgent attention. My journal showed a new theme of collapse, although I could never say what I was going to collapse from or into. I was simply overwhelmed by a sense that I was going to fall to pieces. I'd lie in my bed at the weekend and imagine stop signs all around my house facing out, as though I couldn't handle any more of anything. When I walked my dog I thought I was being followed. Even though I knew it wasn't a real person, it was eerie. I felt that if I stopped suddenly this thing would bump into me. I hated those times. I felt I was on the edge of a breakdown, but had no idea what was causing the feelings. That sense of having something right behind me was like a black shadow. It was as if that blackness I'd earlier experienced on my body had become externalised and was following me around ceaselessly. I was frightened and terribly alone. I wasn't brave enough to turn around and face this blackness, whatever it was. I wanted to escape, but there was nowhere to go. It was a part of me.

These experiences intensified every time we had a workshop, and particularly when Neil visited. My sense of peace and togetherness shattered at the end of every workshop. I was back to sitting in my emptiness trying to stave off whatever was trying to break in …

I was cooking one Sunday, not long after a workshop, and as I reached for a pot, a memory flashed in front of me. I could hardly bear what I saw and withdrew to my bed. I kept saying 'No', over and over. I wanted to wipe it out, to erase it. I didn't want to know. In the following weeks I looked at the photographs of my childhood that I had tucked away. Why hadn't I noticed before that there were tons of photos of me as a baby up to about a year or eighteen months, but that there was nothing between then and the age of eight or ten? I slammed the box shut and put it back on top of the cupboard behind the blankets. That was enough, I didn't want to see anymore.

Humpty Dumpty. That's exactly how I felt. It was like I was getting worse, not better. Instead of feeling empty and depressed, I felt I was in a million pieces – totally fragmented, totally broken. The despair was deepening. I couldn't bear to tell anyone what I saw that day and yet I couldn't bear to contain it. I felt I needed to face the fact that I was damaged beyond repair. The image I had at that time was of wanting to go somewhere where you hand yourself in. I don't know exactly why, but I wanted to go to some authority and say 'Okay, I give up. I know there's nothing anyone can do to make me better. Let me live without memories of who I am, but please, please just take away the pain'. It was as though I wanted to strike a bargain; I knew I couldn't cope much longer and I wanted a reprieve.

None came, and the image followed me constantly. It surprised me that people couldn't see I was actually in a thousand pieces, floating around in space. One of the dreams I had was of a delicate pink vase being smashed to the ground and a man patiently trying to piece it all together with glue. Just as he'd get to the last few pieces, something would happen and it would crumble into tiny pieces once again. I knew the only person I could even begin to speak to of this was Neil. It was all so fragile. *I* was so fragile. I wrote to Neil and asked if I could see him when he came in two weeks' time.

As the time of our meeting approached, I became more anxious and began to wish I hadn't written the letter. A big part of me just wanted to ignore the whole thing. Perhaps he didn't get the letter; perhaps he wouldn't have the time available, I hoped. But it wasn't so. As soon as I arrived he said he'd see me at 4.30 when he'd finished the last supervision. What a day. I don't know how I stayed around. Eventually he came out and got a cup of coffee, and we went into a room that was quiet, very quiet. He didn't prompt me or push me, he just sat there at ease. So I began, and it felt as though I'd die at any second. The pain that arose in telling what I saw was horrific. My body felt tortured; every cell was screaming not to bring it to consciousness.

I told him I had remembered a scene from when I was about eighteen months old. I saw everything in vivid detail. I had on a blue dress with pink flowers around the bottom, white socks and brown shoes. I was sitting on the floor in the kitchen, banging pots and pans loudly. I had a real bodily sense that I was safe, and I was playing with great enjoyment. I looked up and saw my mother walk in. She had on a brown and yellow flowered dress and her hair was done up on her head. I recall her face – she looked so pretty. Then she walked behind me to light the gas stove and there was a horrendous explosion. My mother was suddenly on the floor beside me, her clothes and hair on fire. There are no words for what was happening inside me – my whole world blew up. I was totally frantic. I crawled over to her, but I didn't know what to do or what was happening. I just screamed and screamed and screamed. I remember colours of red and white; the ambulance officers, I guess. I recall looking up at a woman in white with red around her shoulders. I remember trying to meet her eyes, but she turned away. Then my mother was taken away.

A man came over to me and put a brown leather bag beside me. He opened it, got something out and then stuck a needle in my left arm. As I was telling Neil, it was as though it was happening right then: I could actually feel the exact spot where the needle went in, and it hurt. Soon afterwards my father appeared, and I started crying loudly. Oh, to see my father's face! Somehow the world was being partly reinstated; the horror of my other half of the world was unbearable. He picked me up and hit me. I stopped screaming. I guess that's what he intended. Somehow he had to stop this hysterical child. But the repercussions were enormous, far more than I could possibly know. He put me in my cot, and that's all I remember.

I sat in my chair, exhausted. An hour and a half had passed and yet it could have been years. It was timeless time. I timidly raised my eyes and all I saw was compassion. I know that at some deep level he had just gone through the experience with me, he had been right beside me in the kitchen. I was aware of his voice in the distance throughout, although I couldn't recall his words. After some silence he said 'And no one even held you'. I started to cry again, a different cry of finally finding someone who understood; a cry of letting go. The experience was horrific, but the real horror for me as a child was that no one picked me up and held me. That was the vase in a thousand pieces – that was Humpty Dumpty.

I trusted Neil with unfeelable feelings and unthinkable thoughts and he contained them. He did what hadn't been done before: he created the space that held the little girl, so that she could say how it was and feel the pain. He also helped me see how I reversed everything. As I spoke about the experience he pointed out that all along I kept saying how awful it would have been for my mother, but I continually left myself out and empathised with her. He was able to give me a new perspective – yes, it would have been awful for my mother, but hers were real, outer scars; people could see her pain and do something about it. Yet I was treated as though nothing had happened, as though I had escaped untouched. He gently made me see it from my own perspective and to understand that the unseen trauma was devastating for a child. What was even more damaging was that no one understood or even spoke of it. I began to get a glimpse of how I had created an outer Me that did not match the inner Me. Is that when the black hole took hold?

I hardly remember leaving the building that day or driving home. I crawled into bed and slept and slept.

I talked to James about the memory of the gas stove, which I had recounted to Neil. He listened, but it was as though he didn't really understand the profound impact it had had on my life. It made me wonder what effect my inner hidden self had had on people all along. When therapists began to go beneath the surface, did they pick up my intense anxiety? Is that why they backed off, prescribed drugs and tried to make me more functional? But Neil's calmness and sense of containment made me feel accepted and acceptable, and also gave me a deep sense that since he didn't fear my falling apart, I needn't fear it so much either. Finally I could see what wasn't helpful for me.

Before I had had no yardsticks and believed that I was immune to cure. But through the experiences with Neil in self psychology, I knew there was another way. I also knew I needed to leave James and did so not long afterwards.

It had been almost three years since I'd started therapy with James. Yet it's strange to look back to that time. Very little stands out for me. The main feeling that arises is one of aloneness. His room seemed like a wind tunnel. He sat in a huge high-backed swivel chair next to his desk overlooking a large window with a view of the building next door, and I sat in a leather-like deck chair near the door. He said very little. I mainly recall the sound of his fountain pen scratching on my file. A lot of the time it felt like I was having a conversation with myself. But the most unsettling memories were when I'd be lost in my blackness. I recall a few times lifting myself out of my tears to see him staring out the blank window. Only now can I see there was no emotional connection at all. No relationship. I realise that the absence of memories of this time was not only due to the drugs, it was also the emotional stagnation. My feelings kept running like a tap, but they were never met, never responded to; there was no movement, no resolution to them. They became just ink on lined paper. Nothing happened – inside or out. I left, unaltered from the time I started. The only visible growth was my file and the list of drugs I'd been prescribed. Leaving felt like a very positive step.

A few weeks later I received a letter from my father. I had written to him and told him I'd remembered the gas stove exploding. I wanted to know why no one had talked about it or even told me I was there. As I sat holding the unopened letter, a myriad of feelings flooded through me. A part of me hoped he'd say it never happened, it wasn't true. I think that although I knew that being unable to remember one's childhood is a sign of the pain of the time, I had always wished that I'd had a normal childhood with loving, caring parents. I wanted what I felt everyone else had. Another part of me knew I needed the truth in order to understand myself. That part of me knew the reality of that memory; it knew it couldn't be made up. So I opened the letter cautiously.

It was still a shock to hear my father acknowledge that it had happened just as I'd described. He said he was astounded I could remember back that far. He also told me that I had gone to stay with my grandparents. He couldn't recall exactly how long I was there, but it was over the time my mother was recovering in hospital and then later when she had plastic surgery. He said the damage had been mainly to her arms and face. When I read that, I suddenly got a flash of the painting I did for Anne. It seemed to explain the two images I had of my mother in that one day. A pretty face and then the horrific 'scream'.

From that point on I got a lecture from my father. He told me he didn't think it was at all good for me to go delving into the past. 'You've always thought too much about things,' he said. 'It happened long ago – it's over, just forget it.' He went on to say that the way he handles such things is to just sweep them under the carpet and that there's no point dwelling on them. So, this was my family and how they dealt with pain! Just as the day my father reached out to shake hands with me at the airport I saw that touching had been such a barrier for me, now I saw that forgetting was also a family inheritance. It was with mixed feelings that I put the letter away. The validation was important – I could feel that, but the lecture on forgetting sat uneasily with me. It was quite a while before I could reply to him.

I didn't see any connection at the time between my inner and outer lives. However, as I gained a perspective of that period of time I realised my inner issues were pulling me in a specific direction at work. I was responsible for the psychological services at several hostels, but there was one in particular that claimed most of my attention. This hostel had been a maternity hospital about thirty years previously. It was a large, rambling wooden monster. It was cold and uninviting with clearly delineated spaces, like an army barracks. Very functional. It was an awful place for children to call home. There were about fifty children with moderate to severe handicaps. Several of the children were autistic and I tried to understand them more. There was no doubt from my in-tray bulging with requests for behavioural programs that the autistic children were seen as the most difficult. The staff wanted me to do something about their negative anti-social behaviours. It took me a while to immerse myself in the environment. I moved my office from the safe central office to a spare room in the hostel. I listened to staff and spent as much time as I could with each of the children, just being there, trying to understand them and not recording their behaviours (as staff thought I was). The message from the staff was: 'Find a way to get these kids under control. Stop them from screaming, kicking, biting, hitting, smashing, banging their heads, masturbating, throwing their food, scratching their bodies, and hurting other children and the staff'.

When I first arrived I thought from reading staff requests that the place was filled with monsters, not children. But after observing these 'monsters' I felt sure that if I lived there, I'd be screaming endlessly too. The noise was horrendous. There were no carpets, just bare floorboards with children racing up and down, throwing things; it was a ceaseless din. There were no toys, the 'reasons' for this being that they might injure themselves and also that they didn't know how to care for toys. These children were to sit and have a quiet breakfast, then quietly sit in front of the television or on the front lawn until they had lunch, and so on.

Most of them went to schools for the handicapped. One of the staff's major complaints was that the autistic children were so aggressive when they got to school. They wanted me to implement a time-out program in the school. I went in early one day and followed the schedule. The children were woken at 5.30 a.m., given showers (which were cold), dressed and given breakfast. At 7 a.m. I was standing out the front with the children, waiting for the school bus. We got to school at 8.40 a.m. By then, even I was ready to kick the driver and bite the principal, who waited sternly in the driveway, expecting the worst. What astounded me was that the school, which I'd often visited, was actually fifteen minutes away from the hostel. But because the driver had to pick up children from all around the city, and this was closest to the depot, they set off at 7 a.m. These were autistic children who couldn't handle many stimuli, who needed things quiet and in order, yet there they were going through city traffic with all the noise and visual input imaginable. They certainly deserved time out, but not in a dark cupboard or corner; not as punishment, but as a reward. I doubt any teacher could have arrived with their sanity intact after that ordeal. Once I'd seen the impact of this schedule on the children, I decided to order a bunch of taxi vouchers from head office. I told the staff that the autistic children were to go to school by taxi from now on. That meant they could sleep in almost an extra two hours, and then have a quiet, short ride to school. Their behaviour changed dramatically. I had no further requests for time-out programming for them.

I found it hard to believe that no one had bothered trying to put themselves in the shoes of these kids. From then on, staff were really on my side. I think initially they thought I was pretty weird not doing behaviour programs; not stopping the violence and the hurt. Soon they, like me, began to see these reactions as understandable given the conditions. They saw that they too would scream, kick, yell and carry on at living in such a dump.

Our next step was to develop proposals to the government to establish group homes – real homes with four or five children and two house-parents. We put an enormous amount of time and effort into these and after a year or so we, too, had the experience of banging our heads against brick walls. The view was always the same: this hostel was to stay. That came from the top, so we felt pretty defeated. Then one day I was having coffee with the hostel supervisor, who was saying how derelict the place was, and how several years ago the fire inspector had reported it unsafe. I jumped up – that was it. Safety – a basic human right; Maslow's first hierarchy of needs! My dilemma was that I knew the authorities would ignore further information on safety if they had ignored the inspector's report, and yet for me to go outside the system could threaten my job and that of the supervisor. It was a ruling that one could not speak publicly about internal government matters. The next morning I worked from home, so to speak. I made some anonymous phone calls to newspapers and also to the fire department. A few weeks later I was looking through the local newspaper and came across an article on the hostel with the heading 'Children's Hostel – Fire Trap'. Something was happening!

I gave a lot of my attention to the other hostels until things quietened down. Then one day there was a message for the hostel supervisor and me from 'on high'. Could we please present our proposal including cost estimates for group homes?

That was September third. On December first I had the absolute pleasure of entering a beautiful five-bedroom home with new, bright furniture and lots of toys, plus a cosy garden and swimming pool. It was so quiet and the children were a delight to watch. This was the first home, and many more were to follow. Self psychology was teaching me so much about understanding children.

CHAPTER 7

Fire and irises

I was in the basement of my childhood home. It was completely dark. There was a man with me hammering nails into a wooden pole that supported the house. I heard footsteps on the stairs and thought it was a man coming to harm me. I went to grab the hammer to attack the man, but the man with the hammer said 'No – he won't hurt you'. He said 'It's important just to keep hammering – it's the sound of the tapping that's important'. The man coming down the stairs walked over to me. He was dressed in black leather and initially looked threatening, but as he got close, I saw he was such a beautiful man. His face was filled with compassion. He said to me 'You must understand the darkness, you must understand the black hole, you need to know the gravedigger's book'. Then he turned around suddenly and left. I ran after him up the basement stairs. I raced through the house. All the lights were on and it seemed really lovely. I ran onto the front porch and he was gone. I looked across the street and saw my father and a group of men standing in a circle. In the centre of them was a pile of wood, like you have for a camp fire. It was unlit. The men were chanting something I didn't understand. Then the wood caught on fire by itself. Out of the fire burst a huge bouquet of irises.

That dream had so much power and energy, it literally knocked me out of bed. No other dream has ever come close to it in the physical and psychological impact it had on me. I was forty years old when I had that dream. Since then I've tried to understand it in different ways and at different levels. Each time I learn more. I had an intuition that embedded in the dream was the essence of my life. It contained my story, hidden for the first forty years. It also seemed to hold the keys to the second half of my life. The dream told of my liberation from the basement, the darkness, and the black hole of my childhood. Although my journals still spoke of the emptiness and darkness I knew so well, there were times when I sensed the inner flowers.

Externally my focus at home turned to gardening. It gave me joy to plant flowers and trees. I didn't really see the growth then; that was taking place both in my garden and in myself. I'm aware that it was truly a time of tilling the soil and planting the seeds. They'd take a lot of nurturing, but it was, I believe, the beginning of my life. It's as if those seeds had been left dormant for forty years, waiting for rich earth, water, sunshine and, of course, the gardener.

Around that time I gave Neil a gift to take back with him after one of his visits. It was something I'd had for years and wanted him to keep. It felt like a part of me went with him. It made me feel that the sense of disconnection and abandonment on his departure was not quite so final. Maybe it was to ensure that even if I couldn't remember the bond in his absence, he might remember me. My gift was like a paperweight of egg-shaped, thick glass with a blue flower in the centre. He was very accepting and appreciative, and commented that there seemed to be a flower wanting to emerge in me.

My dreams began to have a depth and a richness to them. They all weren't inspiring and positive, but they were a beginning.

I was walking up the steps with Ray, a colleague of Neil's. He looked very tired and haggard. We were going into Neil's office, where he and Neil worked together. All three of us, as clinicians, were trying to help a baby, who was lying on Neil's desk. I knew the baby was me. As I walked in with Ray he said 'I've assessed this baby for the past twenty-two hours. I've done every assessment I know and I can't find anything wrong with her'. He seemed very despondent. Neil looked at Ray, hoping he'd found something, and then said 'This baby had been taken away from her parents because someone reported them for neglecting and abusing the baby'. We were all trying to find some concrete evidence to ensure the baby was not returned to her parents. Neil said 'Well, we can't find any evidence. The baby is okay. There's nothing wrong. Today the judge will make a decision as to whether she will be left with us or returned'. He looked very worried that the baby would be taken away. He then said 'There's just something we can't see. Something is eluding us about the parents' treatment of this baby. I believe it has something to do with suffocation or strangulation. But she must not be returned to her parents – she would be in great danger'.

I found it quite distressing, particularly seeing myself as a baby. She looked sad and forlorn. I wondered what he meant about suffocation. In past dreams similar to this, the baby had been either dead or severely handicapped. In this dream, the baby at least seemed as if she had a chance and there was also a change in emphasis. Previously the baby was damaged irreparably, but here they were saying there was nothing wrong with her – it was only the way she had been treated. I trusted it signalled movement and growth.

I wonder how much of our outer life is a reflection of our inner life? Over the years of working for the health department, I'd gone from working in the multi-handicapped area to working with autistic and severely handicapped children. Now I was transferred to the pre-school early intervention team working with handicapped children from birth to the age of five and their families. Our aim was to give these children every chance to reach their full potential. We were fairly successful in getting them into regular schools by the age of six. The strengths of these babies and infants usually outweighed their handicaps. Perhaps most significantly, these children were all wanted by their families, whereas all the others I had worked with had been abandoned and lived in institutions. Maybe that was it – these babies all had a real home, a real family. I didn't know precisely what it meant, but I enjoyed the shift in perspective.

Throughout this time I was also seeing more and more clients privately. Since I had specialised in my research on maternal grief, paediatricians were referring to me many women whose babies had died. I was becoming more visible professionally. I began presenting papers at conferences, conducting seminars and running training courses for doctors, nurses and social workers. I was also on the professional advisory committee of a community support group for women and their families who had suffered the death of a baby. A maternity hospital had appointed me to a board that had been established to address a wide variety of issues related to the care of bereaved women. My interest in and dedication to the area of maternal grief developed quite a momentum. I had never before had the experience of being so enthusiastic about anything.

I also became politically involved, lobbying for a project to initiate wide-ranging changes in the health system for bereaved women to be understood and to receive appropriate services. I put in several submissions to the government and health department, and lobbied for the project for many months, but to no avail.

Perhaps it was going through that experience that provided me with the determination to write my first book – on maternal bereavement. It took me about a year to complete. I'd wake up every morning at about two or three o'clock, write until seven, and then get ready for the normal working day. I suppose this was my first taste of passion. Nothing could stand in the way of my writing. On completion I sent it off to many publishers and received multiple forms of rejections varying only in their degree of politeness.

My growing sense of belief in myself inspired me to send it to a publishing agent. Within weeks I had a contract for *Loss of a Baby*. A year later it was out in print, and that experience remains a highlight of my professional life. Little did I know the book was to lead me even more out of my shell.

Over time, my visibility on this issue continued to increase. In writing my book I gained some self-confidence, at least in relation to my work. A few months after completing it, I had a dream that I resigned from work. The feeling of the dream was so light and joyful I began to realise how much I felt mismatched with my work. In my heart of hearts I really wanted to become a therapist. The following day I wrote a letter of resignation. I felt shaky, but I knew it was the right decision. I wasn't sure what I was going to do afterwards, but that problem was solved within the week after I left work. Ruth rang me to say she'd decided to leave her government job and was going to start a private practice. She wondered if I'd be interested in joining her. We started our practice in a lovely little house imbued with peace and tranquillity.

Initially I worked part time, until my practice built up. I was wondering what to do with my new freedom when I saw an advertisement for painting classes at the local art centre. Thus began my other form of expression. When I opened my tubes of oil paints I was totally seduced by the smell of the paints, the vividness of the colours, the texture of the oils. When I was painting I was transported to a high that surpassed anything I'd ever known.

Our first task was to do a painting of the art centre. It was an enormous, complicated building. I wandered around for ages trying to get a perspective to begin with, and was overwhelmed. Eventually I felt a strong pull to do one window. When it was completed, I was more than satisfied with it. I loved the colours, the light, the shades, the reflections in the glass, the tree that caressed the window. Yet, how scary it was for me to show or acknowledge my creations. The art teacher was quite pleased with my work, but somehow that didn't sink in. I really wanted to get it framed but the agony I went through in getting it in the door to the framers was unbelievable. I sat in my car terrified. I was afraid that if I took it in, they'd laugh and say 'You've got to be kidding: you're not going to waste your money framing *that*, are you?' Finally, I got myself in the door holding the painting towards me, so no one could see it. Then I had to put it on the counter so we could look at the choice of frame. It was a big step. There were no attacks, no humiliation. As I turned to leave, he said 'If it's ready before you come to pick it up, do you mind if I put it in the window?' 'No, that's fine,' I said, and I felt a smile come from deep within. I've done quite a few paintings since that time. Each entry into the framing shop challenged my fears and they gradually began to lose their power. It did highlight for me though what a negative self-concept lay inside.

Whatever I did, I felt it wasn't good enough. That applied not just to what I did but to who I was. One of the most disorienting experiences I ever had was at the hairdressers'. My hairdresser was drying my hair and I was drifting off looking in the mirrors in the salon. Since the room was oval and the mirrors were not opposite each other the images were askew. It was quite unnerving. I was looking at the reflections of the six or eight women around the room, wishing I had that one's face, or this one's hair. Then I glanced over and saw a woman's reflection and thought to myself: why can't I look like her? I took another look and gave a startled jump. The woman I saw was me. I was so sad and shaken afterwards. I had been viewing myself all my life through black glasses I wasn't even conscious I was wearing. Why was I so hard on myself? Did I see myself only through my mother's eyes?

When I was looking at my painting one day I remembered that the art teacher had told us the art centre was originally a prison. My painting was of the window of a cell. That is how I often felt. I'd been in prison all my life and just never knew it. The presence of self psychology in my life had created a window. Now I was beginning to see the world in a new way and there was light entering my darkened cell. Yet I was still well and truly inside the prison walls. I got brief reprieves with each self psychology workshop, but they were only temporary and were confiscated within a week or so. I had a dream at that time which links me more deeply to this sense of imprisonment.

> *I was let out of prison but it was really scary, so I tried to get back in. The guards refused to let me back in. 'You're free,' they said. I didn't know where to go or what to do; all I knew was being in prison.*

My life was a paradox. On the outside it seemed to be blossoming, but the time between workshops was horrendous.

There was no doubt self psychology was affecting me at a depth and in ways I couldn't comprehend. I now worked with all my clients using a self psychology framework and I witnessed their growth and transformation. I could see this form of therapy had a beauty to it that surpassed all others. It seemed simple: to listen to my clients and tap into the feelings beneath their words; to help them see their own selves. To witness them hearing their own inner voice was such a joy. In many cases it was clear that this was their first experience even of being aware there was a self to listen to. It seemed to work very well with bereaved mothers as well: perhaps because they were so vulnerable in their grief the voice did not have as many barriers to break through.

Self psychology was part of my daily life; I was steeped in it. I was involved in an after-hours course in self psychology. My study group held frequent meetings where we discussed self psychology literature and the books by Heinz Kohut, who developed this form of therapy. The essence of what he was saying was so powerful. What moved me most was that his understanding came from listening to his patients, rather than imposing models on them. Unlike other forms of therapy, this one actually evolved from people in pain, people who had not been understood in other models. I rejoiced in a therapist who treated his patients this way in order to relate to their feelings and perspective. There were no rules, about either assessment or intervention. One did not get labelled and there wasn't a prescribed path on which to take the patient. No rush, no vast leaps, no heady interpretations. It was an equal, even-keeled relationship. Each person was seen as unique, with an individual story. By listening you saw they knew not only where they were, but also the path home – they held all the keys. The therapist remained unaware of the specific course of each client's journey. I also appreciated Kohut's belief that the therapist should not evaluate a therapy until it was complete. That, too, seemed wise. Just to be with your client, to try not to pre-guess every move as though you were playing chess. It equalised the power in the relationship. This new way of viewing people and the inner journey never ceased to touch my heart. It was about providing a safe, contained space where a person could become their natural self.

Besides the study groups, we also met in small groups and presented tapes of our sessions with one ongoing client. In addition there were formal monthly meetings where we organised future visiting lecturers and supervisors, and our own training programs. In that time I had been on the executive and was now vice-president and head of the training committee. I cannot look back and say which aspect was having the greatest effect on me. Whatever the combination, the result was that my childhood memories and feelings were continually being invited to surface.

I had so many dreams I couldn't even begin to write them all down. The fragments of memories that would surface were all over the place. Often I'd try to push them down; other times I'd talk to Sophie. My main feeling was of being overwhelmed. It was certainly different from nothing; almost the exact opposite – it was too much. Each time we'd have a workshop, new images and feelings would emerge. This would happen even in the workshops when Neil wasn't there. When he was there to supervise, though, something more happened. It was powerful to hear him supervise someone else and their client. It was that undefinable depth of understanding and compassion for the child. It brought me together and ripped me apart at the same time. I was reassured to see that Sophie and other people in the group were crumbling at times as well.

Each time Neil visited for another training workshop, I could feel the growth of my inner garden. When he left, it continued for a while, but then things would begin to wilt and

I'd be back with the 'nothing', the desert. I seemed like two different people – total opposites. When Neil visited I felt together, happy, enthusiastic, and life was filled with colour and vitality. When he left, the blackness began its gradual re-entry. It was terrifying at times. I'd often wake, startled, and feel the presence of this black amorphous mass. Sometimes when I'd be wandering around the house, I'd feel as though there was this death figure right behind me. I recall one morning stopping suddenly in the kitchen and turning around to confront it, but there was nothing – no one. What was happening to me?

It was summertime and Neil wouldn't be returning for four or five months. I tried hard to distract myself, but it was useless. My body began to develop other symptoms. I developed a nervous rash and spent many nights scratching, unable to sleep. There was a battle going on inside of me. There were two dreams in particular that really distressed me:

> *I was running away from my mother. I was my present age. As I ran away, she flashed a whip that caught me around the waist and pulled me back. The whip was a rattlesnake, so I was not only caught and dragged back, but poisoned. My mother said 'No matter how far away you get from me, I'll find you and bring you back'.*

The other dream I had was about a law that had been passed that declared anything that went wrong or anything bad that happened within a hundred-kilometre radius was my fault.

I was so tired of this relentless inner battle. I'd be fine for a while, then something would happen and I'd be back in the hole. The dream that it was all my fault was so real. I felt this badness inside me, like a black mark that could never be erased and that would show everyone that I was basically bad. I began to wonder if anything could be done. Did I simply have to live like this? Was there no real escape? In my dark moments it seemed that I would have to either accept the way I really was and throw myself on a junk heap, or live a deadened, token life.

On Neil's previous visit I had given him one of my paintings. Words were still difficult, but painting seemed to convey what was happening for me. It was of a brightly coloured kite flying over the ocean. The string from the kite came down to the shore and across the beach. My sense was that there were two people there – myself and Neil – who were holding it. I painted a similar one for myself. That is how I felt when he was there, but his departure heralded a crash and I didn't know how to get the kite up into the wind again on my own. I was trying hard to knit these experiences of the little oases together to make myself 'better', but I just couldn't. Neil's presence provided the glue that mended the pink vase completely, but he took the glue with him and I didn't have the formula. The image I had was of a little girl working hard trying to build a bridge between California (where I was) and New York (where Neil was). She was out in the middle of the desert and the bridge was almost half completed, but she was so tired and exhausted, she just threw down her tools and lay down. She knew she couldn't do it on her own.

Sophie was the one person who really knew about the darkness and the little girl's struggles. Eventually she asked 'Why don't you ring Neil and talk to him, maybe even arrange to go over and have some sessions with him?' I thought she was speaking another language. It seemed inconceivable to ring Neil, as though when he was gone, he just disappeared. Yet he'd said years previously that if I wanted to ring him, that was fine. Why couldn't I hear or remember that? I rang first thing in the morning and told him I wasn't coping. I asked if I could come for a week and have a session each day. He said 'Yes!'

I went to New York for two weeks to attend a conference and to see Neil in the second week. I felt the bridge come together as I traversed the country. As I walked to Neil's office for my first appointment, I could sense my nervousness. In fact, I felt as though I needed to dress up just to go there. I must have expected something palatial and grand because as I approached his place, I almost thought I'd got the wrong street. There was a fence with a gate, and a garden with plants and trees. I went to the waiting room, sat down, and closed my eyes to catch my breath and calm down. I gradually opened them and looked around. What an ordinary office! Just regular chairs and a desk, a computer, a fax machine and a photocopier.

Neil came in and greeted me, showing me the way down the hall to his room. Then he followed me. He told me to sit wherever I liked and waited until I'd chosen a place before he sat down. He didn't seem to have a chair that was his. I sat there looking around astounded by how plain and ordinary it was. There were a two-seater black leather couch, two black leather chairs, and an old brown couch at one end with a brown blanket on it. At the other end was a cabinet with different objects on it. I saw my flower and began to cry. He hadn't forgotten. He did have a space for it. That meant so much to me. It was a long time before I spoke, for I was still taking in the ordinariness and readjusting my fantasy. It felt good. Neil seemed more ordinary too, dressed casually in shirt and trousers. I realised it hadn't been necessary to dress up. It was less than I expected, but instead of being disappointed I was relieved.

All these sessions seemed to centre on the feeling I had about everything being my fault. The memory of the gas stove still haunted me. Some awful guilt had seeped into all the cells of my body. I'd been carrying an enormous burden and had been punishing myself all my life. How could it have been my fault?

I started to remember my mother saying 'If it weren't for you I'd be happy. If it weren't for you I'd be pretty. If it weren't for you I could play the piano. If it weren't for you I wouldn't be in this marriage – I'd be free'. I hated remembering. I didn't know why she used to say all these things to me, but it seemed that she blamed me for the accident. I knew she'd played the piano, even though I'd never seen her touch it. She said her fingers were too scarred to play. I recalled her showing me a newspaper cutting from the time when she was a young girl and had won a medal for playing the piano. All these memories were mixed up. Sometimes, she'd be telling me the story and it was all okay. Other times she would fly into this blind rage about everything being my fault. I recalled that when I visited my grandparents as a child, I'd sometimes sit and play the piano. If just Auntie were there, Auntie would lift the lid and play something for me. At other times, when my mother was there, my mother would slap my hands if I touched the piano. As I spoke about these memories I began to feel pain in my hands. I didn't know what was happening. I felt I should cut them off, like I'd done something so terrible. Through my tears, Neil's voice reached me. 'It must be hard to know those hands can create beauty.' How that went straight to my heart. Beauty? My hands? Could I start to allow that into the depths of me?

Each day I'd go back to the hotel and sleep for hours and hours. Then I'd wake with more memories. They seemed unrelenting. It all felt overwhelming. Too many secrets, too many unanswered questions, too many unopened doors. The inner turmoil was reflected in a dream:

> *I am in the centre of a tension bridge. It's very high above a river. I'm stuck in the middle. Buses go in both directions to each side. I go to a bus, but find I've been robbed. Someone has stolen my purse. I have no money and no identification. The bus driver won't let me on until I pay or until I can identify myself. But I can't even remember who I am. I have amnesia. I also don't know which side of the bridge I'm heading for or where I'm going. The bus driver takes off and I'm stuck there in the middle. I look over the side into the river and wonder what I'll do.*

This dream was similar to my image of the little girl desperately trying to build a bridge across the country to maintain the connection to Neil. He said he felt that I'd shown great courage over the past four years dealing with all this on my own and also that it took courage to get here. The little girl in me felt proud that she'd actually got here, even if there was still the bridge to be built inside. She now had hope.

On the last day I noticed my painting of the kite on his wall for everyone to see. He wasn't ashamed of it. He hadn't discarded it or put it away in a cupboard somewhere. I was moved to see it, and said so in the session. 'It's beautiful,' he said. 'I see it every time I walk into my room and every time I leave.' I was overcome with feelings. I said it felt like it had been such a struggle; that it had taken me four years to get here and I felt exhausted and battle-weary. 'Yes,' he said, 'and yet you can see that a part of you was already here.' At that moment I knew I wanted to move to New York and have therapy with him. He agreed.

At the end of the session Neil picked up the two rocks I'd brought along. It had been one rock that had been cut in half so that the two pieces were a mirror reflection of each other. Inside the hardened lava were different shades of pink crystals in the most delightful patterns imaginable. He held them both in his hands and said 'If it hadn't split open you would never know what beauty lay inside, and it came out of fire'. Why hadn't I seen all that in this symbol I'd handed him? Perhaps inside of me wasn't just emptiness. I felt like one of those seeds in the forest with such a hard outer shell that it takes a fire for them to germinate or for the inner seed to blossom. Therapy is like a lifegiving fire, I thought.

It took me a year to finally get back to New York. Whatever obstacles could have arisen did arise, and at times I despaired that I would never get to the other side of the country.

Three months before I was to leave, I dreamt I was a child in the primary school I used to attend:

> *All the rules were crazy. I asked why there were these rules and one of the teachers said that the principal (who was my mother) needed to change and understand children. Then everything else will change, for she sets the rules.*

About three weeks later I dreamt:

> *I was standing in a group of hundreds of people. A voice said 'You have to take care of the needs of all these people before you provide for your own needs'. I felt so forlorn and downhearted. I'll never be able to give enough to them all, I thought, so I'll never ever get what I need. Then another voice said 'Neil has the power to change the rules'.*

I knew these dreams were telling me the truth. Deep inside I realised I couldn't live under this tyranny much longer and no one else had ever come as close to reaching me before. To not go on would be death; I knew it was a life-or-death decision. I finally rang Neil and made the specific arrangements for starting. It was settled.

There were three other dreams that were significant for me at this time. I had never had repetitive dreams before so it felt that the three repetitions meant I needed to listen. There were slight variations in each which enhanced the impact.

> *There was a knock on my front door. When I opened it Neil was there. He handed me a tray with a book on it. I looked at the title and it said 'Fire and Irises'.*

Then about five or six months later I dreamt:

> *There was a knock at the door. When I opened it, Neil was there with a tray, and on the tray was the book* Fire and Irises *and beside it was a big bouquet of irises.*

In a couple of months – as though my subconscious wasn't sure I'd got the message – I dreamt:

> *There was a knock at my door. I opened it and there was Neil and an Indian woman dressed in an orange sari. They came in and guided me to my desk and sat me down. Neil put in front of me a tray on which were a typewriter and a bouquet of irises. The woman put the irises in a vase. Neil put the book,* Fire and Irises *(with my name, as the author) beside the typewriter. I looked up and said 'No, I can't write another book – I've just finished one. I'm too exhausted. No, I don't want to'. Then Neil said 'Don't worry, it's already been written, you just have to put it on paper'.*

CHAPTER 8

The
lost child

Although I was feeling tired and depleted on arrival in New York, it seemed that my inner self couldn't be more delighted at being there, as was reflected in a dream I had at the time:

> I got into the front of a two-seater plane. The teacher, a man, was sitting in the back. I said 'I never thought of flying before, but it looks like fun'. He said 'Just start it up and take off.' So I did. We flew over purple tulips and then over the streets of a city filled with water like swimming pools, where children played.

I had rented my house in California and organised a delightful apartment to live in. I found the right school for Michael and we began settling into our new lives.

Along with my excitement I was surprised to become aware of the ambivalence that emerged in my first few weeks of therapy. It was no wonder I'd chosen the two-seater couch to sit on during therapy sessions. It felt like there were two Me's present. One Me felt very positive and enthusiastic about entering my inner world; the other was absolutely, totally and utterly terrified. My dreams were filled with scenes of being chased by authorities as well as of poisonous rattlesnakes. Having begun therapy, it became apparent it was not just the bond with my Auntie that was emerging, but also the bond with my mother. I'd never have guessed that the therapy I'd longed for would become so unsettling.

Doing therapy three times a week was far more demanding than I had ever expected. It felt like constant processing. The day before a session, issues would arise that needed a voice. Then there was the session itself which brought up new issues and new links in the chain. I'd write some of them down. It seemed I'd turn around and there would be another session. It felt like I was running a marathon. There was so much coming up inside that there never seemed enough time in the sessions. At the end I'd feel totally wrung out.

The turning point came one day as I sat with my journal and dream book beside me. I picked up my dream book and flipped back to the point I'd reached in the last session, which was a dream from over a month previously. For some reason I'd decided to keep my dreams in order. Yet there was also a deep sense of frustration that I'd never catch up, because I was recalling more and more dreams each night. It seemed like the story of my life – always so much to do, so much backlog, so much past that there was no room for the present. A part of me insisted I get my dreams and therapy 'right'.

This need to keep things in order was a way of warding off the underlying terror. It was one thing to know I'd explore the bond with my Auntie, but to sense the arising issues about my mother was frightening. I had one foot inside the door and one outside, just in case I needed to run. I could see it was one thing to commence therapy but quite another to hand yourself over to the process. I was scared of what I might find. Eventually I understood that the real dilemma for me was commitment. Did I really want to fully enter the space? It was something I needed to think about. The next twenty-four hours felt like hell, like the inner army, navy and airforce had been activated to stop the emerging commitment.

As I walked to the session the next day, I felt the inner 'Yes'. Once I was clear that I wanted to bring all of me into the space, to commit myself to the inner journey, I felt a huge sense of relief. However, this relief was followed that night by a most distressing dream that showed the huge step I'd taken and the underlying terror in letting go and trusting:

> *I was being attacked; I can't remember the pictures, only the bodily feelings. It was like I was being strangled, like I couldn't breathe. The necklaces around my neck were being pulled tight as though someone was trying to murder me.*
>
> *Suddenly I was looking out over the ocean – everything was okay. Then without warning I saw a huge tidal wave coming towards the shore. I stepped back and there was a canal with huge brick walls on each side. On the wall was a strong iron bar. I stood beside it and then heard a voice saying 'Hold on tight to the iron bar and don't worry, it will be all right.' So I held on and the tidal wave dissipated and flowed up the canal.*

The experience of putting all of me in the space brought up a tidal wave of fears. Initially I was disheartened by the presence of another tidal-wave dream, since the last one seemed to signal to my therapist that she could no longer help me and that I required drugs. But this dream spoke of a new way of dealing with my fears, a new therapy that connected me to a real anchor, which meant I wouldn't be overcome by the subconscious. In trusting and handing myself over, it felt like the process of therapy could begin to find an inner self to hand back.

Visibility and hiding were the other themes that emerged at this time. The following dream conveyed the hiding experience most vividly:

> *I was under a bush at night in front of my house, which was a beautiful pink colonial home. I was watching this white stallion running free. I said to Neil (who seemed to be there, although I couldn't see him): 'If the authorities find out that the white stallion belongs to me they'll take*

it away', So I made a bowl of vine leaves and filled it with
water so the stallion could be taken care of until I owned
it for real.

That dream triggered deep pain about my invisibility. Shortly
afterwards, I wrote in my journal:

I feel lost
I can't find the words
I feel the real me shut down, went underground at eighteen
    months
For forty years I've been hiding
Now it feels like the light and the bushel have equal energy
Either the real me comes out
And the bushel burns
Or the bushel hardens
And the light and vitality dies
I just can't bear the tension much longer
Why can't I just be me?
After forty years, couldn't I just come out?
Just be?
It is the fear that freezes me
I'm so frightened to be myself
For me
To be visible
Is death
The contrast between who I've been taught I am
And who I am
Is enormous
It's like a leap to the other side of the bridge.

I've been taught:
I'm ugly
I'm stupid
I'm uncoordinated
I'm not feminine
I'm untalented
I can't paint

I can't write
I'm not musical
I'm nothing
Unwanted, unloved, unlovable
All of me has had to be denied
To avoid my mother's wrath
If I showed any of my inner or outer beauty
It reminded her of what she lost
And I was punished
Every time I got something
She took it away
The only way I've been able to create
Is to pretend it wasn't me who did it
But most of the time I live in my own world
I feel so lonely
Couldn't I just come out?
Say what I think?
Express what I feel?
When can I have my life back?
What needs to be done
To claim my natural inheritance?
I want to be me.

Around the time I wrote this, I recalled telling Neil about a print I had at home called 'The Lost Child'. The child was in the middle of a forest with her head down, looking forlorn. He helped me see that for me to know I was a *lost* child meant there had to be an experience of 'home' deep inside. That picture, and his reassurance that there was a home inside me, became an anchor that would enable me to fly.

The idea of 'home' took me back to memories of the summer holidays I spent at my grandparents' as a child. I remembered sitting on my Auntie's lap in her rocking chair on the front porch. As the rocker creaked back and forth she told me stories or sang songs, or we'd just be still.

I also remembered the lemonade we made together. It sat in a jug with two matching glasses on a table next to us. I could almost taste it. Then the colours began to return. They came with such vividness: the vine leaves that grew around the porch, and the soft filtered light. Oh yes, and the smell of lilacs – it was right there in the room. It seemed that when I sank into the memories, I relaxed into my Auntie's arms.

I then remembered a dream I'd had the night before:

> *I was in a big room. Someone was trying to kill me. I ran from one place to another until I got to Sue's house. She asked me for some help to do with her femininity. I gave her a box of pine cones and said for her to burn them as a sacrifice, but then I realised there needed to be gold in the sacrifice. I thought of the five gold objects I'd been carrying around with me all my life – I'd never known what they were for. I then realised they were five gold nibs for the pen my grandfather had given me. But I'd thrown them in the rubbish when I was being chased. I went back to look for them.*

I awoke feeling anxious about finding them again.

When I talked about this dream in therapy, it was the pen nibs that grabbed my attention first. They seemed connected to my book *Loss of a Baby*. I began to see that unless my childhood had been the way it was, I couldn't have written my book. It was like turning grief into gold. It seemed that these gold objects were the most precious things I owned. Then Neil asked who had treated me as though I were precious. 'My Auntie and grandfather,' I answered. Yes, the pen my grandfather gave me was precious to him and he gave it to me. Neil suggested that the pen nibs had some other significance: perhaps there were some precious things I wanted to say, perhaps there was a wish to write the words. It seemed it all had to do with feeling valuable and that what I had to say was worthwhile. At home I didn't feel precious at all – I felt just like rubbish. The two Me's and the contrasts of the two homes were to be in my dreams a long time. Was I precious or was I rubbish?

The next important part of my dream was about the woman named Sue. She was someone I'd known years ago. She had always struck me as sexy, but she never seemed to be feminine. In talking about her, I came to understand more about what being feminine meant. The pine cones helped link me to my own personal understanding. I realised I felt feminine just by being natural. It then occurred to me that I'd stopped wearing my jewellery. It was almost as though I just didn't need the external silver and gold. That's what my dream was telling me: be precious on the inside, be natural – be who I am. This sense of naturalness took me back again to my Auntie. Even in her eighties she was the most beautiful woman I've ever known in my life. It was her presence. I began to see that although I didn't have a model of young femininity, it could emerge from the inside out. I didn't have to do anything. I just needed to be myself.

For that to have happened I realised how crucial my commitment to therapy was. That step established a home base in which I could grow. I felt solid and peaceful inside. I realised how painful the past month had been. I knew I'd been through a sort of hell, doing battle with my inner bonds, and with trust and mistrust, love and hate.

The foundation of a home was cemented. I learned that trust is the most crucial issue in therapy. When a baby is born, trust, safety and security must all be provided. To really find the inner lost child one cannot be both the guard and the search party. Nothing could evolve until I'd totally let go. Yet I will never forget what a risk I felt I was taking. The core issue was whether I could trust Neil with all of me – the good, the bad, the parts I had disowned and disavowed for over forty years. If he really saw all of me, perhaps he wouldn't like me. The inner question was 'Will he go away?' If I started to be who I am, what would happen? Did I have to be good and nice and figure out what to do in this space and not make a mistake? At a deeper level there was a more frightening unspeakable question: 'Will he die?' Trusting Neil intensified the powerful connection with my Auntie. I knew she saw me and loved me just for who I was, but because of the circumstances I never got enough to feel the ground under my feet. It was always a ripping and tearing of the heart, a coming together and a going apart. This commitment to therapy revived these experiences of love and separation. It also linked me to the death of my Auntie. I never had the chance to grow up, to say goodbye and go into the world naturally. It all seemed too painful.

The symbol of the tulips that emerged in my dream about flying in the two-seater plane reappeared in another dream that helped me to understand my journey ahead:

I was wandering around a school where there were lots of objects – objects that helped people remember the bond of love. There were all sorts of things like cups, teddy bears, flowers, tulips. There were hundreds of things that in themselves didn't seem special, but that helped take people back to the memory of being loved for who they are. I was there with other children who had lost something and were trying to find it so they could finish their schooling. We wandered through several rooms. The real difficulty was that none of us could say in words what we really felt was missing, all we knew was that something was missing. We kept going from room to room choosing objects, and as we walked down the hall there were kids dancing in the hallway. It was a very loving, carefree school.

My dream seemed to be telling me that symbols would lead me back to the long-forgotten memories of love. I was trying to find my way through these wordless uncharted waters. This time I had chosen the right school and my therapist was there as an anchor so I could wander at ease. What made it even more vivid for me was that one day soon after the dream I saw some purple silk tulips in a shop. I bought four of them, and put them in a vase on my window in front of my desk. They seemed to be there to remind me of the bond. I needed to remember and trust. I also realised that they were silk flowers that wouldn't die. These flowers were everlasting and indestructible.

I wrote in my journal in large letters: YOU NEED TO FEEL SPECIAL AND HELD, BEFORE YOU CAN FEEL ORDINARY AND HOLD YOURSELF. The bridge needed to be built before I could use it to travel more distant, unknown lands.

CHAPTER 9

Speaking my own truth

What enthrals me about doing therapy in self psychology is how it allows issues simply to unfold. From my experiences in other forms of therapy, the therapist always had questions – questions connected to the last session, questions connected to outer events in my life, questions connected to times in the past. Always questions. On some level this was reassuring. If someone is asking you leading questions you assume they must lead somewhere. I recall that feeling of security derived from this verbal direction. But because they are all logical, linear, left-brained pieces of information, they lead absolutely nowhere. There is no opportunity for the true self to emerge in a space brimful of question-and-answer dialogue. I can see how this makes things 'comfortable' for the therapist and the client. It appears that something is being done, something is being explored, someone knows where to go and someone can follow. If it was only that simple, therapy would be fast and efficient. But it is suffocation by words.

The self psychological space is vastly different. My sessions never started with a question; in fact it was always me that began. There was no direction, no lead-in, no prompts from my therapist. This was also reflected in the way he always came to the waiting room and held the door open to the hallway and then followed me. I led the way. That's how it needs to be. Self psychology isn't 'comfortable', isn't easy, isn't clear-cut; it isn't anything but an open, safe space where I can say whatever is inside me at the time. Once I'd really decided to trust in that space there was a natural flow. Perhaps the most important thing I learned in therapy was to trust my own process, my own way and my own expression. They've never let me down.

About two months into therapy I talked about the times in my life when the bond of love had been broken. For the first time I realised how many separations and losses there had been that I hadn't ever really acknowledged. There were separations of one form or another, at least every two years, as well as a continual breaking and reconnecting of the main bond in my life with my Auntie. This realisation was to lead me into darkness, not so much through the telling of my story but through the exploration of my reactions to the story I was telling.

I started by explaining that my mother had told me I was a very difficult and sick baby, so my Auntie came to live with us and cared for me for the first year while my mother went back to work. Then my Auntie left and went back to my grandparents. After the accident with the gas stove I stayed with my grandparents and Auntie until my mother had recovered. I then went back to my parents, and my Auntie came to help with me until I was three-and-a-half or four years old. My mother then told her to go, after they'd had an argument.

As I was describing this, Neil, who had been sitting forward in his chair, leaned back. It was such a simple, ordinary thing for him to do, but inside something snapped and I became very distraught. We tried to understand what had happened, but all I could say was 'I don't know'. I felt heavy inside and sad. I also sensed that this blackness was going to get worse. I told Neil I wished I had a happier story to tell. He reassured me that it was my story, that I needed to tell it, and that whatever it was I had to go through, we'd share it together. It had been too much for me to deal with on my own. It was healing to have him say he'd be there.

When Neil had moved back in his chair, I'd seen this as a sign that he wasn't interested or that I wasn't good enough. Deep down I felt that if I told him the rest of my story, he'd go away. My mind had been going a million miles an hour trying to work out what I'd done wrong that had caused him to move away. I feared that if I didn't make my story better, I'd break this bond, which felt so fragile. I couldn't stand another loss.

My misinterpretation opened pathways that had been blocked for a lifetime. No questions could have led me to these memories and insights; the process always shows the way. The next day I gained a deeper understanding of my distress at his moving back in his chair. About halfway through the session I mentioned that I'd had more nightmares about suffocation and attack, and recalled the dream about the tidal wave being twenty-five feet high. There was the link – twenty-five. I remembered I was twenty-five when I saw the first psychiatrist. I knew that I had needed help then, but all I was offered was hospital and sodium pentathol.

With almost every entry I'd made into therapy, the result was the same. I ended up on drugs. I was just questioned then put back to sleep. I finally believed it was my fault because I was overwhelming. Whatever this blackness was, it was just too much. All the therapists moved away from me in one form or another. Nobody, till now, was able to handle my pain. The message was 'just don't talk about it'. It was only when I started training in self psychology that I came off antidepressants for good. Whenever I hit a low or a tidal wave, the first response had been to medicate so I would forget the underlying pain. My dreams of suffocation became understandable. My deepest fear was that as I told my story it would be blocked, as it had been in the past; my words would be stifled. I had never really had a chance to talk about how I felt and how the world felt for me. No one had listened. I remembered how difficult it was being an only child. There was no other person to share my reality.

Not long afterwards, more memories started to break through. They stood in front of me; I had to face them. I remembered that it wasn't just the hall closet my mother put me in. She used to lock me in the basement in the dark. My whole body shook in uncontrollable spasms as I said it. The pain of bringing these memories to consciousness was horrendous. I was torn – half of me had to say it and the other half had to stop me.

The nothingness. You can't see. There's nothing there. It was terrifying. No power. I never knew what the punishment was for. The rules changed all the time. I had to tell my mother that whatever I had done wrong (which on any other day would have been okay) I'd never do again. I'd have to tell her I loved her, before she let me out. I had to condone her abuse, or I'd stay there. Madness.

The importance of my dream of the abused baby being assessed and how there was nothing wrong with her apart from the way she'd been treated, became clearer to me. The results weren't physical, they didn't show on the outside. Nobody knew. I couldn't speak about it. I didn't even remember it. It felt like all the therapists along the way didn't want to look at the inner cellar, because they could sense too much darkness. It made me feel that I caused people pain and that the only answer was to be nice and to have a nicer story. If I had had to go through it surely someone could have listened. Now I was finally somewhere where I could speak.

The entry into the darkness had been made, without my having any idea of what it meant or what lay ahead. A step at a time. That night I couldn't stay still, my anxiety was so great. I was awake half the night trying to soothe myself. The next day I had a strong urge to buy a teddy bear. Although I had several, I needed a big bear for comfort. I went to the teddy bear shop before my session and bought Gus, the biggest teddy I'd seen and excessively huggable. I sat in the waiting room with Gus in the chair beside me. Neil's eyes widened and he smiled. The teddy was there for a very good reason, which I was to find out. He would be the key to understanding my inner blackness.

I told Neil I'd been feeling as anxious as I had when I remembered the gas stove exploding. For the previous three or four nights I had tried to sleep with my light off, which made me realise I always left lights on in my apartment, particularly my bedroom. The darkness had always been unbearable. When I turned them off and woke up, I was stricken with horror. I couldn't move and I felt I was going to be attacked. I had no sense of my own boundaries. I knew there was nothing in the apartment I feared. But that day the anxiety was severe; I could really feel it in my stomach. I felt like I was going to break into pieces and go crazy. I didn't know what was happening or what to ask for or what to do. The prospect of leaving the session that day seemed daunting. I was so terrified, I just kept repeating 'I don't know, I don't know, I don't know'.

Memories of the basement then began to come to me. I always disliked it. Sometimes there were floods in the spring and the sewage would back up, and the basement would get flooded right up the steps. Sometimes rats would float on the water. When my mother put me there without a light, I never knew what to expect. I would sit on the top step, huddling next to the door. Although I had no visual pictures, my whole body contracted and told the story. I began to shake again. 'It must have been cold in the cellar,' Neil said. 'Yes,' I answered. 'Cold and damp.' I remembered the pain in my stomach at the weekend and then I didn't feel anything, as if I in the darkness, I didn't exist. It seemed that from my waist down there was nothing. The shaking got worse; it felt like a pressure cooker inside. All the memories were trying to surface and I couldn't bear to see them.

I picked up the teddy bear and tried to stop shaking. It was then that I realised I'd had my dog with me in the basement. That was it. I held onto him. The parts of my body that would be touching something alive were my chest, stomach and arms. The rest was cut off. My lovely cocker spaniel. The teddy was about the same colour. And past the right size for a little girl, Neil added. The anxiety receded, and I sat back in the chair holding Gus.

It seemed a very long time between sessions. At times I didn't know how I'd survive. My anxiety was so high I felt I'd explode and everything would come crashing down inside. I began my next session describing the night before. I'd wake up three or four times a night; I never allowed myself a deep sleep. I'd wake if I heard any noise at all. I recall one night waking up at about 11 p.m. when I heard a door bang. It was someone coming home next door. Later that night I awoke with a vivid image of being locked in the basement. I started to say the words but my whole body began to shake as though I were having a convulsion. I couldn't stop it. It was like my body had a voice of its own, and I had no control over it.

Eventually I was able to talk about another memory that emerged during the night. I was four or five years old. I was sitting on the floor trying to put together a very big, difficult puzzle. There were hundreds of pieces. I tried hard to listen to the music on the radio to cut off the sound of my parents arguing. My father slammed the door and left. My mother suddenly became angry with me. Everything escalated and I was put in the basement. I understood why it was so dark. If it had been daytime, there would have been some light through the windows. There was only darkness and she'd gone away. It seemed forever. I kept returning to the image of the puzzle. I was left to work out what I'd done wrong. I didn't know why I was in the basement and what I wasn't supposed to do anymore. What was wrong with me?

I don't know how many times this happened or for how long I stayed in the basement, but my whole body felt frozen in terror. I couldn't get out and I couldn't go down. I stayed on the top step. No one was on the other side of the door. I don't know where my mother went or why my father wasn't there. I just fell asleep and when I awoke I listened for the sound of someone coming home, of doors banging. There was the connection. That's why I was always startled by any sound in the night. At the age of forty-four, the terror was still hiding beneath the surface. I hadn't known what it was.

What had surprised me about the anxiety over these days was that I overcame it. Instead of sitting with the anxiety, I did something: I rang a friend, I wrote letters to other friends – I was finding ways to open the door. I couldn't bear sitting still.

Sometimes I played some music and danced. The anxiety dissipated. It was liberating. Movement was the key, both inside and outside. I was beginning to speak and to take action. I didn't have to sit frozen in fear.

These sessions marked the emergence of the real Me. The little girl had found a safe space to tell her story. I can now see how all those childhood experiences have shaped my whole life. In my search for love I'd always tried to fit into what I thought people wanted or liked. It was such a waste. So many years of trying not to be myself; so much energy spent trying to deny my pain, my story. I didn't know who I was, nor could anyone else know. I was a mirror for others, and I shattered as easily. But now I began to see in the dark and although what I saw was agonising, it certainly wasn't nothing. I was beginning to know my own self and to claim my history.

Following these sessions I became despondent and angry about the previous therapies that never came close to touching the core issues. It seemed that many therapists in the past repeated the abuse of my childhood by trying to make me more functional. I felt sad about the journey and how long it had taken to get here. I wondered what my life would have been like if I'd had this therapy twenty-five years ago, but I knew that self psychology just wasn't around before. I felt grateful for Kohut's courage in breaking the barriers. How angry I was with all the old models of therapy that try to be clever and understand other human beings through the mind. The clever mind knows nothing of the heart and the lost child within.

This anger inspired me to write to the self psychology group back in California. There had been major battles over the models we were supporting, especially when we joined a national body. We'd moved from a total focus on self psychology to a more encompassing approach. As head of the training committee I had tried to retain the self psychology orientation but it was a losing battle. The national group (which didn't recognise self psychology) said we needed to be trained in the more traditional Freudian, Kleinian and Object-Relations models. It was going backwards. I mailed to each member a letter expressing my views.

I knew my views probably wouldn't suit some members. It was an important step for me now to speak my own truth.

The essence of my letter was about how valuable I believed self psychology to be in validating and supporting the growth and integrity of the individual. I wrote about how it provided a safe and trustworthy space in which to speak, to be listened to and to learn of one's unique potential. However, what concerned me most, and was the impetus for writing in such strong terms, was the prospect of mixing the traditional models with self psychology. From my experience, self psychology was a two-person egalitarian model where the therapist followed the client and invited him or her to go into the depths of their being to the point of early childhood trauma. If the therapist used those aspects of the model for the client to open up, and then adopted a judgmental, authoritarian, intellectual stance, the previously protected secret self could be destroyed. The very cause of the need to hide in childhood could be re-enacted. Bringing the traditional models into the self psychological space could actually cause more serious harm than could a traditional model alone. The client would never open up to the depth of their true self in a space that didn't feel trustworthy. At the end of the letter I stated that I wished to resign from the group, for I could not support their new direction.

About two weeks later I got a call to say that my letter inspired two other members of the executive to write with similar views. They then had a meeting in which a vote was taken and the consensus was that the group would go back to self psychology. I had written the letter not just out of my own pain, but from my attachment to what I knew was a healing therapy. I also knew that I liked the people in the group and what we had shared together, and I wanted them to hear me. I saw that the letter was an expression of my passion.

Around that time I dreamt I was visiting two different schools with two different principals. One was authoritarian and tyrannical, the other egalitarian, creative and dynamic who saw the inner wealth of his students and invited it to come out. This was how I felt about self psychology and my therapy. It allowed the Me inside simply to unfold in my own way. No rigid rules, no specified plan – just being in a space where I could be myself and gradually find the words to tell my story.

In a later session I recounted my dream of the two schools. Neil helped me see that I'd used 'principal' as if it were spelled 'principle'. I appreciated the significance of what he was saying. I was a woman of principle, and like the egalitarian school in my dream I believed in fairness, honesty and integrity. This was what my letter had been about, and people had listened. Something grew inside. I felt stronger, more alive and proud of myself. I knew that while the responses of the group were validating, what was more important was being true to myself, being authentic and saying my truth, undiluted.

That was the first step to knowing my own self, a step I will never forget.

CHAPTER 10

Symbols led me home

Buffy went to hospital one morning. He'd been sick all week. I helped him into the vet van. Before the door closed and I reached out to say goodbye, a hand gripped my heart. Why did it hurt so much? The vet assured me he would be okay, as indeed he would. But as I stepped inside my apartment I remembered another Buffy, the dog of my childhood, who was my companion in the basement. A beautiful cocker spaniel with big brown eyes. I can't bring him vividly to my mind, but I can feel his warmth and softness. My body had a picture of him.

As I lay on my bed, my sense of desolation told me more. It told me how important my childhood Buffy had been to me. I know I could not have survived the basement without him. But then another memory surfaced – one that I didn't want to see. I felt the terror of being down there without him and of having no one to hold onto. Buffy was on the other side of the door – the free side, the good side. Is that what I ended up believing as a child, that I had less value than the dog? Is that the pain the child within was telling me about? Is that why my heart froze that morning?

Later that day, the vet rang to say Buffy had settled down and he'd be leaving him overnight. 'Will anyone be there?' I asked. 'No.' That's when everything got blurry; time and space merged. I didn't know if it was the grown-up me or the little girl talking. When I got off the phone I once again drifted back to my old Buffy. I began to understand why a child has no option but to dissociate from pain. Here I was, a woman in her forties with enough intelligence and insight to separate past and present, yet I was swamped and overwhelmed. What chance does a child have who hasn't yet developed any boundaries or any power or a sense of self? What can a child do with such intense emotions? Push them down over and over with all the other unfelt, unspoken hurts, until it is simply too dangerous to dip into feelings, images or an inner language.

Painful as all these childhood memories were, I knew they had to be revived and relived emotionally. A dream reassured me of my path:

> *I was at a railway station waiting for a train. Many friends were there. Trains would come and they'd tell me to get on, but I knew it wasn't the right train for me, so I waited. This happened several times. I was carrying hundreds of photographs – photographs of my childhood. I was holding them over my stomach, like I was pregnant. There were so many, I just couldn't hold them all. Some would fall onto the train tracks underneath the train that was standing still. A man in a white suit kept picking them up and giving them back to me. Eventually he and I got on the train where we sat side by side. That felt good. We began to look at the photos. I knew I was finally on the right train.*

The unconscious paints such clear pictures at times, which capture much more than words. The first part of the dream reminded me vividly of my years of searching for a model. Throughout the Master's course and the years that followed I was hungry to find a way of understanding others and myself. I remember my colleagues saying this model was great or that model was the best, and going off trying this or that. I remember comparing the philosophies and underlying principles of different models, but it was of no help. None of them spoke of the truth. Even though it seemed like everyone had a model, my whole being rejected them; they didn't make any sense to me. They weren't models that worked for me as a person or as a therapist. They weren't therapies that took you to the centre of yourself. They were like plastic surgery – good for surface problems. They didn't touch the emptiness. I remained a therapist without a model. When I entered the course in self psychology I recall my supervisor asking me what model I used. Hesitantly, I said I didn't have one. 'That's a great advantage,' he said. 'It's very hard to disengage yourself from a model and deepen yourself naturally into self psychology.' I knew self psychology was my train. It was the right train tapping the right brain, allowing the memories to flow.

The dream also helped me understand that the memories contained my self. Having repressed most of my childhood, I was a lost child with no history. I was like a person with amnesia. Who was I really? This dream gave me hope – hope that by allowing memories to surface, I could find my lost child. Dreams like this were anchors that secured me while I delved into my childhood photographs. Of course, the waiting at the train was the time before starting therapy. The man in the white suit was Neil. We had begun to look together, side by side. The dream also told me it would take a while.

It did.

Each therapy session was a surprise to me. Between them I'd write about what was happening within me and think about it. By the time of my next session I was back in a pit. As I walked to the office, I'd often think 'What's the point? I don't know what to say. I don't know what's going on, how can anyone else? I'll feel just the same afterwards as now. Nobody can help'.

Then I'd enter the space – the still space. In the dream, the train was standing still. I knew it was going where I needed to go, but it was standing still while the others were speeding off. How essential is the stillness in self psychology, especially the stillness of not being asked questions. Questions would have locked me into the pit of my mind, spiralling down, taking me nowhere. By not activating or encouraging that cognitive part of my brain, it left space. After a session I was always amazed by my shift in mood and my clarity of understanding. Everything fell into place as the pit evaporated. I was connected to myself.

One day I bought two little bubble gum machines and filled them with jelly beans. I remembered seeing these machines in my childhood. It seemed nice to have one you didn't have to put money in, and the jelly beans were so colourful. But when I got home I wondered what had drawn me to them. Why had they 'spoken' to me in the shop? I simply knew that I wanted to take one to Neil and to keep one in my kitchen. That was the extent of my awareness. By this time I had learned to trust my subconscious, to act on my intuition. The gifts I gave Neil – the painting, the flower encased in glass, and now the bubble gum machine – were the only way I could provide the clues to so many locked memories. Symbols painted pictures more effectively than words. Every step of the way, symbols in my dreams, in my paintings or in external objects led me home.

I arrived for my therapy session with this gift for Neil. The significance of the bubble gum machine still eluded me, so I went on to talk about going to a kite festival on the weekend. Michael and I had gone with friends and taken a kite I'd had for a long time. We'd had such fun. I realised that the exhilaration was in sharing the experience with someone. Then I mentioned that I'd seen a purple kite just like the one I'd painted. The kite connected me to the exhilaration of being with my Auntie. I realised that whenever I smelt oil paints I feel as high as a kite. The smell, the colours – they take me back to love, to loving and to being loved. It was at this point that I understood why I'd chosen to paint a kite flying over the ocean. That was the bond that brought me this far and that is what I brought to therapy. I realised too that I must have painted with my Auntie a lot. I have the sense of being side by side with her. It was interesting that I couldn't remember painting with her through my visual mind, but I could remember through the colours of my senses and emotions.

I had also taken some music that day to play in my session, for it seemed to convey the feelings I had for my Auntie. The song was 'Carry me (like a fire in your heart)' from the album *Flying Colours* by Chris De Burgh. As I played it, the words seemed to touch that long-ago bond: '*You must take away the pain/Before you can begin to live again/So let it start, my friend, let it start/Let the tears come rolling from your heart/ And when you need a light in the lonely nights/Carry me like a fire in your heart.*'

In listening to the music I became aware that even in the black times in my life, when I felt that there was nothing to live for and my only option was suicide, there was always a flicker of light. Once again I was struck by how important the love from my Auntie and grandfather had been. I began to understand the other side of the bond. I never before realised that it wasn't just that they were loving. Neil helped me see that they had carried me in their hearts – I thought it had been me holding *them* in mine all along. Something grew lighter inside. I was lovable. It turned things around so much.

I also saw that the love wasn't because I was my grandfather's granddaughter or my Auntie's great-niece. It was *me* they loved and they would have wanted me to have as much in life as possible. 'They would have wanted to give you the world, not take it away,' Neil said. If I suicided, that would be taking it away, I thought. That was what my mother wanted. The ancient message of my mother buried deep in the chasms of my mind came bursting through: 'I wish you were dead'. I felt sick. It was as though I was right back in the time she'd said it, or that she was right there in the therapy space. I hated these times when I'd go back into childhood and have no sense of also being an adult. Unlike the positive memories of my Auntie, when I hit this blackness with my mother I felt there was no protection. But I began to learn that in the safety of my therapy I could retrieve memories or words and feel that Neil was attuned to what was happening to me. Then we could view it together.

All my life I hadn't believed in the feeling of being loved and lovable. When people conveyed it, I had thought they were just being nice. I remembered how difficult it was to leave my friends

– especially Sophie and Mathew – when I came to New York. Sophie had given me a present and a beautiful card. On the card she said she'd miss me enormously. I had felt so shocked at the words. 'Do you really mean enormously?' I asked. 'Yes,' she said. 'Honestly?' 'Yes,' she said again. I knew I'd miss her, but it didn't register that she'd miss me.

The card and the words were the next link to my Auntie. I would have liked to have written a card like that to my Auntie, to say goodbye. I talked about my Auntie's death and the funeral. How robbed I felt of goodbyes. Then I remembered that when I won the fellowship and went back to Canada, I'd visited her grave. I took a pottery brooch of blue and white flowers on it, like the corsage. I buried it at her grave. But as I was retelling the story, my mind went back a step further. I recalled that I'd taken the bus to the town where the cemetery was. I hadn't been there for over twenty years. As the bus got closer, I became hotter and hotter, as if I were on fire. That is how I used to feel when my parents' car approached my grandparents' house. I came alive; my energy just couldn't be contained any longer. Right then, right there, I was transported back to my childhood … I opened the car door. My foot touched the kerb and then I was off – up the front path, up the steps. Grandma was standing on the porch, and I gave her a quick peck on her cheek. 'Where's Auntie?' I sang, as I passed through the front door, not waiting for her answer. As I ran upstairs, I felt my legs stretch like elastic bands: two, three steps at a time, up, up, around and up. The last four I took in one very big step. There she was! She was coming out of her room. I threw myself into her arms. I was home. All was right with the world. She held me, caressed my hair and gave me a kiss. 'How's my little girl?' That's it, I was her girl, her child. Only to the outside world was she my eighty-year-old great-aunt. In truth, she was my mother. She had my heart and I had hers. This was the bond. This was my natural home.

I stepped back and looked up at her. She had that twinkle in her eyes. 'Now I wonder if I've got anything for you.' She put her finger to her chin and looked bewildered. 'Let me think. My memory is getting so bad. Did I get something?' I saw the tease.

She always had a treat for me when I arrived, something tucked away on her. I went in search. Her myriad of apron pockets revealed nothing – just a few tissues. So on to the next layer. I exhausted the dress pockets as well. Maybe she did forget, maybe it wasn't a joke. My disappointment showed. Then she tugged at a string around her neck. 'What's this?' she asked, pulling it as though it were hard work, as though she'd had no idea there was a string around her neck. I took the hint and pulled on the string necklace. Up came a little cloth bag. I stretched it open and poured the contents into my hand – jelly beans! I loved jelly beans! They were all different colours. 'Well, my goodness,' said Auntie. 'Now how did *they* get around my neck?' 'Oh Auntie, oh Auntie!' We laughed together. That's how it was: love, hugs, warmth, fun, laughter and jelly beans.

When you feel loved you feel in love with life – you feel your own vitality, your own energy. It's like having an inner rainbow – you just feel and feel. Feelings are the bridge that take you home to your true self. I understood the depth of meaning that the song 'Carry me (like a fire in your heart)' had for me. I felt that I was connected to my Auntie right from birth. Her love was real and unconditional. It was the fire in my heart. When I reconnected with the bond to her I began to find my inner passion for life, my inner belief and my love for myself. I started to see that I had locked that precious love away so it would never again be questioned or harmed. In an adjacent 'heart room' I also locked my grief – her death. The loss I felt was too overwhelming for me to experience on my own. The song gave me hope and courage. I felt it spoke to me of a deep truth. It was essential to go through the pain, and only in doing so could I find my way home and begin to truly live. I began to view pain as a guide, as something to be embraced rather than avoided, and that therapy, although painful, contained the seed of my life. My Auntie was the flame that for forty years staved off the ice from entering the inner sanctum of my heart. I remember being loved.

After this session I bought an easel, some big canvases and new oil paints. The creative spark had been kindled.

CHAPTER 11

I was a secret

ophie came for a visit. We didn't plan anything specific, we just let things happen. The days flowed with conversation. Closeness and joy were abundant. Even now I can recall the bushels of laughter collected over that time. But during the fourth night of her stay I awoke with such sadness. I closed my bedroom door and wept. She would be leaving in a day and I found this so disturbing that I almost wished she had never come. Saying goodbye ripped me apart. As I lay on my bed feeling empty, I noticed the photos on my bedside table. I picked up the frame and looked at the pictures of my Auntie and grandparents. Suddenly I realised that I didn't have the same feelings of devastation and loss about my grandfather. Why? There was a clear path between us. It wasn't like the loss of Auntie. I thought back to the time before his death. I realised his death was different from Auntie's because I had had a chance to say goodbye.

My grandfather had been sick for several months. He was in a hospital bed in the parlour in his home. I was there for the summer holidays and spent a lot of time with him. I used to pick flowers from the garden, put them on a tray, and carry in his meals. He liked the flowers. But mostly I remember sitting on the bed listening to his stories. He talked about his life, about his favourite pastime of fishing and about his dog. I remember reading the poem he wrote about his dog. I liked his stories.

Then something happened. Perhaps he got worse or perhaps people began to hear that he was ill or maybe he knew he was dying. Suddenly the house became very busy. I remember men with briefcases. They'd sometimes leave them in the hall by the hatstand. They all seemed to be very busy, business-like, important people. I think it was related to grandpa being the Grand Master of the Masonic Lodge.

I recall grandma saying these were Lodge men and I wasn't to interrupt them. So the parlour doors were slid shut. I hadn't realised until then that the parlour had doors that disappeared neatly into the wall. I felt lost. There was an endless stream of strangers. My mother and grandmother told me not to bother my grandfather because after he had visitors he needed to rest, and I would make him tired. Once again, I felt like it was my fault – it was I who was too much. But this time I didn't take their word for it. I talked to grandpa and asked him. He said I didn't make him tired. He loved our talks and said I was much more interesting than all these Lodge men. So we made an arrangement. He suggested I come down early so we could have a chat before the day started. I think he probably meant about 7.00 a.m. I would go down well before dawn. We had a nice, quiet time. It was an even better time to talk for no one was around. I'd then go off to bed before anyone was up and go back to sleep. No one knew. Another secret. I felt like my whole life was a secret. All my loving relationships had to be conducted without my mother's knowledge. I had to pretend that I didn't have a close relationship with my grandfather, that I didn't matter. Being loved, being valued, having space to speak – I had to believe that was all 'not me'.

When grandpa died I felt pure grief. It had a beginning, a middle and an end. We had said our goodbyes. I had told him how much I loved him in words and in little ways. He too had shown me I was loved by him and that I was special. Before he died he gave me his pen, which he treasured. Everything was sorted out between us. After he died his body wasn't taken to a funeral home; the coffin was in the parlour. For several days I was able to go into the parlour, just as I had with him in the hospital bed, and sit beside the coffin. I'd talk to him and touch him. That experience allowed me to see death as ordinary. It was also a time of more stories, great stories. As people came to pay their respects they'd sit down, have a cup of tea and talk about my grandfather. I grew richer knowing more and more of this man I had only known as grandpa. I felt proud to be his granddaughter. By the day of the funeral, I felt an inner peace.

I recall being in the car, following the hearse to the cemetery. What astounded me were the people lining the streets. It was a small town and grandpa was well known and obviously well loved. Shops had been closed for the time of the procession. It seemed like everyone was out on the street. I can still see the faces of old men with their hats over their hearts standing on the bridge on the outskirts of town. I saw their respect. The service at the graveside also had a sense of completion. We were encouraged to drop a flower in the grave after the coffin had been lowered. That, too, felt important. After the funeral, people came back to the house for tea and cakes. There were more stories. I just lapped them up. I was learning so much about grandpa and what a fine man he was. I saw how much people loved and admired him – as a businessman, a Mason, a fisherman, a friend; but mainly as a warm, loving, gentle man.

After people had gone, grandma started sorting out flowers. Some were to go to the hospital, and to different groups and organisations. There had been so many. Grandma loved organising everything and everyone. The next thing I knew, I was going to the cemetery with my Aunt Ellen and my mother in the car filled with flowers. Grandma had decided that some of the nicest bouquets were actually on the grave. She wanted us to take these lesser ones and exchange them for the 'bigger, better' ones. It was so silly, but so typical. Grandma was such a snob; she was always aware of what other people thought. Seeing her and grandpa together was like seeing polar opposites. Grandpa would be around the house in his old fishing sweater and slippers, but grandma was always one hundred per cent proper – neat, tidy, well dressed, and well groomed. She always wore jewellery, and was always straight-backed and severe.

So here we were caught in one of grandma's social whirlwinds. We got there just at dusk, which I think was a relief to us all, for we weren't very comfortable with our task. We put one small bouquet back, and took a big one with white roses, and so it went on. We were carrying them to the car when we stopped in our tracks. Straight ahead on the previously clear path were gates that were padlocked. After exhausting other ideas, I was boosted up onto the wall to climb over to the keeper's house to get the key. I think this was the one time I recall laughing with my mother. At this point we were splitting our sides laughing. We kept saying if only grandpa could see us now, stealing flowers from his grave and being locked in the cemetery at night. He would have enjoyed that. That's how the memories of that day ended. Yet I had had no real access to these memories until now. They were filed under 'loving', which had become 'not me'.

Although I'd lost these experiences along with those of when Auntie died, I realised they were the wellspring of my knowledge in grief. I often wondered how I knew about those rituals that help people resolve their grief and those that impeded the grieving process. I'd written papers on this topic and counselled bereaved people. But I was not conscious of where the depth of my understanding had come from. When I wrote my first book, it was hard for me to acknowledge my own wealth of experience. It comes as a shock to me, now that I think about it, that the whole theme of my book was unresolved grief and how to deal with it. Did I teach what I most needed to learn? Of course. Because my Auntie's death came after my grandfather's and I was never able to resolve that grief, all those memories of the bonds to both of them were blocked.

When Sophie left I thought I'd be okay, but I wasn't. Sophie had a lot of the qualities of my Auntie that I loved so much. She was fun, easy to be with, loving, open, creative and she enjoyed playing. Her presence had opened my heart and my wound. I talked about Auntie in my therapy sessions for a long time afterwards.

The most poignant memory was the last time I had seen Auntie. On Christmas Eve, we walked to the local church for the late service. It was particularly special because the two of us went together. This was treasured time for me. It was a bitterly cold night and we walked arm in arm. Standing beside her in the church in the warmth of the candle glow and the sound of the Christmas hymns was unforgettable. When we came out there was a gentle snow falling and we stopped to look at the stars. When we got home we had hot chocolate, then Auntie was off to do 'a few things'. When I went to bed there were always some presents under the tree, but by morning it was abundant. I knew Auntie collected little presents all year long for the children in the family and tucked them away. I'm sure she was up most of the night wrapping them and each was a work of art. I also recall the sound of sleigh bells. To signal that Santa had been, Auntie would get the sleigh bells out and jangle them outside the window, which was next to my bedroom. The sound was pure magic. On hearing it I'd race down the steps and there in the living room was the tree, all lit up and engulfed by presents. I'd race up to wake Auntie and she'd be in bed, seemingly oblivious.

My memory of her that Christmas was filled with joy and closeness. I never imagined that this would be the last time I'd see her.

Not long after her funeral I helped clean her room and sort out her belongings. I found bundles of letters from a long time ago, tied with ribbon. My grandmother explained that they were from the man Auntie was engaged to when she was in her twenties. He had been killed. She said that Auntie never really got over it. There was never anyone else in her life but him. I wanted to open them and learn more about her, but it just didn't seem right – they were too private. So we burnt them. I never knew if that was a good idea or not, for I would have liked to understand more of her life. When I talked about this in my therapy I saw that I didn't know a lot about Auntie as a person, other than the way she was with me. I knew the essence of her. I knew her loving. We began to explore this thread that was to lead me to understand more and more about secrets. I had only one dimension of her in my memories. To me, she was perfect. When I said that word something clicked inside. I realised it had been impossible for me to let in anything negative about her.

I began to understand that the image I had of my Auntie was a barrier to my seeing the people I loved as they really were, warts and all. I had this picture of a perfect person which I placed over those close to me. Perfection – the one thing being human excludes. It was an untenable yardstick, both for my friends and for myself. For me to try to be like my Auntie was to be faced continually with my own flaws. It was a very distressing awareness, for I'd loved Auntie dearly, and held onto the memories I had of her like a drowning person holds onto a life raft. But I never knew of her grief, her disappointments or that she had a dark side.

In having only positive experiences with Auntie I missed out on learning about the ups and downs, the highs and lows of an ordinary relationship. This was reflected in my therapy. If there was any disruption, I just fell apart. I was hit by the enormity of the contrasts – all good or all bad, white or black. No greys. I was aware that I needed to reconcile these opposites. I needed to find a world that contained them both. It would take a long time before I could tolerate any inner rearrangement.

The destructiveness of secrets became clear. I began to understand that children only begin to know their own self by their reflection in their environment. I had two separate mirrors, two separate lives: one with my parents which was mainly negative and filled with abuse I couldn't tolerate enough to remember, let alone tell anyone about; the other with my grandparents which was fun and peaceful and playful, but in which there was no room for pain. I couldn't speak of my life at home. The mirrors felt like two circles, one black and one white with no overlap. I was totally different in each space. I had some intimation of this huge contrast before now, but I couldn't comprehend the secrecy that kept them both out of my consciousness. Perhaps even more disturbing was the fact that there was hardly a space where I could see my reflection. Where was I? I was mainly a reflection of the two circles. Secret reflections.

After these memories of my grandfather and Auntie surfaced and I was able to express them, I felt a huge release of energy. In the days that followed I did two paintings which reflected the two circles. The first painting was of a daisy growing in parched and arid soil. That was how I felt at home: trying to eke out some existence, trying to gain enough sustenance just to survive. But I did find nutriment beneath the harsh soil. The daisy's roots went deep underground and tapped another space, another experience. My hidden oasis. The other painting was about the love and abundance I felt with my Auntie. That one was of brightly coloured nasturtiums – oranges, yellows, greens; vibrant, alive, exhilarating. While the paints were still wet, I took a rag and gently wiped it downwards so that the colours smeared. When it was completed I knew I was trying to convey that while I had all this, I could only remember it through my tears and my grief – my Auntie's death. Now I wanted to reclaim what I had with her: I wanted my vitality back.

As the secret Me became less secret, it seemed I opened up more and more to my own creative self. It was as though a weight had begun to lift. I felt lighter. I think secrets are a heavy load. By bringing these powerful memories to consciousness, by making them real and sharing them, I was becoming more real. I was beginning to claim my own history. I wasn't a total secret to myself. I no longer needed to pretend that I wasn't loved. More importantly I began to feel lovable. I was catching the other side of the bond. Out of Sophie's departure came a growth that I couldn't have predicted when the blackness was crashing in on me.

Soon another secret emerged. I remembered what a friend of my mother's told me when I was about twenty-one. She said she could never figure out what was happening when I was born. She lived close to my parents and saw them regularly. However, she didn't know that my mother was pregnant. When my father came to tell her I was born, he said, 'We have a new addition to the family', and she said 'Did you get a dog?' I gather that was all she could think he meant. When I recalled that, I shrank inside, for I really felt that that was exactly how my mother treated me. That was all a secret too. I began to cry in despair. All my life I'd felt like a secret, but it seemed it really started before I was born.

I didn't want to keep remembering. I hated it. It hurt too

much. It was hard to understand that it was only when each door was unlocked and I could see what was behind it, that I could begin to claim my freedom. Locked doors kept me a prisoner. But I still wished I could unearth memories of a normal family. I felt so ashamed of things I never did. My sense of worthlessness was overwhelming. To feel that you have no intrinsic value, that you're just a nothing, is unbearable. I can see how children believe they are as worthy as their parents deem them. They love their parents, trust them and accept their appraisal. That's why all my life I've had a sense that deep down inside there was a black mark against me. No matter how hard I tried to be 'good' and to be liked, there was an underlying belief that if anyone really saw the Me inside, they'd see the blackness, the badness that I didn't even have any words for.

Over the weeks that this was all surfacing, an outer reflection of my pain was occurring. For some reason there were trees being cut down in my area. Each time I walked to therapy I saw either a tree being cut down, or the sawdust remnants of another. Ironically, it was all being done under the platform of the beautification of the area. Eventually I mentioned to Neil how distressed I had become over these lovely trees. He helped me see that it related to innocent growth being cut down, for no reason. They just seemed to be in the way, that's all.

I called every organisation I could think of to stop the trees being cut down. It was as if I was trying to be a voice for the trees. Then it became clearer that it was like all the secrets I'd been keeping. I could no longer remain silent. I needed to speak. But I also needed protection so I wouldn't fear being cut down again. I wished there had been someone in my childhood to stand up for me; I had been powerless as a child. Maybe the trees were about my own growth. Perhaps I still couldn't believe I could just grow without anyone stopping me. Neil wondered whether the book in my dreams – *Fire and Irises* – had something to do with speaking out. That clicked with something inside. I sensed it was very important for me to speak, to tell my story.

I then remembered that since my last session I'd done two paintings. There seemed to be freedom in the air, freedom to express myself in whatever way I wished. I also realised the essential beauty of self psychology: it was not about simply removing symptoms or becoming more functional. It enabled the connection to be made to one's natural creativity. My paintings, like my dreams, were bringing the secret Me to life.

CHAPTER 12

Broken bones and hammers

By bringing more memories of my Auntie to awareness, the bond of love had been strengthened. I never would have survived without her. For me to have come this far and to have accomplished what I had with my life was due to her presence in my childhood. What she'd given me needed to be substantiated.

Not surprisingly, the next flood of memories to come out of the secret's door (which now seemed permanently open), were to do with all the positive things I'd done in my life. I wrote a long list of achievements I was proud of and took it to a therapy session. It was like a tribute to her. I needed to say out loud how much I gained from her, otherwise there wouldn't have been enough of a self to be able to do anything. When I talked about my talents and achievements, I could feel the discomfort rising. I would probably feel awful afterwards. It felt audacious of me even to consider speaking of the positive aspects of myself. There seemed to be a rule that they were to be kept secret. Competence, talent, achievements, excelling, were all filed under 'not Me'. However, I continued for the whole session, only covering half the list before time ran out.

The memory that stood out most was of an incident in my honours year. All of the honours students were feeling overwhelmed by the workload. I got the group together and organised a meeting with the professor to address the issue. He wasn't negotiable. I talked to the guild president, and with their support, the honours students went on strike. We refused unanimously to write exams. Eventually the professor negotiated with us and we had our course load reduced to what was expected in other faculties. Yet I didn't know whether I had offended the professor by standing up for what I believed was fair. My past experiences with authority figures told me that if you didn't go along with the rules, there would be punishment. This time it was different.

After the marks had come out, I was told that at the meeting about my final mark the vote had been half-half. Half said I should get first-class honours, the other half said it should be an 'A'. The professor had the casting vote, and I got first-class honours. That experience showed me it was possible to speak your mind to some authorities, even though they might not agree. So vastly different from silence. It was a very important memory to claim, for I had put it in the 'forgettable' basket.

Even though it had been very difficult to talk of my accomplishments, at the end I felt my own vitality. I felt solid and proud of myself.

Then came the predictable backlash for trying to claim what was 'not me'. My next memories were related to my mother's abuse. As soon as I showed my aliveness or strength there would be punishment. I hated recalling these memories but now had no option. Most of them were about visibility. The most painful were about just being who I was. I recalled an occasion where someone had said I had very long fingers – like piano fingers. My mother later took a belt and strapped my hands. I remembered wishing so much that I had short fingers. Now I knew why. If people commented that I looked pretty, there would be another outburst. My body remembered the slaps across my face. All my life I'd felt ugly and here was the essence of it. Over and over, my mother's view of me established itself inside. It seemed whoever I was and whatever I did was bad. I felt the terror of living in constant anxiety that anyone would notice me at all. I just wanted to disappear.

My disappearance led me into books. There had been so few things I could do at home without punishment that my limits grew tighter and tighter. My world opened when I could read books, so I read endlessly. Another intolerable memory surfaced. I could feel an inner fragmentation …

By the time I got to my session I wasn't sure I'd survive with my sanity intact. This time I had such pain in my stomach I felt I'd be sick. It took me over half the session before I could say anything. I felt so ashamed. I was back in the experience again. There were times when my mother would fly into a rage about my reading. She'd say I was reading a 'bad' book. I never knew which were good or bad books. There weren't any children's books at home, so I grabbed anything; then she'd punish me. I felt awful about myself. I felt ashamed to tell Neil, as though I were bad for being treated this badly. Neil asked if my mother had said what she'd do if I ever told anyone about the way she treated me. 'Yes – she said she'd kill me.' No wonder each of these secrets had such power when they surfaced. 'Now you can tell me,' Neil said.

Somehow, in breaking that worst injunction of death, it felt like the child in me now had a protector and a safe space in which to speak. What I'd remembered was that when my mother decided I was reading a bad book, she'd give me an enema. The pains in my stomach and the urge to throw up continued. But Neil was compassionate; he stayed right with me. He didn't turn away or make things better. I began to understand that the experience I'd been describing in my body was exactly what happens when you hold an enema. Gradually it began to ease off. Things were making sense and I was okay. I'd come through the blackness again. I knew then why I always got such stomach-aches when I went into libraries.

I often felt as though every bone in my body had been broken, but because no one could see, no one knew. This image of broken bones took me back to when I lived in Vancouver and had had an accident in which I broke my collarbone. I was unconscious until I got to the hospital – then the pain set in. It was ages before I saw a doctor. When a doctor arrived, he seemed truly baffled as to what to do with my broken collarbone. He spoke little English and tried to read the directions for the support I was to wear. He took it out of its box and turned it round and round, looking puzzled. Eventually he cut out a big triangular piece of metal from the support – which he obviously didn't know what to do with – and then strapped me up. I should have known it was all wrong. My shoulders were hunched forward with a knot tied at the front; it didn't feel right. I had broken my collarbone when I was much younger and was told to keep my shoulders back and my back as straight as possible. This was the exact opposite.

However, I didn't say anything, I didn't do anything, and I didn't complain. I went home hunched over and loaded with pain-killers. On Monday I rang work, which happened to be at the same hospital. My boss, who was a senior doctor at the hospital, came to see me a week later. He was appalled. I don't think I could ever have imagined this man being angry, for he was always softly spoken, but he was very angry. Yes, the resident medical student had made a total botch of it. The worst part for me was that the bone had begun to set. An appointment was made with an orthopaedic surgeon. He explained that if I didn't get it realigned it would create a dysfunction in my right arm which could create long-term back problems.

The specialist told me he would have to break the bone again. I gasped at the thought. I looked at his rubber hammer so intensely that it's still emblazoned in my mind. It's one thing to have an accident – you aren't conscious beforehand that you're about to have a bone broken. But to voluntarily sit still and watch your bone being broken is indescribable. My right shoulder flinched as I remembered. It took three strikes, as it didn't break completely on the first two. By the end I was a mess.

This was the memory I recounted in therapy. I saw how I never stood up for myself and how I allowed people to treat me neglectfully, without question. It was as if I could use my intelligence and experience and strength of will on behalf of others, but when it came to my own welfare I became dumb – I rejected my own knowledge, my own inner voice, and bowed to authorities.

This story more than any other seems a perfect analogy for my childhood and then my therapy. I could see how damaged I was because of my childhood. It left many psychological bones broken. The broken bones of my personality structure had prevented normal growth and made me adapt and compensate in many distorted ways. I became 'not me' by hiding what I thought was not me. I tried to be nice, happy, giving, caring and fun. I did anything not to show my broken bones, because people might think they were broken because I deserved it. I tried so hard to make people like me. I did everything I could to join the human race. I contorted myself into a thought. I tried to be who I thought people wanted me to be. I was failing; I couldn't keep it up. Everyone wanted something different. The worst thing was, this false personality structure was beginning to calcify.

I had heard in a seminar that when people reach their fifties, it becomes very difficult to alter the structure of their personality. I didn't fully understand restructuring at the time, but I knew that what the speaker said was true. Entering therapy was like going to a bone specialist. In order for me to have a second chance at my life, those bones had to be re-broken. It seemed a terrible irony. I came to therapy because my bones had been broken. It was hard to appreciate that re-breaking them was essential to have my life back. I needed to keep reassuring myself that pain was healing.

Therapy was a painful process. The pain of the memory was actually worse than the pain of the incident itself. When those exeriences were initially stored away, they were totally dissociated. All that pain had been put aside, inside. It felt intolerable to have to pull up all those memories and relive them consciously. Just as I hated that specialist as he hit the hammer onto my already painful bone, I hated therapy at times and fought against it. I did not like watching the inner hammer approach three or four times a week, uncovering more painful experiences to be relived. But the blows kept coming.

The image of the hammer revealed another connection to my dream of fire and irises which I'd previously not seen. In the dream, a man was next to me in the darkness, tapping away on the foundation of my childhood home. That was how it felt for me in therapy. It was like the old belief systems of endless fears and rules forced on me at home were being broken. My perceptions of life were changing. I had held onto this house desperately, but it was being dismantled step by step. I couldn't keep living under that tyranny anymore. But as well as the man with the hammer there was the compassionate man who knew the darkness, who had the courage to enter it, and who also knew the way out. Only now could I see that in order for me to have my life I needed to let my old self go. Therapy was instrumental in both the destruction and the creation of myself. Hammers and compassion: the tools of healing. I never realised how crucial the hammer was.

CHAPTER 13

An absence of presence

I had read about transference – where one transfers feelings and experiences onto the therapist that are part of one's self, or are related to other people in one's past – and had seen it through the eyes of my clients, but until I experienced it myself, I would never have believed in its power. My link with Neil had begun many years ago, when he supervised the self psychology workshops. But having undergone therapy with him, the link was much more profound. When I walked into his office I was no longer a forty-three-year-old woman, or a psychologist. It was the very young child in me who spoke of her feelings and told her story. It was confusing and disorientating.

It was extremely difficult for me to maintain the connection with Neil between sessions. Many times I just didn't know how I'd make it. I became more and more depleted and sank into nothingness. I didn't like feeling so dependent, but there wasn't much I could do about it. But these minor breaks suddenly seemed inconsequential when the prospect of Neil's holidays loomed ahead.

The feelings about his going away took me to memories of my mother and my Auntie. The link seemed to be that whenever I asked my mother where she was going she'd just say 'out', or if I asked how long she'd be I'd get a non-response like 'I don't know'. When I visited my Auntie, it could be for two weeks or ten weeks – it depended on the whim of my mother. Neil's holidays were bringing up a lot of anxiety related to the distant past. I could feel a deadness filling me as if I didn't care if he went or came back. A feeling of hopelessness was all there was. I felt like I just had to sit still until his return.

The other issue this break brought up was the grief related to the death of my Auntie. I didn't want to feel the pain of her loss, and more than that, I didn't want to remember how much I'd loved her. As soon as I remembered the love, I felt the ache of the loss; they seemed inseparable. I tried to cut off all the feelings, because it hurt too much. I realised I did this not only at the thought of her death, but at all the times I'd have her love, for every time I visited I'd open up and then have to close down again. Each separation signalled a return to abuse.

When I was able to talk about this, it shone some more light on why Neil's leaving was so painful. The only way I felt I would survive the break was to close down and tell myself it didn't matter. Neil conveyed that he knew the break would be hard for me. He then asked me if I had ever spoken to my Auntie on the phone. Such a simple question and such a simple thing to do. The answer was no. That's just the way it was – either I was with her or there was no contact. Neil then gave me his holiday phone number. I can't explain how healing that gesture was. I didn't ring him, but it was wonderful to know he cared and that I could ring and there could be a connection. My stomach calmed down and my heart opened.

I was beginning to understand that when I felt hurt or vulnerable I'd close down and withdraw. My automatic reaction was to say it didn't matter, but that wasn't what the child inside was saying. She was saying it mattered very much. It was very important to express my feelings, to let Neil know his absence mattered. Being silent, being strong and coping wasn't the answer. I was slowly learning to say what I felt, instead of trying to work out what the other person wanted, or what I thought they wanted me to be.

The night before the last session, I was filled with turmoil. I tried to explain my feelings to Neil. The closest I could get was to describe the image I had of a room deep within that contained me. I'd kept it an absolute secret all my life, as that was the only way I could survive. During these months with Neil, I had begun to show him my inner sanctuary. But I still didn't know who I was. The scariest feeling was that somehow Neil now contained me and all my secrets. I also sensed that he could see where I was, as if from the top of a mountain, whereas I felt lost in a fog. 'And you're going away, so how will I remember who I am?' I felt unhinged. It related to the fears I had before starting therapy. The first was the fear that if Neil saw inside me he'd see what I'd been running from all my life; my deep-seated belief that underneath I was actually bad. The second was that if I came for therapy and didn't get better, I knew that was my last chance because Neil was the best therapist I'd ever met. If he couldn't help me, no one could. In following Neil to New York, I'd risked my whole life, because if I didn't come, I could at least have told myself that I might have been able to change. In the background had been this fear that Neil would see me as worthless, stupid, hopeless – all the things my mother taught me I was. Staying invisible had been crucial to my survival. But I was no longer invisible to Neil.

That night I'd had a more frightening insight. I saw that the beliefs making up the foundation of my life had always been that I was bad and that it was my fault. But in the night I awoke and saw that it wasn't the bottom – a trapdoor opened and I fell through to another level, a secret room. When it happened I felt like I was going crazy. I saw in this hidden room a really lovely little girl and woman. That felt scarier than being at the upper level. It felt more shameful to see that I was actually bright and talented than to believe that I was bad. This was the war inside. I thought I'd go insane. I saw no way out of the inner dilemma: if I came alive, I would die; if I spoke up, I'd be silenced; if I showed love or was loved, I'd be punished. Everything life-giving was terminated.

It seemed like such a delicate time. I was still not ready to go out into the world on my own. I needed a safe place, like a chrysalis for a butterfly when the butterfly's wings are forming, and are in need of protection and support. My dreams all started to make sense. They were the connection that led to my special place. For that reason, my dreams and my dream books were precious to me – they meant everything to me. My dreams told me that I needed to stay connected to the positive bond and that bond was with Neil. It didn't even have me in it yet.

I dreamt about my house:

> *I was sitting on the back step, with my goddaughter and my first boyfriend. I was looking across to the next street and saw a big sword plunge into the house opposite. It caught on fire. I could tell it would fall onto the next one and so on down the street. Then it would soon come to mine and it would burn too. I walked with my goddaughter and my boyfriend out to the front of the house. We crossed the street and sat on a blanket on the grass and watched the town burn. I wondered to myself if there was anything I should have saved from the house. But I realised there was nothing I needed from there.*

That's how I had felt the night before, like everything that I thought was me, wasn't. I was afraid to watch it all disintegrate. But as Neil pointed out, I was safe. Maybe with this birth of Me there had to be the death of the old Me, the whole outer structure. I began to understand that the blackness had been put *on* me and was not within. I had no choice. Suddenly, I felt lighter. The little girl had done pretty well to survive. Better than pretty well, Neil added. It felt like a bottle of champagne had just popped inside. The little girl in me felt proud of herself for getting there.

Although this time was disruptive, there were changes happening inside me. That old house was going and the cement was being poured for a new one. The cement was safety and trust.

I realised how these were connected to my own therapy. The more I was believed in, the more I felt my presence. Yet when Neil was away, I mainly felt my absence. The child in me went underground, but the adult Me was busy all the time on external work-related issues. I thought I must decide either that I was hopeless and would never get established here and have enough money, or that I could believe in who I truly was and come out.

The seventeen days of Neil's holiday passed and I was back to my therapy. The dream I had the morning of my first session back was one where I'd been handed seven serpents' eggs, each of a different colour. The different colours of the eggs reminded me of a quote I'd used in my speech at my book launch. It was by the painter Marc Chagall. He said something like: it's important for an artist to use the full range of colours, to paint the terrible as well as the beautiful. But the central colour, he said, is always love. It made me realise that I'd always believed that the outcome of therapy was happiness. But I was beginning to see it was really about being emotionally alive. To be psychologically healthy doesn't mean being happy. It means you feel the colours of pain and sadness as well as the colours of joy and love. My belief seemed to be related to being an only child. I'd always assumed that other people were happy and I wasn't. Maybe people who grew up with siblings see the variations: their brothers and sisters could be happy, sad, angry and loving all in one day, and by night-time everything was back to normal. They knew the ups and downs were simply ups and downs, whereas for me, things were either ideal or horrific.

The idea of the colours made me realise there were two I'd kept securely out of my paintbox – black and red. I began to see that all my life I'd tried to be 'white' – good, nice, compliant, caring; trying to live up to an ideal and to avoid living down to blackness. I couldn't have any of my own colours. I locked out black in particular, because just one little smudge, one little black mark, and I'd be totally in blackness. I then saw the connection between black and red. When I kept black away from all situations and all people, I saw everyone and everything as nice. There was no ability to discriminate and there was also no chance I'd ever get angry at others, no chance I'd express my anger when things went wrong or when I was hurt. Instead I just got angry with myself and this took me straight into the blackness, the depression. It seemed to be related to never having had a protector, someone who stood up and was angry on my behalf.

Anger. That was a very vibrant colour. I wouldn't allow myself even to dip my white paintbrush into that bright red paint.

I spoke with Neil about my previous therapists. It was as if when therapists got into long convoluted interpretations they spoke in a language of their own, a language full of hidden messages. That was when the darkness descended. I couldn't figure out what they really meant; I felt I was going crazy. Instead of saying 'That isn't clear' or 'Tell me what I need to know', I'd go away thinking it was my fault for not understanding. Somehow I believed that if I worked hard enough I could understand crazy language. That's when I'd decided that if I couldn't understand, it must be *me* who was crazy.

'I'm not bad or crazy,' I said firmly to Neil. 'And I don't need drugs,' I added. We both laughed. 'I'm not bad, not crazy and I don't need drugs.' Just to say it and hear it out loud made me feel a sense of lightness. How many years had I unknowingly searched for that awareness, that prison key?

I then began to try to express the feelings I'd had while he was away. The adult in me did a lot in his absence but the child felt wounded. Perhaps the bond had just started to really feel secure. I don't think I'd allowed myself to connect this deeply with anyone since my Auntie, so when Neil left, the child once again felt abandoned. The timing seemed wrong. I hadn't found ground under my feet. I was angry that there had to be this break. The more we explored these underlying feelings, the more I understood how it had been emotionally difficult for me. I was hurt and distressed, but what was hardest to see was that I was angry that there had to have been this break. But my fear of expressing even the tiniest piece of anger was enormous.

It soon became clear that it related to my mother. When I was a child and showed any vitality or rebellion or anger, things got out of control to the point that it could have cost me my life. I was faced with my inner conflict: how could I claim my visibility and also feel solid enough to express anger? It's as though these building blocks were missing. It seemed to me that if I got angry I'd scare the living daylights out of myself and would never do it again. I was also frightened of any disruption to the bond with Neil. My experience was that anger destroyed bonds. Then I realised, with a greater clarity than ever before, that because of my mother's terrible rages I'd probably put anger in the same file as murderous rage. I couldn't risk touching it. This is why I always caved in when someone got angry with me. I wanted peace at all costs!

I then thought back to the saying by Marc Chagall. You need to be able to use all the colours in the paintbox, but the central one is always love. When love is present, none of the other colours are dangerous. There could be no murderous rage while love was at the core. I felt the truth of it. I began to see how love and anger worked together as friends, it was my anger that got me to crawl out of my familiar black hole, and it was love that was my motivation. My love for Michael provided the impetus to ensure I was able to provide for him adequately, and my love for the child within me ensured that I had the money for this therapy that I knew was essential to heal that child. In fact, I wrote on a card that I put beside my bed: 'Decide whether you're valuable or not'. It was like a kick in the pants for me. I was angry at being so financially stressed. Love was the core motivation to get me to jump out and take action.

Another insight I gained about my struggles to come out of the blackness came from an unexpected source. I went to see the film *Parenthood*. In it was a wonderful old lady who said that most people chose to go on merry-go-rounds, but she always loved the roller-coaster. She loved to jump in and enjoy life, with all its ups and downs, instead of being safe on the merry-go-round. Yet for me the roller-coaster was inside, not outside. I wanted to be like the little old lady, free to flow with life, while feeling centred. I had a sense that life controlled me instead of my feeling some groundedness in life. Whatever happens out there changes me inside. When Neil was away it was like I was absent to myself. These experiences weren't little bumps, they were roller-coasters. My emotions were related not to me, but to checking the outer mirror. How I wished I had a sense of evenness inside me. But somehow I'd got that mixed up with deadness. The waiting space, the quiet space for me held nothing. Perhaps the title of my book needed to be *Death of a Mother*, because emotionally my mother had never been there. My primary bond was to nothing, to deadness.

That night I got out my easel and a large canvas. I stood and faced the empty white space and tried to connect to my feelings about my mother without thinking about why or what went wrong. I gave a space for the child in me to say what it was like for her to be connected to her mother. What emerged was chaos. Masses of disjointed, disconnected, thrashing, frenetic strokes of black. Slashed amongst the blackness was red. Not the red of passion, but of intense anger. Hers or mine? I didn't know. When I'd finished I was totally exhausted. The expression had such intensity. It had been crying to come out for more than forty years. It was the statement I could never find the words to express. I put the canvas in the garage.

I began to see that the hole I got into was an escape from seeing this torment. I could see there were two bonds in me struggling for expression and understanding, struggling for power. Was the link to my Auntie strong enough to overthrow the hatred and deadness of the bond with my mother? Who was I really?

I know there are always some significant landmarks in any journey, including the inner one. This was a major turning point for me. In putting all of those feelings about my mother on canvas, something was released inside. Something had been spoken that was beyond words. Some space had been cleared inside and within that open space arose memories of high school.

Even though things were awful at home I seemed to do okay at school. Yet all my school reports were filled with the same comments: 'Could do better', 'Isn't doing well enough', 'Underachiever'. Then like a flash of lightning, my consciousness let in a memory of an IQ test, where once in a while I'd deliberately write down the wrong answer, or purposely leave out an answer I knew. I followed the maze in my mind as I tried to ensure that I didn't do too well. I wondered how the teachers always knew I could do better. These tests seemed to be a give-away. If they found out I was brighter than I was showing, they might look deeper, ask questions, and wonder if something was wrong at home. I felt sick. My heart hurt to see what I'd done as a child to protect myself from being visible.

Neil wondered if my mother knew how much I protected her. I crumbled. That was the first time in my adult life I remembered that I had loved my mother. It was like a thread unravelled back through time. Like most children, I had loved my mother. I wanted more than anything to please her and to make her happy. I desperately wanted the love reciprocated. That's when I hit the bottom line. To make my mother happy I needed to disappear. More and more I began to understand why I had kept everything a secret, including my own self.

As soon as that memory settled I recalled a teacher who refused to let me disappear. When Mr Donahue came to mind, it was like a whole rainbow of memories flowed into me and I realised how crucial he had been to my mental health, my development and my self-esteem. Mr Donahue was the vice-principal at my high school. The principal was a real army major type – yelling orders all the time. But Mr Donahue was delightful. He was the heart of the school. I first met him about two weeks after school started. I had lost my Latin textbook and went to his office to see if it was there. I recall his greeting. He wanted to know my name and where I was from. He asked me how I was finding school and generally just chatted. I'd felt so lost in the school, as most first-year students do. But the key was his acknowledgment of me. He pointed to rows of shelves of lost and found objects. As I went through I mentioned that there was an awful lot of stuff and wondered how he found anything. I must have offered to straighten the shelves, one thing I was good at. He asked me if I'd like to run a Lost and Found stall before and after school. I was happy to feel liked and valued and to have an excuse to spend less time at home. We also decided to charge the students, and give the money to the Red Cross. I set up the stall, put the fees up on a board, labelled the shelves, and recruited a couple of my friends to help. Within a few weeks I'd become president of the Red Cross Society and head of Lost and Found. A big step for an invisible girl.

Once we had a substantial amount of money I took it to the Red Cross headquarters. The people there offered to show me around. I hadn't known that they had a school for crippled children. I met the children and was moved by their cheerfulness despite extreme handicaps. It was mentioned that the Red Cross was always looking for volunteers to read to the children individually. I began to go there two days a week after school. More acceptance. As the staff got to know me, they began to offer other things for me to do. Eventually I went every Thursday evening to help at the blood donor clinic. But the very best part was when they asked if I'd dress up as the Easter Bunny for the kids. I had never had so much fun. It was hard to believe it was the same shy student who sat at the back of classrooms, saying nothing.

Importantly, Mr Donahue was my English teacher. He breathed life into whatever he taught. He got us to see below the surface. I moved from the back of the class to the front. For once, I loved school; I'd race to get to his class. Mr Donahue also encouraged me to join the public speaking group, which he ran after school. At first it was hard because I was anxious, but I grew more confident over the years. In the last year of high school I was in the school finals. The topic I spoke on was leprosy. The untouchables. It seems that even then I was trying to tell people what it was like to feel so unaccepted and worthless.

In a sense Mr Donahue was like an extension of my Auntie's presence in my life. They both showed me there was another way of being in the world. I may have lived under an authoritarian system at home, but I was having wider and wider experiences in a heart-based democracy where qualities of creativity, feeling, passion, spontaneity and caring had highest priority.

Children develop self-respect and self-esteem when they are respected and valued. Both are key ingredients in parenting and education, as well as in therapy. They form the cocoon that creates the environment for transformation. Butterflies always come out in the warmth.

CHAPTER 14

A red Cadillac

*M*ost of the focus in my therapy had been about reclaiming secret parts of myself and dealing with issues of abuse and neglect. Interwoven with my therapy was the issue of my work as a psychologist. Because I had written a book about my ideas on and experience with maternal grief, the professional side of me was being driven to be more outspoken. This brought to the fore my terror of visibility. Since private practice didn't come easily I had to broaden my horizons and ultimately my skills. During the break from therapy I drew up an Action Plan. The priorities were: to establish a private practice; to develop a proposal for the government to develop services for bereaved women and their families; to do some media work on my ideas for this proposal; and to publicise my book which formed the basis of the proposal.

My constant dilemma was expressed in the dream ab
being in the centre of a tension bridge. The question
becoming insistent: Am I going to come out or just
again? Am I going to believe my mother's view of
worthless or my Auntie's view that I was valu

battle was fought over who I was and whether or not I was a worthwhile person. I could see that my tension was related to the fear of attention. I couldn't come out and say what I had to offer, or show my talents without people seeing them. The symbol of the bridge was important. Could the bond with Neil support me enough to enable me to come out without feeling as though I'd die? Attention for me meant attack. With each step towards visibility I was aware of the inner tidal wave, but now I held onto a new bridge, one where I was valued and supported.

One of the greatest difficulties had been to continue to believe in myself in Neil's absence. If I didn't get my act together I wouldn't be able to afford to stay in New York and have therapy. So I worked hard. I sent letters to doctors and developed the proposal on health care services. Having worked in this area for ten years it felt important to consolidate my thoughts and ideas, and to create what I believed would be appropriate health care services for women in the future. I sent off almost two hundred copies with letters to politicians and to the media. It was something I just wouldn't have had the confidence to do before. I felt that I was enough on the positive side of the bridge to feel I could initiate something I really believed in.

From my experiences, I was beginning to see that my views as an individual did have some validity. I also had a growing belief that I had a right to speak out. What I hadn't bargained for was the snowball effect it would have. Within the first two weeks of starting therapy again I got four requests from women's magazines to do articles on maternal grief. Two of them asked if I'd like to write the articles myself. I had never contemplated that. It was a challenge to write in a style that was foreign to me – a challenge I enjoyed. One of the interviews was with a writer from the women's magazine with the largest circulation in the country. I was elated to see my message about women and grief going to such a wide audience.

Then something very important happened. I was contacted by a woman well known for her outspokenness on women's issues. Her call was unsolicited, and it seemed that once I initiated things, validation and response came from all directions. She was writing an article for a newspaper about the effects of the death of a baby on women and their families. She was going to talk about the death of her own son who had died at birth over thirty years ago. She explained that a friend of hers had sent her a copy of my book and she realised that the depression she'd suffered all those years was unresolved grief. She asked if I'd mind if she quoted from my book in the article. She told me that she planned to do a series of articles on the different forms of loss and asked how I felt about talking to her in more depth. We arranged for me to go and visit her in a few weeks. I felt I wasn't such a lone voice in the wilderness anymore. I'd been talking about the importance of this issue for years. But when she spoke, people would really listen because of who she was.

In my therapy, I talked about going to see this woman. I felt my fear rising. As a child when I was excited or exuberant or looking forward to something, punishment followed. I had sensed that my mother knew of the love between my Auntie and me and that the time before I went to visit her could be precarious. I had to be quiet and pretend it didn't matter if I went or not, so that nothing would spark my mother's rage. I began to understand that that was why I was so anxious about going to see this woman. The meeting was at her place, some distance away. There was the link to my past. I was going to see a special woman that involved a journey. (When the article was eventually published, I brought it in to show Neil. I wasn't particularly excited. Exploring my lack of excitement helped me see that as a child I wasn't allowed to get excited about anything, or become too visible. The story made me very visible. The author had mentioned my work and my book a great deal. I also thought that this article would trigger the media attention I'd been seeking. There was a part of me that wanted that and another part that was dead scared.)

As well as the fear of visibility, I went through feelings of shame. I had always seemed to be a source of embarrassment to my mother. I didn't remember the words like that, just the endless string about my being too emotional, too highly strung, too excitable – too *much*. I'd always believed everything was all my fault. I felt so much less valuable because of the deprivation I experienced from my mother. There was an ongoing sense of never measuring up, no matter what I did. I had an awareness that in childhood all my friends seemed to have normal families. Maybe underneath, I felt they deserved them and I didn't. So I kept visiting their houses and wishing I lived there. Then I recalled that there were a few people like my teacher, Mr Donahue, who wouldn't let me keep hiding – people who believed in me. There had been quite a few more since that time, Neil reminded me. Once again I needed to decide whether I was valuable or worthless. Going to see this woman had brought up all these issues. Was I good enough to visit her?

It helped that each of these present experiences of visibility triggered earlier memories. The sequence started automatically: visibility–excitement–attack–blame–anger at myself–terror–shame–acquiescence–depression. How can you, as an adult, stand up, speak out and show your talents, when you've got this film playing its millionth re-run in your mind? I knew that I had to keep doing these anxiety-provoking things that were about visibility and trust, to reinforce that this world was different from the world of my mother. I bought a book that caught my eye around the time called *Feel the Fear and Do It Anyway*. It became an inner motto.

My therapy helped me explore a new way of viewing things. This meeting could be two women sharing something. People are usually helpful and I wasn't going to fall flat on my face. So I went to the meeting with a different focus – which was not based on fear – and it was easy to talk. She provided me with several personal contacts in politics and the health care area, who she was sure would assist me in furthering the awareness of this issue. She also said she'd help promote my work as much as she could. On the plane coming home I felt overjoyed. It was very much a red-letter day for me and would remain so. It seemed like doors were opening for me. However, there was one door I would never have expected as an outcome of this meeting: the publication of this woman's autobiography three years later. In it she spoke of the healing effect that my book and her meeting with me had had on her life. Making real contact with someone always opened doors and made your life richer. It was a lovely affirmation that meant a lot to me.

When I bought the newspaper the following week, her article was front-page news. That did a great deal for my self-esteem, not to mention my book sales. My book and this article substantiated the reality of the loss and grief suffered by bereaved women, and exposed their right both to express their pain and to expect support and understanding.

Early the next morning I got a phone call from my favourite journalist, whose writing I admired enormously. He explained that he'd seen the newspaper article and wondered if I'd come on his radio program for a one hour interview. I got another call from a reporter for a leading national current affairs magazine also wanting an interview. It was all on. If visibility was an issue for me, I seemed determined to jump in the deep end.

That night I had a dream about a red Cadillac:

A friend of mine had given me his big red Cadillac convertible to use. I parked it in front of my house. It was huge and I thought it would be hard to park but it wasn't. I then saw the friend who owned it. He asked me why I hadn't been using his car. I said I'd forgotten he'd given it to me to use. He said well, he did want me to use it, that's why he'd given it to me. I told him I wouldn't forget again.

A red Cadillac was a pretty visible car – bright and fast and perky. Neil suggested that perhaps showing all these positive aspects of myself was being like a red Cadillac. It seemed the furthest symbol from my self-image. I had this belief that somehow 'good' people are humble; they're not showy. For me to show myself in a positive way felt artificial. Yet I could feel the growing sense of my own self-worth. Maybe self-images could be changed, and as Neil suggested, the Cadillac was there waiting for me in my dream.

Feeling positive about myself took me to another important childhood memory of someone who believed in me. Doctor McDonald came to mind – the doctor who delivered me. I'd seen him throughout my childhood and he was another supporter in the background. He had his practice in his home which was halfway between my house and the primary school. As I grew older I used to ride my bike to school and would often drop in for a chat, at his invitation. I also remember that he had a big jar of jelly beans on his desk and we'd always have a few. When these memories flooded back it felt, in a sense, that I had started therapy then: I had someone outside of my home who cared about and was interested in me, and who gave me a space to talk. That connection was more vital to my health than I'd ever recognised. It made me understand that children are pretty adept at getting what they need. If they don't get it from home, they try to get it from somewhere else.

After I failed maths at high school, I was trying to decide what to do. How was I to get out and yet go on? I decided I'd do nursing in the town I lived in which meant I could live in the nursing quarters. I had gone for the interview and had been accepted. I needed a medical certificate, so I took all my forms to Dr McDonald one day and placed them on his desk. He asked what they were and I told him, saying I was going to do nursing. With that, he picked them up, looked through them, ripped them all into tiny pieces, and then threw them in the garbage. He turned to me and said 'I wouldn't have let my daughter do nursing – she's doing medicine. Now I'm certainly not going to agree to your doing it. You're far too bright'. He wasn't going to let me undervalue myself. I see how supportive he was to me, particularly in the words he used, linking how he felt about me to his daughter. I felt that he truly did care. I worked for a year and did my maths exams before leaving to do medical technology in Ottawa.

From that memory leapt another one from around that time. It had to do with the graduation ceremony at high school. I was feeling down, with all my friends getting excited about the ceremony and the dance afterwards. I remembered going shopping with my friend Judy to find her a dress. The really bizarre thing was that my parents went to the graduation. It was as if my feelings didn't matter at all, as if they were celebrating my failure. I'd never talked about these feelings because it felt crazy, like my mother taking all the money from the account for my tertiary education. I ended up not passing – probably both from the stress and from not wanting my father to find out what she'd done because she'd said the shock would kill him. I knew at some level I was as bright as most of the kids graduating and yet I was a failure. Neil could sense how crushed I was by that experience. He helped me realise that considering how devastating that time was to my self-esteem and self-confidence about my scholastic abilities, I hadn't done badly. On the night of the graduation, who could have predicted the list of degrees I'd end up with after my name? As well as a book … and a red Cadillac, Neil reminded me.

I began to understand why my book launch had meant so much to me. I had never attended my graduation ceremonies, even when I got my first-class honours. I preferred to get the degree in the mail – anonymously. I told myself I didn't like pomp and ceremony. It was as though my high school non-graduation had set the scene for 'not graduating' even though I did. It was also about being visible.

The book launch was like all the graduations I never had, all rolled into one evening. It was undoubtedly the peak professional experience of my life. Self psychology managed to get me to start believing in me. Standing up on the podium at the book launch looking at all my friends and seeing my book in displays along the side was something I simply could never have imagined happening. It was the bond, the new way of seeing that even then was changing me from the inside out.

Memories and links kept arising with each step of visibility I took in the outside world. I had set myself up for a fair amount of it too. Several of my sessions focused on my anxiety over an upcoming event with the media and later on with politicians. How important it was to explore the childhood memories first. The inner needed to be separated from the outer and dealt with. There were two Me's in the therapy space. The little girl terrified to be visible, yet longing to be seen, and the grown-up trying to get her feet on the ground in a new city. Dealing with the inner traumas was lightening the load on the adult. The child within was growing and learning that there wasn't anything to be terrified of. The world she'd seen through her mother's eyes was a million miles away from the safe and welcoming world she was coming to know. As time went by I felt freer to speak and more at ease with myself. My tortuous anxiety had been present when I had done promotional work for my book, but at the time it led nowhere. I wasn't doing this form of therapy, so no links to my childhood were made and no understanding came out of it. The levels just went up and down with each interview, like I was on a roller-coaster. This time, I had the opportunity to go to the core issues. For indeed I saw that little of the anxiety was related to the outer events. I think the other important difference was these interviews were more about me and my work and my views on reproductive loss and future health care services. When I did book promotions, the focus was on the book and the interviews were brief and to the point.

The fear of making mistakes and of being ashamed seemed to be the central issues. I well and truly had 'Attention' in the same file as 'Attack'. A refiling was called for. Over and over again we kept trying to understand the childhood terror and seeing that then was not now. It was the spoken word that was such a painful issue, because no one had listened to me as a child. It was also about getting the right answers. I'd imagine all these questions they'd ask and how I'd have to have every piece of factual information at my fingertips. There were a lot of statistics in what I had presented, and I felt I had to have them all at immediate recall, instead of referring to my proposal or saying approximately how much. Even worse was feeling that I couldn't guess what their question would be. At times I felt that I was supposed to stand there and have questions fired at me. That's how it was with my mother – 'Why did you do this?', 'What made you do that?', 'Why didn't you do what I said?' – that's what I felt I was preparing myself for. I felt despairing at times, living in this prison of the past. I'd learnt that it was hard to come out completely when the only way I'd ever known was to try to make everything perfect. I tried so hard to get things right. Only now was I beginning to see that usually what I did was pretty good. Neil suggested it was better than pretty good, and that there wasn't anyone who wanted to attack me. The impression he had was that everyone wanted to learn from me. Maybe I could simply tell my story and share some of the good things I knew with people. That really filled an empty space inside.

The next day, the interview with the current affairs magazine went like magic. She was a lovely young woman and was very keen and well prepared. When she left that day, I really felt for the first time the childhood curse was losing its power. A week later I got a call from her saying she'd spoken to her editor about the interview and suggested it be their special feature, instead of a small news article. She explained that in each edition they chose one person to do a profile on. She also mentioned that in the past year they'd only chosen two authors for this personal interview. She then sent out a photographer. That threw my anxiety barometer a little, but again it turned out fine. It was the best article about my work I could ever have hoped for – four pages of interview. It gave a very accurate portrayal of my work on maternal grief over the past ten years.

What delighted me about the accompanying photo was that it was taken at my desk with a painting of Michael's just behind me. He had also done one of a kite over the water. You could even see his initials in the corner. That felt important because in essence what I was really talking about was the importance of the bond between a mother and a child. When children feel loved they will grow to fly free and high – unfettered by fears, mistrust and self-doubts. If grief broke the bond, there would be no kite-flying.

Each of these experiences widened my horizons. I enjoyed meeting the reporters and hearing their views. My horizons were also broadened by the political work I had initiated. I received about a hundred letters in response to my proposal. The majority were extremely supportive and enthusiastic about my recommendations, although the issue of finding the money to fund such a program was the real stumbling block. I met with several politicians, mainly women who were interested in trying to support these ideas. One woman who was in charge of the area that provided grants for the development of women's health issues suggested I put in a proposal to create a video based on my book that could be available to health care centres. She assured me that if I did, I would get the grant. I did receive it and began to make plans to start on the video. So while not all I had hoped for from my proposal came to fruition, it did provide me with a whole new network and a far greater understanding of how politicians work. It also opened doors I never would have thought of knocking on. When opportunities arose, I said 'Yes', opening up my exciting new world. Perhaps I was getting used to the idea of having an inner red Cadillac – and using it.

CHAPTER 15

Space to grow

A new year arrived, a new beginning. So much was happening externally, and so much was being pushed to the surface internally. I felt that I needed twice as long for all my sessions of therapy. I couldn't catch up to what I'd wanted to say that day, because I was always dealing with issues arising from previous days, or dreams I hadn't mentioned or hadn't finished talking about. I felt like I was caught up in a whirlwind – memories, dreams and insights were all being churned so quickly that it seemed there was little time to gain perspective.

Re-entering therapy felt different. I had a sense of simply talking slower with spaces between what I said. For months I had felt as though I were in a race. This time it was more like a walk along the shore. I had time to reflect and to be quiet; I had less of a feeling of being lost in the middle of the experience. What a relief. There was some growing perspective, not in enormous amounts; but it felt that Neil and I were walking side by side. Before, I was running in circles or trying to race ahead of where I was. This mental realignment seemed to be physically reflected by the fact that I switched seating positions from being opposite Neil, to being in a chair that was in line with Neil's. I had never really taken any notice of the other single chair. It was in my blind spot. When I walked into the room in January it just seemed the right place to sit and it certainly felt more contained than sitting in a space for two. Maybe I'd needed the two-seater for all the baggage I'd been carrying. Whatever it was, it felt different and better to be on the same side of the room as Neil, with the similar view. I also enjoyed looking out through the long windows, to the trees and greenery. All this I'd never seen before. Perspectives were changing – internally and externally.

There were a few dreams I'd had around this time that seemed important:

> *I was on a roller-coaster. It was going so fast, so high and then so low. I was terrified and was holding on desperately. Then I heard a voice saying 'Let go'. I did and it was absolute bliss. I just floated and I felt a peace and joy I had never known before. I was still on the roller-coaster but I was so quiet and peaceful inside.*

The roller-coaster had been such a powerful image for me before Christmas. Then, it was about how I longed to have a solid centre, so I would not be pushed and pulled all over the place, depending on what others felt or wanted. In this dream I had a taste of that centring feeling that I'd longed for more than anything – inner peace, inner constancy. The dream gave me hope that it was possible to roll with life instead of feeling rolled over by it.

Another dream painted quite a different picture about my therapy and also about the power of my mother:

> *I was on a sailing ship. I was standing on the edge, and the boat moved and I fell in the water. It was like a swamp, like green pea soup. I was swimming towards the boat wondering if there were any crocodiles in the water. My mother was on the ship and threw me a pink life-saver which initially seemed reassuring, but as soon as I got it I realised I was swimming okay on my own. I'd been thinking I couldn't swim. Then Neil jumped in the water and swam towards me – that felt great. He helped me back in the boat and lifted me up just as a crocodile went to bite my leg. We were both safely on the boat.*

Initially I was struck by the fact that I'd been standing on the edge of the ship. That was how I'd felt months before. I'd always had a sense of sitting on the edge of the two-seater couch as if so much was spilling out that I couldn't sit back and relax. The green pea soup water was an accurate image of the unconscious waters I'd been in. However, it was reassuring to see that I was actually swimming through it. A most significant aspect of the dream was that Neil jumped in the murky waters with me. I am sure he was the first therapist to actually join me in my pain. Other therapists had kept their clinical distance and tried to convince me not to even enter the waters.

The previous months of therapy had dealt with trust and grief and the terror I'd felt as a child. I had felt very vulnerable during that time. Now my dreams were saying that there had been some consolidation deep within me. This next part of my therapy felt qualitatively different. It was to do with letting go inside. I had a growing sense that I actually liked me and that if I could just be myself, everything would be fine. That was quite a step. The painful part was experiencing my resistance to allowing myself to leave my prison cage.

The more I explored my family, the more I realised that my parents had lived their lives in cages. Neither of them had found a way out; they just made the best of their cage. That was what I'd been taught: just pretend it's not a cage and shine the bars so they look pretty! That's what I'd done in the past – simply manage. Neil suggested that I had a right to more. When he said that, it felt like my whole therapy centred around rights. Did I have the right to exist, to be protected and valued, to grow, to feel free, to say what I thought and felt, to be listened to, to express my talents, to have a space of my own, to have a life of my own? Rights. I did have the right to more. That wasn't what the bars echoed. To me they said it was a life sentence – nothing could change it and I'd just have to stay in the dark. I suddenly remembered I'd been sleeping with my light off and I'd also been closing my door, something I'd never been able to do. It made me understand that even inside a dark room it is never totally black – provided I could see with new eyes. That was the link to the inner shift.

When I awoke in the morning, it wasn't anxiety I felt, it was 'No!' This voice inside of me was saying 'No, I'm not going to do it', 'Nobody is going to make me. NO, NO, NO!' It had to do with refusing to continually apologise to my mother. A part of me now refused to say 'I'm sorry' for all those mistakes I didn't make, like being myself. When the blackness lifted the 'No' was highlighted. Now I could see that the 'No' was my anger which previously had been hidden by fear.

My thoughts during the night had centred around my family and cages. When I returned to therapy, I had known that there was still a lot of pain ahead. What knocked me was the lack of reprieve. It wasn't long before I was back in the basement. It didn't seem fair. I'd forgotten therapy wasn't about making things nice or comfortable, or about avoiding the pain that was trapped inside.

My despair of things never changing or my never changing was reflected in a journal entry entitled 'The Cage of My Mind' written around that time:

> I can't be bothered
> I just don't care
> It doesn't matter
> Nothing matters
> Nothing makes any difference
> Why should I?
> It's boring
> Life is boring
> I'm just not interested
> There's no point in doing anything
> There's no point in living
> Nothing ever works out
> Nothing ever goes my way
> Life is a struggle
> Life is totally meaningless
> Nothing ever changes
> It doesn't matter if I do anything or not
> It will always be the same

There's just no point in trying
No one really cares
No one really cares if I live or die
No matter how much I work I'll never get there
I'll never amount to anything
I'll never make a difference
I'm useless
I'm stupid
I don't matter
I'm hopeless
No one loves me
I'm not lovable
I'm bad
It's my fault
I feel like a motherless child.

So there it was – my cage, handed down from my family. The meaninglessness of life and the pointlessness of action was the matrix of thought from which I grew. This was the subconscious flow that went on and on without my awareness – until now. It was a deep river bed that kept me stuck in muddy waters and blurred my vision of life. Hope was missing, as well as my ability to value myself. If I didn't value myself how could I hope for a change to occur? Did I really believe I deserved more in life?

For some reason I needed to go and look at a bridge. I knew whenever I'd looked at bridges before, they had made me feel solid. But this time in particular, I was simply awe-struck and inspired beyond words. The friend who was with me at the time told me how the bridge had been built. There were two pylons, and all the girders were brought together with a huge pin or bolt in each pylon. Once the girders were connected to that one king-pin, the bridge couldn't fall down. In fact, once everything was in place the pin didn't even have to function.

I was longing for an inner bridge, but at this point in therapy, and in the real world, a central pin was missing from my life. Sometimes there'd be a bridge, but it could be easily swayed this way and that by people or events out there. It could still collapse, and I'd have to start from scratch again. I'd end up on the murky river bed below where there was nothing. Things just swept past me, impacting on me at random, and I just had to lie there and let it happen.

There was more insight. When the bridge was built strongly and firmly, with the pin centred, a whole city opened up. As I looked at the bridge, two intense feelings followed each other, as though they belonged together: the bridge flooded my body with a feeling of *inspiration* that led to a sense of *expansion*. When I felt the bridge internally, I felt my creativity. Once the bridge or bond was in place, the music and the dance of life rushed in; it was the freedom to be oneself. This day was to become an anchor of crucial importance in my journey.

As I stood looking at the bridge, a phrase from self psychology kept going round inside my head: 'An independent centre of initiative'. That seemed to be the core issue, the king-pin. That was what was missing inside of me; the solid rock that held the bridge in place, no matter what happened externally. I began to understand that to have this centre of initiative would mean ultimately that I could determine my own path in life. That's what my aching need was all about. I wanted my own motor so that my actions weren't the result of someone else's push or pull, or other people's needs.

I thought about the image of Humpty Dumpty that had been following me around for weeks. I felt that I was missing an ingredient that most human beings have. Often it seemed impossible to fix. I saw that all Humpty Dumpties sit on walls. The symbol of Humpty Dumpty in pieces on the ground had been with me for years. The other image was of the pink vase in pieces. In the past I had seen myself as a mass of broken bits and pieces that no one could ever reassemble. Now I began to understand at some deep level that it wasn't so much the fear of falling and breaking that was the issue, but rather the sitting on walls, waiting. The image of sitting on walls took me back to the dream of the ship and of standing on the edge of it. No wonder I fell in the swamp. Sitting on the edge of anything didn't seem like such a great idea. In my childhood, the only time I seemed to get a response from my mother was when I was totally distressed or in pieces, sitting on the edge. I realised the point of changing what seemed like an inevitable sequence was to substitute action for inertia.

The image of the river bed then came back to me. Being down on that inner river bed was actually related to my experiences with my mother. That bond led nowhere and made me feel that there was nothing in life. She allowed me no initiative and my actions always seemed to have enormous repercussions. Self-initiation had come to mean punishment. Another misfiling in my psyche! I began to see why all the things I initiated were so fearful. Just to get myself into therapy with Neil felt like a miracle, because all my inner resistances came to the fore. In a sense it felt like I was going to die. By seeking out help and moving, I was going against my mother.

The shift in the therapeutic space heralded an inner shift. Exploring my empty inner cage had connected me to the 'nothingness' in my outer life. Money was the external issue – I was really skating on thin ice. I had extended my overdraft and had a second mortgage on my house in California. The years of not standing up for myself financially were catching up on me. The costs of being in New York were so much higher and I felt I was going under. I felt the stress constantly. I was now finding it difficult just to pay the ordinary bills. Intermingled with all my worries about money and my feelings of despair and hopelessness, something was bubbling away inside. It was related to whether I had rights and was entitled to more. Was I worthwhile and valuable? My monetary state was not a good indicator, and sitting and waiting was losing its appeal. Establishing oneself as a private therapist in a new city was not an easy job. Referrals were so dependent on networks, which I lacked. So I took up an option to do a series of one-day workshops for nurses on grief counselling skills. I designed the workshops and began. I was asked if I wanted to do further workshops, and I said 'Yes'. Later, I was asked if I would do workshops in other cities and again I agreed. Then everything just happened. I did about thirty workshops in different cities around the country from February to June. I have no idea where I found the energy, but I did, and I learned an enormous amount in the process.

Each workshop brought up my fears of not being good enough, of making mistakes and of generally falling on my face. There are only so many times you can terrify yourself before you see that nothing bad happens. In fact, it was all positive. After a month or so I became much more relaxed with myself and with the participants. I really began to enjoy meeting these people and seeing different cities.

Perhaps the biggest bonus was that it challenged me to show more of my talents. I've often been intrigued by the synchronicity of outer events that somehow take you where you never would have gone if you had made a conscious choice. If I weren't totally out of money, I never would have considered doing these workshops. I'd believed it was other people who travelled the country teaching – not me. So ironically my deficit became a benefit. My skills in group work and in teaching in the area of grief would not have developed if it weren't for the absence of money. If my private practice had been established easily, there's no doubt I would have stuck to what I knew and was comfortable with. But there I was in a room full of nurses, doctors and social workers, telling them about my work and conveying what I had learned. I tried to make the day as dynamic as possible and to include everyone there. I knew everyone had a story of grief and loss and each person's contribution was important. There was a sense of equality which I liked so much; we were all working together to share our experiences and to learn more. I made friends all around the country. Life was expanding.

Besides the external advantages and the development of my skills, the greatest personal impact of these workshops was on my inner terrorist. The participants assessed the workshop at the end of the day. All I got were glowing comments. The only 'negative' comments were that it wasn't long enough. Yet my terrorist or tyrant was not impressed with so much exposure, and really sent the troops in to each workshop. I'd hear the voice of doom and gloom: how I was hopeless, how I'd make a real botch of it, people would laugh at me, and then who did I think I was, and how dare I pretend I knew so much! But this time I consciously watched the muddy river – I wasn't stuck in it. I'm not saying it was easy; the nightmares I had when I was away were diabolical. All of them seemed to centre around being caged or being attacked; being robbed; being in wars; being in plane crashes, boat crashes and car crashes. It was literally a war. But I kept walking through it. The terrorist and I were having this one out, with me facing my own shadow.

Over this time, the new inner shift was terrifying me. It felt like treading on egg shells. Even though this was open warfare, I was able to tell myself that change was afoot and that it was understandable that I feel all this chaos.

Dealing with the tyrant helped me to control my anxiety during workshops. I found it extremely difficult not to get any feedback until the end of the day. I saw that my anxiety related to that empty space where the tyrant could come in with heaps of messages about how boring it was and about how bored all the participants were; how it was just a waste of time. What I didn't catch for quite a while was how I projected those negative messages onto members of the group. If I saw anyone look away or close their eyes, or show any sign of not being totally involved, I began to think that they thought I was boring. But I gradually learnt that if I could tell myself to just withhold judgments until I found out what people were actually thinking, my perspective changed totally. I have no idea how many times I used that phrase to myself, but it became a constant companion. It was the sword that kept the tyrant at bay. In fact, the very people I'd picked as the ones who didn't like what I was doing, would inevitably be the ones filled with praise.

I also learnt to say how I felt. This was a giant step. When beginning the workshops I would so often be extremely anxious and yet I'd pretend that I wasn't. My new approach enabled me to tell the group I was feeling anxious. Once I'd said it out loud it would go away. Not only that, I'd be able to joke about it, which encouraged others in the group to talk about their own experience of anxiety. Ordinary. I felt more like an ordinary human being who, like most others, got anxious in front of groups. Later, I found I was also able to ask for feedback during the day which seemed to disempower the tyrant even more. Say it, and it is transformed. Don't say it, and it just gets bigger and bigger. I was finding the tools to deal not only with the world, but with my inner tyrant. The world was becoming more friendly and my tyrant was losing power.

I was learning a new way of life that was markedly different from passive fence-sitting. I could also see that letting go of my fears was no simple thing to do. Even to begin to let go of what had kept me entrapped in my little prison felt at times like dying, but it also seemed I had less and less time for wild fears; I knew I had to do battle to claim my own freedom. The pain at times had been horrific – I never want to go through that form of hell ever again. But I felt I was beginning a relationship with myself. I felt stronger.

Another insight came to me through the film *The Jewel of the Nile*. What struck me profoundly were the words of the Indian man in his prison cell. Staring out the window, he said 'It's not the walls that make the prison, it's the desert'. Once again, all the lights came on inside and for an instant I could see past the cage. I understood that what imprisoned me was not so much that long list of beliefs about my badness and about the dangers of the world; they were just the cover of my terror of stepping outside the prison walls. The terror was of the empty space – to let go, to simply let go of all my inherited beliefs about who I was and who I wasn't; what I was and wasn't entitled to in life; and what I could and couldn't say and do. Who was I and what did life mean to me if I didn't have this burden of beliefs to carry around? The prison walls and the bars were familiar, so much like home. If I really and truly let go, would there be anyone there? Was there a self inside, or just a barren desert? I began to see that there can be no growth unless there is first an empty space. 'Empty' didn't mean 'nothing'. 'Empty' meant fertile space for creative growth.

CHAPTER 16

The sweetness of life

My mother had caused two accidents, two explosions, like planes exploding in war. I was in her house. She was asleep and there was a girl (who was terrified of her) cowering in the corner wanting to escape. I woke up my mother and told her she was responsible for the accidents and also that she was terrifying this child. She said she didn't know what I was talking about. I told her she was unconscious, that she had no idea what was going on. Then I told her I was taking the little girl with me. We left. I was then with my Auntie. She had on a black dress with a silver brooch. She was sitting in a chair. I knelt down and put my head in her lap. It felt good. I knew I was safe.

By exploring that dream I began to see that there had been something about me besides my existence that enraged my mother. Was it because I was a girl, not a boy? Although I'd never mentioned it, that idea had been floating in the back of my mind for years. As a child, I asked my mother why she'd given me a boy's middle name. It seemed strange in my conservative family. She told me that they thought I was going to be a boy. Another aspect of 'not me'.

The issue seemed to be related to hope. If I'd been a boy, my mother might have had some hope for me. Otherwise I was doomed to a life of hopelessness like hers. It seemed that she didn't have any sense that women could have an effect on the world. All women could do, from my mother's perspective, was wait. Women were very passive; men went out and did things.

I began to understand that this swampy river bed I often fell onto was indeed the bond with my mother. I had the feeling that she was extremely depressed and had given up on life so much, that for me as a child, it was like being bonded to death. It was as if she was the baby and I was the mother. I kept doing things to bring her alive, but I never succeeded. That was probably why death had preoccupied me so much. It seemed my life was about death. I had this huge inner conflict: I was terrified of being like my mother, and terrified of coming out of the prison and being fully alive. I knew that when I got into that darkness, that swamp – that 'nothing' – it felt easier to die than to stay alive. Yet death terrified me. To be afraid of dying was like a living death. To live in fear was being half alive, maybe even less. It was just surviving. Terror was probably the most intense feeling I ever had as a child. But even that feeling, as my dream showed, my mother never listened to. To her, I simply didn't exist. I'd come to the core of the issue – existence versus non-existence. The bond to my mother was a statement of my non-existence. The truth was that being my mother's child meant non-existence. I had come to believe in my worthlessness because I held no value in her eyes. To a child who just wants to grow and be who they are, that is a death sentence. The challenge was to get off this river bed and continue with the bridge-building.

Some building had occurred through initiating a new aspect of myself in my workshops. At least, I wasn't standing still or sitting waiting. This step was validating, even if scary. It also showed me further aspects of my creativity and my ability to communicate. By presenting myself to large groups for that length of time, I became more real. I gained more substance.

Although doing the workshops wasn't the real central pin of the bridge, it ended up pointing the way. A new trail of understanding emanated from my visit to one particular city, where I was doing workshops. Each morning and evening I would go for a walk in the area around my hotel. What intrigued me on these walks was one street that had rows and rows of cake shops. I was astounded by the number of cake shops in one street. It's a picture I shall never forget. I felt like a little kid, staring in the windows amazed by the variety, the choices, the colours. The first evening I simply looked. The next day I went in and bought a cake which took me an age to decide on. The third and fourth days I bought several, each from a different shop. The astonishing thing was that I didn't like sweet things, but here I was drooling over all these cakes. This experience was to open many new doors for me. It was as if I'd seen cake shops for the first time. On my home ground I never thought of sweets, but being away brought them into focus – I was taken back to my childhood. I remembered that whenever I went to see my Auntie at my grandparents' place, there were always bowls of candies and chocolates in the living room, on the hall table by the phone, and in the dining room. The bowls were always full. I guess they symbolised abundance. I didn't have to ask for one; they were just there to eat.

There were also two brief dreams I had during this time that helped the flow of associations. I kept waking up all night out of one dream in which my mother was incessantly beating me. I just couldn't stop her. I felt I was going to die, but I knew I really wanted to live. Then the next night I dreamt my mother was made of iron. Both of these were more like sensations in my body than actual visual pictures, but they certainly felt real. In the dream of my mother being made of iron, I felt my body was bruised from head to toe. I'd go to her for what I needed but I'd be battered and bruised instead. There was also a sense of her being hollow.

I was becoming aware that I had little idea of what my needs really were. I then had a dream of a small animal trapped in a cage. Initially I thought it was a dog, but when I looked closer I saw it was a rat. I didn't know whether to release it because I was terrified it would then attack me, since it was hurt. I woke in horror. As I explored the dream I began to see that the rat was a symbol of my own hunger. Since my mother wasn't able to respond to my need for freedom and fulfilment, I had eventually viewed these needs as unacceptable. I felt that I had been treated like a rat. I had made the part of myself that expressed needs, disgusting. The dominos were falling into place again. That was what the cakes were all about. I had told myself I didn't like desserts, I didn't like cakes, so I just cut that whole sweet experience out of my existence. There it had stayed, until I was hit by all those cake shops and realised I actually wanted some. In fact, on this particular trip I would make up in the middle of the night feeling ravenous. I recall what a big step it was even to go into the shop. Almost as though I were ashamed to be buying cakes, or I should be buying them for someone else.

Eventually, I began to understand that the rat didn't seem to be wanting anything except to get out of the cage. It just wanted to be free. That was probably how I felt as a child. It seemed that my needs so overwhelmed my mother that she just put me in the basement until I learnt that I didn't have needs. I was the rat. That was a very difficult image to accept.

However, the image didn't end there – it was to evolve over several weeks. Facing the image of the rat continued to be painful. But one thing gave me courage. I had been listening to a tape of a Jungian analyst on dreams and he was talking about the shadow, those parts of ourselves that we just don't want to own. It grabbed my attention immediately when he said that our real gold is in our shadow. The characteristics we think are our worst often turn out to be our most positive. I took heart.

The biggest breakthrough came when I returned to the image of the cakes one day in a therapy session. I blurted out that I wanted all of the cakes in the cake shop, not just one or two. It was such a shock. It was as if someone else had said it. But there it was. The 'not me' effect following the expression of something I wanted. I felt so greedy to want all the cakes. If I had all I wanted, I felt that others would miss out. I was supposed to have nothing or very little. Neil suggested that I imagine what I wanted without thinking about anyone missing out. The image that came to mind was I wanted all the cakes in all the cake shops in that street, plus the cake shops too! I'll never be able to fully explain the power of the feeling that came with the image, other than to say that it was sheer exhilaration. Neil then said something that went straight to the core and which will remain with me all of my life as vividly as when he said it. He said that perhaps I didn't realise it, but I could be whoever I wanted to be, I could do whatever I wanted to do, and I could have whatever I wanted to have. My heart leapt with joy as tears of release from the prison welled up inside me. I'd been aching for those words and that permission all my life. I needed to clarify with him that if I had a lot, it didn't then mean that someone else went without. Just the opposite, he assured me. If I took care of my needs, not only was I enriched but so too were all those who were connected to me. If I got more, everyone got more, not less. Talk about a new perspective! It felt like a carnival breaking out inside of me. Many times since then I've repeated to myself, 'I deserve all the cakes in the cake shops and the cake shops too!'

Looking back I realise that the effect of the cake shop was literal as well as psychological. For at least the following year, maybe longer, I visited a lovely quiet coffee shop, had a cappuccino, and ate a delicious cake after every therapy session. I'm not sure of the significance, but it was always a very nurturing experience. It also seemed to be a transition time, where I could sit and reflect on what had occurred in the session instead of rushing back home or onto something else. It was taking time for myself and being more attuned to my own needs.

Things began to change. One important lesson came from an unusual source – the dentist. I had told him that I was quite anxious because it brought back memories of the pain of dental work I'd had as a child. He explained exactly what he'd be doing and said that I should have no pain with all the present forms of anaesthetics. I was soon to learn that I had a very strange definition of 'no pain'. During the procedure, he'd ask me if everything was okay and I'd say 'Yes, I'm okay', but I'd be gripping the arms of the chair or tensing up. In the middle of the second visit he stopped everything, raised me up in the seat, and said we needed to talk. He said it was clear that I was still experiencing pain even though I was obviously trying to be strong. He went over the idea again and said that when he said 'no pain', he meant absolutely *no pain*. To me no pain meant that I was able to tolerate the pain. I really felt silly. I ended up with a nitrous oxide injection and classical music on headphones.

The nitrous oxide had me feeling as though I were flying like a rocket through space. I passed shining lights and stars and rainbows of colours. I was doing somersaults in space. I felt light and free. I thought that this must be what it feels like to let go of fears. Maybe if I felt that things couldn't go wrong then I could really fly. What held me back was a belief that if I didn't fly then at least I couldn't fall. I saw an analogy to my talents. I had always cut myself off from experiencing the pleasure of my abilities and creativity. Now I was beginning to show my colours and people were seeing them and enjoying them. It was my vitality I was getting a feel for.

And I didn't feel any pain throughout the entire visit. This experience taught me that there was a big difference between just managing or coping with pain, and being certain there wouldn't be any unnecessary pain. It was a new view of pain.

By June I had made some remarkable decisions about my work. These workshops were my most viable means of making a living, but the woman organising them was making much more money than I was, even when costs were taken out. I decided to organise and conduct the workshops myself. The major task was to get lists of contacts in each city, which didn't take long with the nursing networks I was now familiar with. I designed my own advertising and began. It turned out to be quite successful. I was able to return to a constant therapy schedule, holding my workshops on the days I didn't have therapy. I also made a decision that I would sell my home to further relieve the financial stress. It was a while before I took the action, but the decision lightened my load. I stopped worrying so much. The important house was my inner one. Another big decision was to go to a lawyer and begin to initiate action to receive adequate maintenance for Michael from my ex-husband.

Since I'd lightened up a bit about money, I began to spend some on myself. I had facials and massages and my hair done – luxuriating experiences. I bought some new clothes, mainly dresses. All my professional life I'd usually worn pant suits and sometimes a skirt and jacket, but never dresses. I'm not sure what this desire to buy dresses was about, but maybe it was my letting go and being more soft and feminine: a less severe, responsible, hard-working image. However, just to go shopping for a dress was quite an ordeal, as it brought up old notions of my being ugly. I was aware of a tendency to choose bland colours and baggy clothes. This time I went for clear primary colours and a fitted dress. I had spent years hiding my sexuality and sensuality in a blurry cloud of nothingness. I was used to covering my whole body. This was not the woman in the shop mirror. I could see my legs, waist, bust and arms. The dress was bright blue with splashes of yellow. The inner tyrant was not impressed, but at least I expected the backlash. My other step forward was starting painting classes.

During this time I had yet another dream of a rat:

> I was in a big old room in a house. There was a huge rat running around. A voice inside of me said 'Just be still and look at it – really concentrate on the rat'. I watched very intently and wasn't frightened. It had big yellow eyes and was sitting up staring back at me. Then suddenly it turned into a man, a beautiful, peaceful man dressed in black leather who had entered previous dreams.

I felt great when I woke up. My interpretation was that there was a very powerful masculine aspect to myself that knew I had the right to have my needs met as a child and as a woman. Because of my experiences I had denied his voice, denied my healthy instincts until they turned into something I felt was disgusting – a rat. But there he was, transformed again. I was realigning with my inner protector of rights who led me out of the darkness. I'd say it was love that brought him back to life. A new loving of myself was emerging.

On my birthday in June I wrote the following, which I think highlighted for me the importance of my Auntie's love that had brought me this far.

My mother
Robbed me of myself.
My self-esteem, self-worth, vitality
And so much more.

More than anyone ever guessed
Ever understood.

She took my potential and smashed it.
My fun, laughter, creativity and trust withdrew.
I got left – locked away.

But deep inside was an inner vault
And only I held the key.
She never touched the place in my heart
Where all the memories of you were stored.

And it is that storage of long-ago loving
That has kept me searching for more
Like a distant shimmer of light
In the darkness.

I remember
Painfully
The feeling of being loved.
Just for me
Just because
Nothing more I had to be.

Auntie –
Seventy when I was born.
An old lady.
How did you know
To love so deeply that I could not forget?
That here I am at forty-four
Knowing your love is the only thing

That kept me alive
And somehow kept me believing in life.

In the very act of writing, I felt more light come into the darkness. There was more light around, inside and out. I had been invited to present papers at two major conferences. One of them took me back to California. The exciting part of this trip was that I began producing my video. I hired a producer and cameraman and we filmed interviews with the women and families who contributed to my book. Initially I asked the producer to do the interviews because he had been a reporter. When I saw the first one, I asked if I could do one. The difference was startling. Because I'd developed a rapport with these women and their families, it was easier for them to talk freely with me. But I think also it was the language, the style of questioning. The producer had asked very left-brained questions: 'How?', 'What?', 'Why?', 'When?' 'Which?' I simply sat beside them and invited them to tell their story. I said little, except perhaps to expand on a feeling or to validate what they were saying. Again, I saw how much self psychology had given me. The filming went smoothly and the result was very natural and moving. The experience was a big developmental step. To enter a space where I had literally no experience felt assertive and remarkable. There seemed to be more and more cakes being made in this inner cake shop.

CHAPTER 17

Steps towards understanding

*I*t's strange how a word can change one's entire inner landscape. The word that impacted on me so powerfully came after months of the hunger I felt in the night. It wasn't often an issue I brought to therapy, because I couldn't describe it fully and it wasn't every night. But it never went away. I couldn't tell what I was hungry for; it was a hunger no food could satisfy. One night the pain was so intense I thought I'd go crazy. I felt like a heroin addict or a derelict. There was a monster gnawing away inside me. I wandered around the house holding my stomach and feeling like a caged animal. I didn't know what to do or what I needed or what it was all about. My anxiety was hitting the roof. I desperately needed to fill this empty pit. I just wanted whatever it was so much. I was up nearly all night and I wrote pages and pages grappling with the emptiness.

In exploring this inner monster in my therapy, a word was found for the feeling – 'anguish'. That's when something changed irrevocably inside me. It was a word I had never used; it simply wasn't part of my vocabulary. In the deepest sense it was a word I'd been looking for forever. Anguish is what one feels when the self is crushed. Then there's the anguish and the longing to have the self back. The emptiness was not having a sense of self inside of me. All my life I'd filled that emptiness with something else – working hard, being good, fulfilling someone else's needs, linking myself to someone else's identity. I was now slowing down more, clearing space for myself, and entering the depth of the emptiness that had always been there aching to be heard. That word – all it contained and all it led to – marked a significant turning point for me.

Even though the monster was still there, it was now taking shape and had a name. I finally knew what I was facing. It was so liberating. Having the unnamable named made the child in me feel that finally she had got her message across. I knew that anguish had been what I'd often felt in my childhood.

Later I looked through my journal and at what I'd written throughout the night. Leading on from the sense of feeling like an addict and derelict was my emptiness. I felt transparent, as though there was no substance to me at all. My self-esteem and my self-concept were totally dependent on my perception of how others saw me. These experiences linked me to my father. I wrote in my journal: 'Having faced my mother's chaos, I'm now facing my father's emptiness that is in me'. Memories and feelings then came flooding in. I saw how much I had idealised my dad when I was a child. When I was ten or eleven I used to wait for him at the corner of the street to come home from work. It was a highlight of the day to ride with him for the block home just to be beside him. I thought he was the best. He was such a tall, handsome man, with black wavy hair, and he was always well dressed. He was so different from my mother, who was short and always seemed to wear clothes that reflected chaos. There were other things connected to strength and power that I associated with my father, but not with my mother: his big car, money, activity and work. I recalled going to work with him sometimes on the weekend. He was the manager of a trucking company. I was always overawed by the huge trucks in the repair shop. He'd let me sit up in the driver's seat and I was on top of the world. The size of the place and all the truck parts mesmerised me. It seemed unfathomable, how one could ever know how to put them together. Even the smell of the place – trhe mixture of grease and oil and metal – was different from anything I knew. It was like entering a completely different world, a masculine world.

Along with these early memories of idealising my father came others of disappointment, disillusionment and conflict. I remembered how he'd come home drunk and just collapse in the living room, or sometimes not even make it from the garage. When I was a teenager we often seemed to be at loggerheads. My greatest frustration was failing to find a way to communicate with him. He seemed to just come home, eat, go out or sleep. I wanted to talk to him. So often I tried to bridge that gap. My biggest impetus to learn to read was that my father read the newspaper. But even when I conquered the paper, nothing happened. My father seemed to speak in monosyllables or grunts or groans or sighs when he was home. I recall studying Hemingway's *The Old Man and the Sea* when I was in second year at high school. I asked my dad if he would like to read it as it was about fishing, and I thought he'd enjoy it. He simply said he didn't read books. That was that. The agony of emptiness I went through that night brought up my non-relationship with my father. It hit me with full force that my father never knew me and never really tried to. It was as if, to him, I was invisible.

Once the locked door to these memories and feelings was opened, it led to other locked doors and more painful scenes. Interestingly, most of these occurred when I was a teenager. It seemed I had somehow filed them under 'Just don't think about it'. I had never talked to anyone about my father's anger and rigid thinking. When I was in high school, my friend Judy and I would always go to the school dances held every Friday night. One evening I got dressed and was saying goodbye at the door, when my father asked where I was going. I told him, a bit surprised by his question because I'd been going every Friday for months. It seemed, from the way he asked, that he'd never noticed before. Then he simply said 'You're not going!' I was shocked, because usually my parents didn't seem to care where I went or when I came back. They rarely asked. I always had a sense it was a relief when I left. I asked him why I couldn't go and he said he didn't have to give a reason. The answer was just 'No'. I must have been pretty angry because I swore. Then all hell broke loose. My father came up and hit me across the face so hard I went flying and landed against the couch, quite a distance from the door. I have never figured out what led up to it or what the issue was. It wasn't discussed. I realised that nobody ever talked in my family. I think my father was pretty shocked at what he'd done and at his strength when he hit me. Except for that one night, the issue didn't arise again and Judy and I went to those dances all through high school.

Around the time when that memory surfaced, something else happened which deepened my understanding of the sense of unease that reached right into my life. I had just bought a dress that showed I had a feminine figure. Yet a profound shame arose in me for daring to buy and wear something so feminine, so revealing of my figure. I felt sad, because it wasn't an outrageous dress. Until I remembered being hit by my father that time, I had assumed that my problems with wearing flattering clothes must be related to my visits to Auntie. My grandfather had always ensured I had really nice clothes to wear, mainly dresses. But when I went home, the clothes remained in the closet till next time.

Two different lives. When I was at my grandparents' house, I dressed up in bright new dresses. My Auntie usually took me shopping and her artistic talents were reflected in the choices. The dresses came flashing back to me. One was a sleeveless dress that did up with purple ribbon on the shoulder. It had a white background with purple violets and green leaves on it. That dress always made me feel happy; it was so light and pretty. Another one was a bright buttercup yellow, which I wore with a pair of patent leather shoes. Then there was a bright orange top and skirt with black trim and an orange crinoline petticoat which I loved. I remember feeling like a Spanish dancer when I wore it. They were all such sweet memories. Then there was the leaving that smashed that whole experience, when I had to return to looking nonexistent.

Those memories all played a part – but were not the main key – in fathoming the reactions invoked when I bought dressy clothes. The real insight came when I thought of when my mother got dressed up. These images froze everything inside me. My mother always wore dresses or suits, never trousers. She really did look a bit of a mess – dishevelled and in disarray. I sometimes felt ashamed when I looked at her. It wasn't that simple though: there was another level to these memories which opened out into more complexity. When I thought of the times my mother particularly got dressed up, more fear and shame arose in me than I felt I could tolerate. Eventually I was able to recognise that she got dressed up when she went out at night and that signalled to me the cycle of abuse, the basement, abandonment.

There was even more to it – all the secrets I had to keep as to where she went. These memories were so painful because I still felt that I was a reflection of my family and didn't want yet more aspects I felt ashamed of. I was finally able to acknowledge to myself what had happened. My mother had been having an affair with the man she once worked for. This had been going on for years. It lasted until he died when my mother was in her late sixties. His name was Eric, but I had to call him Uncle Andy. He would sometimes pick me up at school and give me a ride home. I also remembered that when I was very young I went on a holiday with my mother and him. It felt awful to remember it all. He would call our place often and if my father answered, he'd hang up. If I answered, I had to pretend it was someone else and get my mother. There was a long list of threats from my mother about what would happen to me if I ever told my father. I'm sure my father knew, but he never let on. I also have no idea where Eric thought I was all those nights my mother went out with him. No matter how you looked at it, the end result was the same – my father went away to get away, my mother went out to get what she wanted, and I was left with no one. So, getting dressed up had a powerful impact on me by bringing up those repressed memories.

When my mother went out in the evenings to see Eric, she looked relatively nice. She found some of her dress sense, maybe because she felt valued. Through my therapy, I was beginning to get an idea of what might have happened inside my father that night of the dance. I had just bought a new outfit: a black tartan skirt that was above my knees, with a green mohair sweater. I also had make-up on, which was unusual. I remember looking in the mirror and thinking I looked nice. Perhaps my father projected all the anger he had with my mother onto me. He had no power over her dressing up and going out and what that meant to his self-esteem, so I got the full impact of his rage. I don't know.

I do know that all the fights I had with my dad in high school seemed to be centred around my growth into a young woman. The less I idealised him and the more I questioned his authority, the more fights we had. The closest I got to standing up to him was when I became angry with him in an argument about my driving the car after I got my licence. I got beyond his range and told him what I thought of him and then went to stay with a friend's family for several weeks.

As a result of these forays into my past, I was drawn to read a book on child development. It was a wonderful validation of what I'd been experiencing. What hit me first was the statement that it wasn't the childhood abuse that later caused the neurosis, but the repression of the trauma. I knew that intellectually, but now I was living it. The abuse that occurred was not what all my pain was about – it was that no one validated it; no one ever spoke of it, or spoke up to protect me. Everything was a secret. The other notion that was conveyed was the notion that a child's development is dependent on the way the mother experienced the needs of her child. It went on to say that many people have gone hungry all their lives, but not for lack of food. Our society has not yet acknowledged that a child's psychological nourishment really comes from parental understanding and respect. This connection to needs and hunger was a most important aspect for me, as it summed up my hunger and my anguish. As soon as I read it I knew that what I'd longed for always, as a child, was my parents' love and respect. My lack of being seen, acknowledged and valued, was the painful emptiness – my gnawing monster. I wanted what every child has a right to. I did feel there was some bond between my father and me, but he never really showed that he loved me; therefore I couldn't feel valued and respected.

Another echo of what I'd experienced for so many years in therapy was Alice Miller's suggestion that there was a tendency for therapists to use strategies and to deny the significance of childhood traumas. That certainly was what all my training was about. Therapy, as the quick fix, was the way to go. The effects of childhood were not really worthy of consideration. Yet what really made my heart leap was her acknowledging that if a person tried to talk to a therapist about these childhood issues, that person would often be given drugs. The rationale, she suggested, was that it was to spare the patient distress and agitation, but it was actually to spare therapists from facing their own unresolved fears buried in the past. Real change came by uncovering the truth. Both liberation and the ability to love came from experiencing the traumatic childhood events and the feelings of despair and anger. It felt wonderful to read this; it seemed like the story of my own journey. Therapists turned away from my pain, just as everyone in my family had done. They had closed the door and left. Truth – that is what I sought and what was the most taboo subject in my family. I knew I needed simply to keep going.

Around that time, I wrote a saying on three cards which I put on the doors of the kitchen, the bathroom and my bedroom: 'The Only Way Out Is Always Through'. Reading it constantly gave me encouragement that I was on the road home. I was reassured that the pain and the revival of all those childhood memories was a statement not that I was damaged, but that therapy was working. I was growing and changing with each truth I claimed about myself and my family. Pain in therapy was not a signal of danger, but a road map to freedom.

I soon came to realise it was extremely important for me to go back home and talk to my father, who was now eighty-seven. I wanted to try once again to communicate with him. It had been impossible to really talk in letters or on the phone. I needed to understand much more about my childhood because I had learnt that understanding was the key to my recovery.

Since I still didn't have much money, I thought of trying to cover costs by organising a workshop close to where my father lived. One day, while looking through a psychology journal I saw an international conference advertised. It had a strong focus on research relating to the impact of early childhood events. Even though they had all the papers and workshops detailed, I wrote to ask if they would like me to do a workshop one afternoon. I received an immediate and very positive answer. I did have a new view of life. It seemed I was beginning to believe that anything was possible, and that doors were worth knocking on. If I didn't knock I'd never know, and if I did, I was often pleasantly surprised.

About three weeks before I was to leave I got a call from the professor of psychology who was organising the conference, saying that their keynote speaker from Sweden was unable to come due to a family crisis. He asked if I'd consider taking his place and give the keynote address. I took a deep breath and said 'Yes'. The bonus was a significant honorarium. One knock on a door had opened up a new and totally unexpected dimension. To speak to this group on the issue of 'the impact of the loss of a sibling on the surviving and subsequent children' really forced me to expand my understanding of maternal grief. In a sense I did what I was beginning to do in therapy. It was like turning the coin over. Instead of focusing on the mother I was now entering into the understanding of the impact of grief on a child. It took me almost two weeks to write the paper. (Well, I actually wrote it three times.)

My paper incorporated my research findings on the effects on women's mental and physical health following a reproductive loss, and my findings on the effects on surviving and subsequent children of the loss of their sibling. I also presented my ideas on the development of the mother–infant bond, some recent research on infant development, as well as a self psychological perspective of grief in children. It was indeed a huge undertaking, but it was essential not only for a deeper understanding of myself, but for what I wanted to convey to other health care professionals.

There was one dream in particular that really helped me complete the work:

> *I got into a new, fast green sports car. I drove along a straight highway and it was wonderful and exciting. Then I came to a stop at the base of a mountain. It was as if it was a dead-end street. I got out and looked up the mountain. It was terrifying. It was a sheer mountain face of shiny red rock. I thought there was no way up, but I knew I needed to get to the top. I felt overwhelmed with despair. Then a man appeared and led me around to the side of the mountain, and said 'Look at the green grass and the easy slope. You can just walk up'. The grass was the brightest green imaginable, the same as the car. It was sunny and beautiful. I knew it would be an easy stroll.*

The dream seemed to be encouraging me to see obstacles, not as insurmountable as my parents did, but as something to be dealt with, calmly and easily. I also felt the dream was about my despair as to whether I could ever piece together all my ideas for this paper, and about my fears of presenting it to such a large group. It seemed I'd taken on too much. Then something shifted in therapy. I realised that the main thing was to speak from my heart, out of my understanding and caring. Suddenly, the whole load lifted and the mountain shrank. There was so much I wanted to say about children and grief. I had created an enormous amount of fear by believing that in order to be acceptable, a keynote paper had to be jam-packed with a mountain of facts and knowledge. I realised most of my real knowledge came from inside of me, not from external sources.

There was one other important insight I gained from looking at the dream. I realised that that was how I had felt as a child, looking up at my mother. Suddenly her face flashed in front of me – cold, hard and with no emotion. Yes, that was the truth. I saw that that was what was so terrifying for me as a child: to look up to my mother for love and warmth, and to be met with nothing.

The night before I went away, I awoke at midnight and wrote until morning. The revised version of my paper just flowed from me; it took on a whole new energy and passion. The revision didn't alter the content – it still encompassed the five main areas I'd started with; it just emanated from a different space. In the past I'd used my research data and other factual information in my talks to try to prove the importance of maternal grief. This time the heart had the reins and the facts were there as support. The symbol of the red mountain was the central issue of my life and my therapy, and it was now transformed into the foundation of my paper. The symbolic blank-faced mountain was all about what happens when a baby is born to an emotionally dead mother.

The main focus of the new paper was that grief is a completely emotional experience, and that if it didn't have any expression or any validation, the person suffering the loss is forced to cut off all feelings. I saw from my own experiences that feelings are not all separated into nice, neat categories. They all flowed around in that deep well within. Thus if grief is cut off, all other feelings are censored; there is simply no contact with one's own emotions and vitality. This is what I saw over and over again as a therapist working with bereaved mothers. In our society the loss of a baby, which many mothers described as the worst grief imaginable, is often considered a nonevent. This attitude deprives a woman of virtually any acknowledgment of her loss or grief. The only option open to her is to disconnect from her feelings, for in the truest sense her reality has been totally denied. The toss-up is between her sanity and her feelings.

That was what most women conveyed to me when they came for counselling. Their worst fear was that they were going crazy. It was understandable, because everyone around them was telling them they should be over their grief in a couple of weeks. After all, it was only a baby; they could just have another one. It seemed like a logical explanation, but it made no sense to the heart of a bereaved mother. She had just lost the most important person in the world to her, a person who was not replaceable or forgettable. Her sense of going crazy was caused by the total discord between her feelings and her mind. The majority of women who suffer the loss of a baby are unable to resolve their grief, because of the absence of support and understanding from those around them.

The tragedy is that the mother herself becomes deadened; the granite-faced mountain. She copes and carries on, but without her heart. And that tragedy is magnified in her surviving and subsequent children. Children cannot grow and blossom without their mother's emotional availability. If a mother has cut off from her own emotional needs, she is unable to be aware of the needs of her children. In essence she is bonded to a dead baby and has no space or time for life. This means that her surviving children will have the experience of a profoundly absent mother, which will create in them a sense of emptiness and have long-term repercussions on their psychological wellbeing. They experience a sense of abandonment, even though the mother is physically present. I suggested that these children are likely to develop apathy, or autistic traits to cover the feeling of rejection underneath. Ultimately, this detachment from the mother could lead to an inability to experience their own feelings. As such children grew to adulthood they would tend to develop a false outer self, with their true self imprisoned in a state of isolation.

I was able to see that the children of emotionally unavailable mothers were open to abuse, for when a mother has nothing to give, children wither from a lack of emotional nutrients. I knew it was also more than that. When intense feelings, like grief, are being repressed in a family, it is the child or children who express the unexpressed. Children *are* emotions. They know the truth of the heart, no matter what is being stated logically. My training in family therapy had shown me that if children express emotions that the mother herself does not want to feel, the children will in some way be punished or silenced. The pain is just too great for the mother to bear.

All these insights for my conference paper were interwoven with an increased awareness of my own childhood experiences. It was as if I could see things from the top of the mountain. I saw that no one was to blame. It wasn't the mother's fault, nor was it the surviving children's fault for trying to reawaken or enliven their emotionally absent mother. Everything just goes off-track and only empty chaos remains. We live in a society where feelings have a very low priority, particularly those of grief and more particularly over the loss of a baby who is not considered worthy of any significant grieving.

To write about all of this was terribly painful, for it was the first time understanding was dawning about my own mother. What she did to me wasn't conscious. I also realised that I had thought that I needed to be forgiving in order to get any sense of resolution about my mother, and that I couldn't imagine forgiving her for the abusive way in which she had treated me as a child. The mountain-top view showed a whole new picture. I saw that forgiveness was a moral or Christian-based principle about good and bad, but that understanding wasn't value-laden – it was just seeing things the way they were. When that clarity of vision hit me in the middle of the night I was filled with sorrow, for then I knew my mother had had no choice. She didn't have a therapist to help her find her way, as I did. The other important insight I gained through reflecting on my own experiences in therapy was that when one is filled with pain and an unbearable sense of emptiness there is a tendency to think it's coming from outside. I understood that she would have thought her pain and her sense of imprisonment was due to me.

It was sad for both of us. It all seemed such a waste of two lives. I sensed that she never really saw me at all; I was hidden behind all her layers of projections of who she thought I was. Strangely enough, I had a feeling that if I hadn't been my mother's daughter and she knew me as someone else, she might have liked me.

In thinking about the absence of a relationship with my mother I recognised that what led me into this area was my interest in the mother–infant bond. The thread that ran through my paper was the statement of how crucial it was for health care professionals to understand the depth and intensity of the mother–infant bond. This again was where self psychology had greatly increased my understanding. I found through listening to the stories of bereaved women, that they were all different because the baby had a different meaning for each mother. Thus her experiences of loss, her intensity of feelings and her needs were all unique.

The major cause of so much unresolved grief in women was that maternal grief was denied not only by society, but also by psychology and psychiatry. My research showed that a woman's grief following the loss of a baby affects her mental and physical health as profoundly as the death of a husband. Yet none of the stress inventories or psychiatric assessments even consider it worthy of inclusion. This form of loss had become surrounded in silence, even though my statistics showed that it applies to most women at some time in their lives. How could such a profound trauma that affects almost all women and families be virtually ignored until the past ten or fifteen years? That made me think of Freud's original contribution to this area. He suggested that the intensity of a person's grief was dependent on the length of the relationship with the deceased. This meant that a baby had virtually no impact on the mother and the ensuing grief would be negligible. It seemed to me that Freud had put all the focus on understanding adult bereavement. When reading about Freud's life I had discovered the interesting fact that his brother died in early infancy, when Freud was nineteen months old. It made me wonder how much this trauma affected his later ideas about grief. Was this his blind spot that psychology had inherited?

From listening to bereaved mothers I was certain that the mother's bond to her baby developed long before the baby's birth, even before conception. I felt it actually arose in the unconscious hopes and dreams of young girls as they developed ideas of the family they wished for. I tried to show that the form of loss was not what determined the grief response. Whether it was a miscarriage, abortion, stillbirth, neonatal death, the birth of a handicapped baby, cot death, or infertility – the length of time a baby lived or the gestation period were irrelevant to understanding the mother's grief. What really mattered was the meaning that particular baby (or hoped-for baby) had had for the mother.

I had seen a documentary on the life of Vincent Van Gogh a few weeks previously. What had struck me was that his mother's first-born son was named Vincent, and he had died. The eerie thing was that Vincent was born a year to the day after his brother's death. His mother took him each week to visit his brother's grave – with his name on it. Again, I wondered just how much maternal grief affected people. Van Gogh produced such beauty, yet one gets the feeling from reading biographies about him that he was never happy and lacked self-esteem. Perhaps as a child he had been trying to live up to an idealised baby – a dead baby. Perhaps he had had no chance to develop his own identity.

In developing this conference paper something significant had happened. I was overcoming the idea of things always being my fault. I certainly didn't want to carry this burden with me either to the conference or to my father. With my work and with this paper, something positive was being created out of my experiences as a child. My underlying hope was to change things for future children. 'Nothing' was being turned into 'something'. Perhaps 'fault' could be transformed into 'contribution'.

I felt anxious about giving my paper. It brought up all that old stuff about being attacked for standing out in the crowd. When that mountain of fears of not being good enough and of making mistakes began to surface, I wondered what I could say to soothe myself. Then everything fell into place; I developed a new perspective. My home had never been a place where my heart felt at home, so I gave it a new name – 'not home'. The mountain was the image of my mother and that was 'not home'. When the mountain rose I kept saying to myself 'this is not my home', and it shrank – no sheer mountain faces, only grassy paths. Just as I had separated Me from 'not me' I was learning the difference between home and 'not home', and I could choose to be on the other side of the mountain – the 'home' side – where acceptance and nurturing and sunshine were in abundance.

Before I knew it, I was standing at the podium giving my talk. It went smoothly and I conveyed all that I'd hoped to. My conclusion centred around self psychology. I said that my past seven years of working within a self psychological framework was most valuable in assisting bereaved mothers to a healthy grief resolution. I acknowledged my appreciation of the truly transformative power of self psychology, where I saw women gain a heightened appreciation of their living children, as well as a sense of how precious they were and of how precious life is. I had come to see that through mourning their loss, the women ultimately found that the foundation of grief is love. Grief is a testimony to the depth of our love. Thus the journey always ends back at love of self, of others and of life.

My presentation included excerpts from an unedited video I had made of a bereaved mother talking about the impact of the loss of her third baby on her life and on the lives of her children. I had indeed spoken from my heart. The reception from the audience was warm and enthusiastic, and in thanking me afterwards the professor said there had not been a dry eye in the auditorium. Several invitations to do workshops and present papers at conferences resulted from my presentation. The whole experience did wonders for my self-esteem. I also knew, even if no one else did, that in a sense I was actually telling my own story. That, in itself, seemed healing. By being able to put words to the grief I'd felt as a child, and being able to explain those experiences through my work as a therapist with other women and their families, I felt an inner and outer sense of connectedness.

Later that day I rang my father and told him how well received my paper had been and how enthusiastic everyone had seemed about my work and ideas. I should have expected it, but even at forty-four I was still hoping for some acknowledgment from my father. 'Oh yes, that's nice,' he said, then went on to talk about the weather. I felt crushed. You can gain the attention and appreciation of many people in your adult life, but if it isn't freely available from your parents you just keep on hoping and doing more to try to get it. That was what my incessant hunger or craving was about. Through my disappointment I recalled that Neil had said I was going to do just fine. So I focused on my own pleasure of having done well. I knew that Neil would be delighted and pleased for me. His voice was already changing my inner dialogue.

The combination of my talk and Neil's belief in me brought me to a new level of awareness. It was related to adequate parenting. I hadn't touched a self psychology book or paper since I started therapy. I had just entered the process and never analysed what was happening. In re-reading my self psychology books, and in looking back to the times Neil used to visit as a supervisor, I became much more conscious of the powerful idealising bond I had with him. What I never really accepted until now was the power that the bond had to heal me. It felt like total re-parenting. I began to see that children grow from the base of the high ideal they have of their parents, and eventually feel proud to be themselves, to be excited about trying new things, and to show their talent. That just didn't happen with my parents. That's why I had seen Neil as extremely talented and competent. Not that he wasn't, it's just that I added mine as well. These were aspects of myself I'd placed on him because I'd been unable to own them. They'd been 'not me' because my parents had never mirrored them back to me. That day I saw how Neil was helping me replace old mountains with easy pathways. The fascinating thing was that he didn't use some unfathomable, indefinable method or have an unequalled talent – he just saw the real me and encouraged me to come out by responding when I did. The encouragement needed only to be minimal, like his simple statement of 'You're going to do just fine', not 'fantastic' or 'wonderful' – those were different mountains, equally insurmountable. 'Just fine' for me meant I would be good enough. The icing on the cake was that it went very well. But I could see that I was now aiming for the middle road. Something more ordinary was happening inside. I felt so much more solid. I'd grown from a seedling into a tree, continually growing new branches and instead of fearing being cut down, I was enjoying being seen.

That sense of having something solid inside was very important for me to be aware of before my visit to my father. The four days I spent with him knocked me around a lot. Even though I really knew it was important for us to talk and for him to shine some light on those experiences in my past, I still wasn't prepared emotionally for what he told me.

We spent several hours on the front porch one afternoon. It wasn't easy to get him to reflect, for he really did believe the past belonged under some imaginary carpet. But I persisted. I asked him to start at the beginning of their marriage. That outlined the whole story. My mother had been engaged to an Englishman who was killed in a train crash. Dad met her not long afterwards and they married within a year. Grief began the relationship, in a sense; there is no way my mother would have recovered in that time. The saddest thing was I didn't get the impression that my father even really loved her. I asked him if she was pretty, or fun to be with and he just said 'No, not particularly'.

So why marry? It just seemed like a good idea. I asked him about children. My mother was forty-two when I was born and my father forty-four. They'd been married sixteen years. I'd always wondered what had happened. He said my mother did not want any children. She just wasn't interested in children. In fact, she had had several abortions before I came along. I wondered how he felt about that. He said he had wanted to have several children, but didn't know my mother was against it. Didn't they talk about it before they were married? No, no talking. He went on to explain that their marriage was all right for about eight years, and then she started having an affair. He told me that several years before I was born, he saw my mother out with Eric one evening when he went for a walk. They were walking arm in arm. He sounded so depressed and defeated when he spoke of it. 'So what did you do?' I asked. 'Nothing,' he said. God. Nobody talked, nobody expressed feelings and nobody did anything in my family. He told me that people had, over the years, asked him why he did nothing, but that he 'couldn't fight'. I asked him what that meant. He said that he just couldn't hurt his family – they'd be so ashamed if his marriage hadn't worked.

'What had my mother wanted?' I asked. She was always wanting to get him to give her a divorce, but he refused. Why, oh, why, oh why? He felt it would embarrass his family and my mother's family. No one in the family had ever been divorced. I was astounded. 'You mean you both lived ruined, empty lives just for the sake of what others thought?' He just said 'Yes' and turned his face away. My dad no longer seemed big or powerful and in control. I felt so sad for him and for my mother – an empty marriage and two 'nothing' lives. Neither of them had valued their own personal hopes and dreams in life, or those of the other.

I summoned my bravery and asked about the time my mother was pregnant with me. He said he'd never forget the day she told him. Apparently he was just leaving to go to a Lodge conference for a week and she stood at the door and told him she was pregnant. She also said she had tried to have an abortion but it had failed. My heart sank. This was the family I was to enter, unwanted and unwelcomed. He then told me that he simply said to her it was impossible that he was the father and slammed the door. I wasn't expecting that one. He then added that the news ruined his conference. My heart sank again, a ruined conference seemed minuscule compared to how ruined I felt by my mother. 'So you're not my real father,' I said. He shook his head. 'I'm not one-hundred percent sure, but I don't think so,' he said.

I then asked him whether he knew my mother was crazy and when it happened. Before he answered, I asked whether it was when I was born or when the gas stove exploded. 'No,' he replied. 'Neither of those things changed her – it happened long before that.' But he said he didn't know what had caused it. I'd really convinced myself that it was either my birth or the accident with the gas stove. Then I remembered Neil saying to me that he was sure it wasn't either of those things; I had probably hung onto them to find some event or reason as to why my mother didn't love me. To just not love me was too much for me to bear. Then I asked my father a very important question. I asked why my mother had hated me so much. He said he didn't know. Then I asked whether it was me and my personality or whether it would have been the same with any child. He said it wasn't me and it would have been exactly the same with any child, she just didn't like children. He then leaned towards me, his voice taking on a firmness as though he were about to sort something out once and for all: 'Listen, your mother never wanted you, never loved you and I don't know the reason why'. That was it. That was the knowledge I'd spent my life running away from, and years of therapy trying to uncover. By this time there was every emotion I'd ever known, plus a few more, coursing through my veins. But somehow the solidness remained – I wasn't engulfed by my emotions. The gratitude I accorded to self psychology and to Neil for helping me find my own truth, my own story, was immense. I knew there would have been no way my father or anyone else would have told me unless I had first discovered it myself and pursued the truth. I felt validated and devastated at the same time. I also had a real understanding of why I was a black mark to my mother.

I think the most painful aspect of our talk was the subject of my mother abuse. He talked about finding me in the closet. He said that when he found me I was unconscious and that when I came out of it I was terrified and in shock. He'd never seen anyone so frightened. I asked him what he felt or what he did afterwards. Well, he was pretty upset with my mother, he said. That's when the child in me wept and wept. 'Upset' – that was the impact. 'But it didn't stop her from doing it again and again,' I said. 'No, I never had much influence on her,' he replied. I felt empty inside. Here was my big strong protector. He did nothing. I had come in search of the truth and that was what I found, but I still wished it could have been a different truth.

At almost every meal my father and I had together, we got into conflict. He was adamant about what I was to eat and would get angry if I didn't share his views on my tastes. He would try to insist I ate what I didn't like. It had so much to do with power and control. I had these awful pains in my stomach, like a hand was clinched around it. I realised later that the hunger I'd felt before was somehow related. What I had needed was the real psychological food of love and appreciation, not to be force-fed what I didn't want or need. That was the missing ingredient. In the time I was there my father never asked me anything about my life or my work or where I lived or how I was going. Perhaps the hardest thing was seeing my book on the china cabinet and asking my dad what he thought of it. He said he hadn't read it, because it seemed to be about women.

On the last day my father went out for a few hours and I had some time alone in the house. It was strange. It seemed so small, almost as if it had shrunk. I had a wander through the basement and walked up the steps slowly. I counted them. Eleven steps that at one time in my life had seemed to lead to total blackness. I got my journal and sat on the top step, writing about the conference and the talk with my father. It felt important to do it from there. I was honouring the little girl who had spent so much time sitting in the same place, frozen in terror. I was saying to her that I would never forget what she had gone through and that I would continue to listen to her story. I told my inner child that although it had been horrific, she had learned so much, and I was using that knowledge to help others understand children's grief.

There was something else I needed to do before I left, but I wasn't exactly sure what it was. I wanted to make a symbolic gesture in memory of the child I once was. The next morning before leaving for the train, I went down to the basement again. I stood at the bottom of the steps and suddenly I had an image of a blue daisy in my hand. I walked up and laid the imaginary daisy on the top step. As I did so I said to myself 'May the child who sat here be healed'. That was what I hoped for more than anything.

CHAPTER 18

Seeing red

I had no idea how disturbing the visit to my father had been until I got back to therapy. I could not process all the pain on my own, so I carried it as excess baggage, just as I'd done as a child. At least this time there was someone to talk to who would understand. It took many sessions before my feelings had a voice. In the first session I talked about being with my father. There was an enormous sadness attached to my father telling me that my mother had never wanted me. While what he had told me had validated my dreams and my awareness of not belonging and of not being loved, the pain was awful. I felt dead and devastated.

Perhaps the worst hurt was in the realisation of just how ineffectual my father was. His response to finding me in the closet was like an observation: no real feelings, no outrage at what had been done; just impotence. I thought about how angry I got if my son was hurt, even in a minor way; I have a lioness inside me when it comes to Michael's welfare. But no parental protectiveness had existed for me. I knew that you don't really get angry about anything or defend anyone unless love is present. My father's story of my mother's announcement of her pregnancy opened all the wounds of feeling unwanted. I saw a mother who didn't want a baby and a father who said he was not my father and who went on to explain how the news of my forthcoming arrival ruined his Lodge convention. I was again encapsulated in glass, frozen, unable to find words to explain what was going on inside. As I recounted my experiences at home, I found a name for them: 'horrific'.

I spoke with my friend Mathew not long after I got back and told him what had happened. He felt my sense of devastation and said that I probably would have preferred invalidation to being told I wasn't wanted. Yes, sometimes the truth hurts too much. The pain was once again about contrasts. I had known what it was like to be loved and I was gaining a renewed sense of myself and my own worth through therapy. Going back to my childhood home brought with it an overwhelming sense of emptiness – an absence of love. It reminded me of the handicapped children I'd worked with. Were the ones with bright minds that could fathom that they were trapped in totally unusable bodies better off? Or were the ones with severe brain damage better off because they were unaware of their plight? I didn't know the answer. I just ached. It was very costly to become conscious.

The other aspect that saddened me was that everyone had missed out on love. There was no joy, laughter or excitement in life at all. It reminded me of the time I had rung my father to tell him about my success at the conference, and he had given no emotional response. I began to see the connection with my findings on bereaved mothers: when people are disconnected from themselves, they're disconnected from all feelings. Any intense, enlivening feelings like excitement and joy were particularly threatening to someone like my father.

Excitement and joy are what most parents normally feel at the announcement of a pregnancy. It should herald great joy. My forthcoming birth signalled unhappiness and despair; I was a nuisance. I had indeed written my first book for a good reason: it was about mothers who were grief-stricken instead of delighted. Obviously something had gone terribly wrong in my mother's life. Whatever it was that happened to her, the end result for me was a deep sense of never belonging anywhere, of being unwanted. Then the memory of my Auntie came to me. Yes, she was the one who pulled me through. I'd forgotten this since I'd slid back into the black hole, but going back home had made it even more vivid for me. With Auntie I had experienced feelings of excitement and joy, and particularly love. My grandfather had loved me as well. I recognised that it wasn't that I was unlovable – it was only that my parents couldn't love. It was a very big difference.

Another dream highlighted my feelings of being with my father. I dreamt I went with someone into a walk-in freezer, like those at a butcher's. Then the door locked and I couldn't get out. I woke up in absolute terror. I felt I'd been treated like a piece of meat when I'd been back home. It was as though I had no existence or identity of my own. My father decided what I wanted to eat and what I did and didn't want to do. He never once asked me anything about myself or about what I wanted or felt like doing. It was as if I were a 'nothing'. He was so rigid; he had to be right all the time. It was a blow to me after feeling so valued at the conference. It was like crossing the border into the frozen zone, not unlike the border between my grandparents' home and my parents' place. I had gone home hoping things would be different, that there might be some relationship there. But it was very cold. I began to see how my mother may have felt being married to my father. There just seemed to be no warmth in him. I could understand why she would look to someone else for love. He truly was a mechanic. Being with him revived all those old feelings. I again had a sense that I was born defective. I had that deep-down feeling that if I'd been good enough I would have been loved, and that since I wasn't, I had no value. It didn't make sense logically, but that was the awful feeling I had.

On the same night I had another dream:

I put all my valuables into a safe in the wall in my home. It was filled with jewels and money. I then went back to take them out and it was filled with ice. I knew the valuables were there, but I couldn't get to them through the block of ice.

I associated wall safes with richness: big houses and lots of money and valuables. What had happened to my valuables? The flower was back in glass, protected from the outside world. Yet the protection was also a barrier that stopped anyone seeing my value and kept me feeling worthless. Presenting my ideas at the conference had been a huge step forward for me. I had never really exposed my views so openly and so passionately. To have both myself and my presentation warmly received gave me a new sense of acceptance. What I had to offer was valued and appreciated. Yet something happened to take it away and put it on ice. One aspect of this was my father's lack of response. The other was the part of myself that feared success. This was very dangerous territory – positive experiences were painful. Success spelled out the things my family didn't or wouldn't stand for – visibility, openness, speaking your own mind, expressing your own feelings, being proud of yourself, valuing yourself, being loved and accepted, and having money. In going against the family system I'd made myself extremely vulnerable. I was hiding in the basement.

It took a while for my anger to arrive. In the time I was with my father and just afterwards, and later in therapy, I had felt no anger – only pain and distress. My personal paintbox was still depleted of the most vibrant colour. I knew black inside out, but bright red had remained fairly taboo. I began to understand more clearly that if you value yourself, it is healthy and natural to be angry when someone doesn't value you. I had always thought it was only love that melted the ice. But this was a new dimension of love – this was the lioness. I'd had a lot of experience with it in standing up for principles of fairness and rights for others, even for trees. If I could be angry on behalf of others, could I not be angry on behalf of myself?

I had to look at this repetitive theme from the inside. My lack of anger with my father was only the outer reflection. It was vital for me to catch the parental voice within, which would not allow me to claim and show my own wealth. I could not change my father; I had to let that go. To face the inner 'Ice Man' was truly horrifying, yet I knew that my depression would never really go until I stopped making ice. The greatest irony was that the fear that had frozen me most was actually the fear of my own anger.

I'd get frightened if I sensed even a spark of anger in myself. It was directly related to the bond of love. I was always concerned about disturbing the bond in any way. It had been broken so many times in childhood, it felt as though it were a precarious and fragile thing.

Instead of the bridge being made of even stronger stuff than steel and iron, it seemed more like delicate silk. It was my responsibility to make sure it didn't get damaged, so I was always cautious. That was reflected in my relationship with my friends, with Michael, and in therapy. I thought that anger blew up bridges. I didn't know it actually made them stronger. I soon began to learn that the availability of anger strengthened relationships with oneself and with others. The image that came to mind was a sword, a sword that cut through falsity – internally and externally. When you felt strongly about yourself and what you believed in, anger signalled your boundaries. Anger had a defining quality. It turned a wishy-washy, appeasing self into a person of depth and clarity. It gave shape and form to who one was. You couldn't be stepped on or taken for granted. It meant that living unconsciously or being a victim would no longer feel like a safe home.

What I hadn't bargained for was how much anger had been stored behind the floodgate. For weeks I felt little else. My paint repertoire suddenly reversed. Red splashed everywhere. My temper also seeped into ordinary things on the outside. I was not always pleasant. I'd often be frightened of the intensity of my anger, but I just kept encouraging myself to find the words to express it. So it just kept flowing and eventually words came.

The energy anger gave me was unexpected. It wasn't just that I slept less and fell into fewer holes, but that I didn't know what to do with all this new-found energy. That's when it really hit me that much of my anxiety was energy demanding to be expressed. The basement and the closet door were being kicked open. I'd had niceness up to my ears. In fact, I had been drowning in it.

So what do you do when you have this wild horse racing through you? What do you do in the middle of the night when you feel you'll explode? What do you do with twice as much energy as you've ever had? Well, that's when I started running. It was hard at first, because I was so unfit. But eventually it felt wonderful. I took my dog Buffy on such long runs that after a while even he was beginning to wonder what was happening. Soon it became a routine. I ran with a friend every morning at dawn. It was great. It cleared my head, cleared my emotions and made me feel much stronger. Now it felt I was running towards something instead of always running away.

The other way I channelled my anger was through my tennis racket, not by playing tennis, but by beating my bed with it! There were times when the anger would just swell up and my body felt overcome. I had to do something, even though I often didn't know exactly what the anger was related to. I'd put on loud music and beat the hell out of my bed. The music really did have to be loud because with each blow I'd yell or shout or swear. Usually some image would surface at that time so I had some understanding of the focus. I was beginning to trust the wisdom of my body and the wordless truth it contained.

It is hard to explain the specifics of my anger, because it was really about everything and nothing. Initially it was anger about my father and his lack of support and protection. It was also about my mother. But really it was about life and unfairness. It wasn't about my mother or my father or their parents or every generation back. And yet it was. I was angry that nobody had a chance to be themselves. No one seemed to get what they wanted in life, so no one could ever show me how to live life fully.

The core of my anger was really the pain I felt about being a woman. Intermingled with all of this was my personal anger about my life. Although some of it was still about my childhood, most of my anger seemed to be about my adult life. These issues had really started to bubble up around my birthday, but I'd put them in the too-hard basket. Turning forty-four seemed more of a mid-life crisis than forty. It brought up all the grief I faced in the realisation that I wouldn't have any more children. This was the very message I had conveyed at the conference about understanding women's grief. Over and over I had stressed how important it was that health care professionals understood the hopes and dreams of bereaved mothers, rather than simply assessing the reality of their situation. If a woman had wanted five children and the fifth child died, she would experience profound grief. While people would tell her she was lucky to have four, it was not the quantity that mattered; each child had had a special meaning for her. That woman would be totally different from one who had hoped to have child and did, and later found she was infertile – she had fulfilled her dreams. The reverse situation was also very important to understand. If a woman had wanted two children and had three, she would experience a significant grief that the outside world would probably find difficult to understand. If that grief was not dealt with, the relationship with that third baby could be quite unhealthy and detrimental to the child.

For the production of my video, I had interviewed many little girls from the ages of four to twelve and was surprised by how clear they were about the number of children they hoped to have. Without much hesitation they would say 'Two boys' or 'Five children and it doesn't matter if they are girls or boys'. All seemed to have a picture. It helped me acknowledge that I had always wanted two children, one girl and one boy. I knew that grief had been there for many years. With each year's passing since my divorce, my grief compounded. My hope for the family I wished for faded, but the grief didn't. Part of my anger was for what might have been.

What I hadn't expected as my anger grabbed hold of me was the uncovering of a memory I had totally buried. My whole body retracted, and all I heard inside my head was 'No, no, no, no – don't look. Don't say it. Don't talk about it'. But I took a deep breath and allowed the memory – that had burned inside me for twenty-one years –to emerge. I was living with Mark in London at the time. I could see myself coming home from work and walking up to the house we lived in. It was spring and I was eating some strawberries that I had just bought. Mark met me at the door and I knew that the look on his face spelt disaster. I had tried to forget that he was going to call the doctor about the pregnancy test; in fact, I'd tried to ignore the whole issue. All I knew was that something died right there, right then on the doorstep. Without his even saying anything, I saw in his face there was no way he'd consider marriage or taking responsibility for a baby. Later we talked, but I didn't ever really understand why he was so adamant that I have an abortion. Maybe it was, as he said, just bad timing. I allowed the decision to be made for me. I didn't see any options, nor did anyone even talk to me about my feelings. As I came out of the anaesthetic, I felt a screaming emptiness. The nurse told me that the baby had been a girl. That would always stay with me. Soon afterwards Mark walked in – hockey stick in one hand, flowers in the other. He seemed happy and relieved. More than a baby was terminated that spring.

It was anger that had taken me back, and anger that had allowed the unexpressed feeling in my body to make a statement. Anger also allowed my grief over not having a second child to have some space. It led me to an awareness I hadn't expected. I realised that although that had been my hope, it was for a distant past. I knew that if I'd been able to have another child, even by the age of forty, I would have chosen not to. It had to do with energy. When Michael was born I'd just turned thirty and the timing was exactly right for me. His birth had filled me with joy. But by forty I knew that things were different. I couldn't have coped with a new baby. I'd entered a different stage of life.

Once again I was back on the mountain-top gaining a new perspective. I had some understanding as to why my mother would have tried to have an abortion when she had found herself pregnant with me. She had never had a dream to have children. She was forty-two when I was born. Her age had never really registered with me. From this new perspective I had some growing empathy with my mother. She should not have been made to have a baby, and of course that left me out of existence. Yet something did change inside of me and I was more able to separate myself from my mother's pregnancy. It would have been the same with any baby. It wasn't me she hated, it was having to have a baby she didn't want. She simply had felt more and more trapped as she lost whatever her real dreams in life were.

My anger seemed to have dragged me mercilessly to all the wounded places in my body and my psyche. It was like a laser beam that homed in on the points of pain. I was feeling the anguish of being a woman in my family. But like a stone cast in a lake, I also saw the reverberations. I could see my anguish was really about the abuse of the feminine. I'd begun to understand more clearly from my reading in psychology that the so-called feminine part of the self comprises the feeling, emotional, relating, and nurturing aspects. It was similar to the idea of the inner child. Children are truly in touch with their bodies and feelings; emotions are their natural paints. Feelings tell children the truth. I saw that the 'child-like' or 'feminine' quality of a person was not just in women but in men as well. Then I realised the trap my father was also in. I remembered what I'd conveyed in my book: that when a person's feelings don't have any validation or expression, the person has two options. One is to cut off completely and the other is to go crazy. I knew that whatever had happened to each of my parents, it had led to their own emotional death. My mother's craziness and my father's coldness were the results. I didn't know which came first or why, but I was no longer stumbling around in total darkness.

The monster was a symbol of my anger at the way I had been treated as a child. I grew to have an enormous respect for this monster. I realised that the anger I'd kept at bay was a very healthy part of me that was enraged at being devalued and crushed as a child. The monster was my lifeblood, and without it I was handicapped. The very emotion I had always been terrified of had befriended me. It was the part of me that made me determined to survive and determined to find my way back.

I knew that if my parents had ever claimed their anger, all our lives would have been different. They both had lived in terror of what other people thought or expected of them. Patriarchal rules were what controlled them. Their emotions and their lives were the sacrifice.

The other thing I realised was that when I got in touch with my anger my heart opened. What I felt angry about was what I cared about, what mattered to me. So for the first time I saw there was a lot in my life that mattered. In breaking the ice around my heart I began to feel compassion for my family and for myself. It eventually led me directly back to love. In all my grief work and therapy I had always shied away from this emotion.

Believing more in myself seemed to be gathering momentum in my career and in my personal life. I was about to have my claim for maintenance heard in court. This was a major step for me – to stand up for my rights with regard to money instead of just accepting the unacceptable, as I had done for ten years. It seemed like such an ordinary thing: to want to receive maintenance for my son that was considered reasonable by the court. Yet I hated every moment leading up to it. Conflict did awful things to me. As the time drew closer I once again felt the vulnerability of being a woman, particularly in a family where women never seemed able to stand up for their rights.

Not long before the court date I had a dream that brought back memories of my Aunt Ruby, who was married to my mother's brother. She was different from all the other women in the family. She was independent and spoke her mind, so everyone thought she was bossy and hard to get along with. I found her to be lots of fun and full of energy. She certainly was well loved by my uncle. They seemed to have the only relationship in the family that was healthy and loving. She was manager of a chain of shops and led a busy and active life. Ruby was probably the only woman in my family of my mother's generation who was actually true to herself and emotionally alive. The memory of her brought a new energy into my life, a new way of seeing myself as a woman. I held onto her image over the time of the court case.

My hypnosis exams were scheduled for the week before the court case. I was very close to not doing them, because I felt anxious about going to court. It was the dream of Aunt Ruby that stopped my postponing them. I'd been studying for three years and wasn't going to let the impending court case stand in my way. It was important to do them. These exams marked the end of formal study and of being a student. I wanted to have a sense of completion and of moving onwards.

The day in court produced a satisfactory result. What surprised me most was that I had been able to do it. When you are not stood up for and protected as a child, it is almost impossible to stand up for yourself as an adult. You don't have the experience to know what it's like.

It had been very important for me psychologically to finally be able to stand up, not only for my own rights, but for the rights of my child (even though I knew that the legal costs would probably offset this gain considerably). Afterwards I was aware that a significant strengthening had developed within me through my therapy. Being believed in really did help me believe in my own self and in my entitlements in life.

The next day I turned up at my workshop. There were over fifty health care professionals in attendance – all women. It felt great not to be in court and to be surrounded by people who cared about women and children. After I stood up and introduced myself, I said 'The bond that links a mother to her baby is the most powerful of all human bonds'. Although I'd said it many times, this time I said it with such passion and conviction that I began to cry. It surprised both me and the people there. I didn't usually start off a workshop crying, yet what I had gone through over the past months and in the court case overwhelmed me with emotion. I didn't know whether I'd lost or won in monetary terms. What I did know was that the bond was more important than anything. I knew that love was what mattered. I also knew that women who love their children would never forsake that relationship. For an instant, I had a profound and wordless understanding of what women went through when that bond was broken or challenged. I felt the full impact of all I had written in my book on maternal grief. I felt both the pain and the richness of motherhood. I was filled with gratitude for my delightful son and for the presence of my Auntie in my life. I knew it was the bond with her that enabled me to be the mother I'd always hoped to be to my child.

A week or so later Michael went to visit his father for the Christmas holidays. Before he left, we had a little Christmas celebration. When I say 'little' I mean 'little' – it was financially the worst time I'd ever had. What saddened me most was that I couldn't afford any presents for Michael. I remembered a game my Auntie and I used to play about imagining, so I called Michael into the living room and said we were about to have a Christmas celebration. His eyes lit up. I asked him to help me imagine a tree in the centre of the room. Then we decorated it. I told him that he could probably see there were ten presents for him and ten for me under the tree. He was just great; he caught on immediately. We picked up presents and tried to guess what was inside. We unwrapped them and went 'Ooh' and 'Aah', and 'What lovely wrapping paper', and 'Isn't that wonderful?', and 'It is just what I'd hoped for!' So it went with all twenty presents. We laughed so much. We both got exactly what we wanted for Christmas. 'Nothing' had truly turned into something wonderful.

In my next session I talked about being upset at not being able to get any presents for Michael and also what we ended up doing. At the end, Neil said 'You know your Auntie gave you the greatest gift any child could receive – your imagination'. That day as I walked home, I felt like the richest person on earth.

CHAPTER 19

Shattering the blackness

The time over Christmas and New Year was spent soul-searching and reviewing in order to set my priorities. I had learnt more than I ever dreamt possible during the previous year. Now I was much clearer about who I was and what my values in life were. Most striking was the realisation that I hadn't been depressed for quite a while. I'd had my disappointments and my moments of resurging fear and despair, as well as all that anger and rage in the later months. As the year came to a close there were two things I was absolutely certain about. I knew that love and the people I loved were what I valued most in my life. I had a deep love for all aspects of my life: my son, my friends, my work, my writing and my painting. I also had a greater appreciation of the inner journey and of my therapy than ever before.

In a sense I felt I had jumped off a cliff. The court process had made me to see who I really was. In forcing myself to make a stand, I had to find a self worthy of standing up for. That experience, combined with the impact of having no money at Christmas, taught me the true meaning of wealth. It was as if the external forces had pressed so hard on my belief structures that they had collapsed, and I found a more solid structure underneath. I'd created the cliff in order to shatter the outer shell. I broke through the wall that had separated me from my heart. The picture I had of the cliff was one I'd had a few times in therapy. I'd be standing on the edge and a voice would say 'Jump' and I'd say 'No'. This would go on many times, then a hand gently pushed me and I jumped – and then I flew. That's exactly how those moments of insights made my heart soar. The 'old' me who wanted everything to be the same would just stand there with her arms crossed saying 'No way, I'm not letting go of my fears. It's not safe out there'. But in opening to my inner world I'd see the fears were all manufactured in my mind in ancient outmoded factories. At those moments where therapy just flowed, the hand of understanding pushed me over to a new experience, a fearless way of being. I'm not saying that these moments stayed long or that the fears had gone, but I was feeling fully alive and that was new. A patchwork quilt was being made, piecing together my life and me and moments of freedom and the joy of being alive. It gave me hope that one day those patches would be sewn together into a whole new fabric of life. Christmas had been a time of gifts, and the greatest had been my own sense of self.

Inextricably linked to my new awareness of self was an acute awareness of the importance of becoming attuned to my needs. I had learnt that if I didn't care for myself and listen to my needs, I couldn't give of myself freely. I'd always tried to work out the needs of others, but this was born out of need, not out of equality. Connected to my belief of not being good enough was an insistence that I compensate for that deficit.

I had to face the issue of power. In the past it had been impossible for me to openly value myself. I had to look powerless and helpless in order to have my needs met. I had constantly underplayed, devalued and dismissed my contribution in my personal and professional life. This increased an already overloaded belief system that the power was outside of me, that other people were talented, healthy, happy, valuable and powerful. Now though, I was grappling with the new idea that I could actually be in charge of my life. I wanted to be a participant, not a passive watcher.

The image that hit me was of being split in two. Part of me had lived under the dictatorship of my mother and the other part emerged from the loving bond with my Auntie – two opposites. I could see that my false self, or mask, the Me who degraded herself and feared every step in life, was all in my mind. It contained endless injunctions, rules and punishments; a court of no appeals that was harsh, strict, and unrelenting in its demands. Whenever I managed to get out of my head and reconnect to my feelings, the judge disappeared and life was sweet. But the battle was ongoing as to who was actually running the show. I knew that whatever the answer was, it was related to staying out of my mind.

I then began to get a picture of the machinery in my mind. It was like a vast construction site, with earth movers and cranes and forklifts. I saw how I kept the whole thing going. These machines kept the fear going round and round in never-ending circles. That was my state of worry. Over the years the actual things to worry about changed, but the dynamics didn't. So much of my energy was spent trying to work things out and worrying about each step, past or future – it didn't matter. Things I had done or said, or not done or said – I got a critique on every movement. I'd just drift into this space of nothingness and the mind would begin its chatter. Once I was in the dead space, I just had to sit there quietly and listen.

I saw how my fear machine affected my outside life. I saw how it created crises, dramas, chaos, giving me a feeling I was in backlog – always trying to do too much with too little as well as doing too many things at once. Too little time for fun or play, too little time for the child. I saw the messes I had created in all of my juggling acts. It had to stop. I could see that if I was ever going to find out what my real needs were, I would first have to disengage this mechanical monster. I needed to deal with the inner issues and to initiate some real outer changes. To me, that meant sorting out the messes around me, especially my financial ones.

I was tired of the battle, tired of undermining myself, tired of working hard at being someone I wasn't in order to fit in, and tired of trying to live out a blueprint manufactured in the mind of my mother. All my life I had tried to make people love me by doing things to please or impress them. It took me forty-four years to learn that love did not come as a result of how much you did, how good you were or how much you tried to please the other person. Love happened simply for being who you were – no strings attached.

My mind had kept me not only a prisoner but also a guard, constantly on duty, watching to see that it was safe. I felt the exhaustion in my body and I knew I couldn't keep living on adrenalin. I had touched the eagle's heart in leaping off the mountain of my fears, and I could no longer keep going back and pretending that I lived in a cage. Flying was vastly different from living on the craggy precipice locked in ambivalence and mesmerised by the dialogue of endless fear: 'Will I do this ... No ... Imagine what will happen ... What will people think? ... Well, maybe I'll do that ... No, it won't work ... You'll make a mistake ... You'll make a fool of yourself ... Maybe I'll write ... or paint ... Don't be silly, you have no talent ... Well, maybe ... No, no, no ... You know you're not good enough ... It's not good enough ... No, no ... don't do it, don't do it ... It's too risky ... Just stay here, stay here with me ... Be good and quiet and nice ... I'll protect you ... Well, maybe ... '

No. I'd had it. No more dramas, no more stresses, no more chaos, no more poverty, no more abuse. My anger was at hand. Last year it pushed me into action, now it was there as an impetus to change my relationship with life. It clarified my need to sort things out. What I didn't know was that sorting out would be the theme of the whole year ...

My three weeks on my own were coming to a close. Michael was due home in two days and my therapy was to start again. I began to see that the spaces in between therapy were as healing as the therapy itself. They gave me time to stop and see where I'd been and where I was going, time to consolidate. They also allowed me to feel the full impact of the stress in my life. My house still hadn't sold and my debts were screaming at me. Living through the intensity of the stress forced me to take off my blindfold. Whatever lay ahead of me I knew that stress had to be removed. I saw how unconsciously I had kept the tyrant alive in my life – by connecting to men who didn't value me and by creating situations where authority figures like bank managers became millstones around my neck. I had to see once and for all that the real enemy was in my head and that's where the revolution needed to begin. If I had created these situations of poverty, indebtedness and abuse, surely I could dismantle them. I was adamant I'd become debt-free and claim my freedom. I knew I had the skills to be an advocate for others who had their basic rights threatened. Surely I could attain my own peace of mind and guarantee my own safety and security. Maslow's hierarchy of human needs – was I entitled to them?

The other important discovery I made over this break was that I was able to process what was going on inside of me through writing in my journal and attending to my dreams. It was as though an inner therapist could enter the blackness, and calm the terrified child without becoming lost or overwhelmed. That inner therapist seemed able to go into the dark places and write her way back out, bringing something of value to the surface each time. My writing was my greatest asset.

However, as I walked to my session I had no idea what my new resolve would bring into the therapeutic space. What I hadn't expected was my body making its own statement. When I walked into the room, I stood motionless inside the door. My body refused to sit in the chair I normally sat in. I wanted to sit in Neil's chair. Even though the choice had always been mine, once I'd moved from the two-seater couch and chosen the chair on the left of the door, I had made this a routine. Today I wanted to change. Could I get the words out? Eventually I asked if I could sit on 'his' chair. He smiled. So I did. It was the strangest experience. I had a whole new perspective. It symbolised my claiming authority over my life. The whole session went smoothly. It was great to be back and to have a sense of moving forward.

What I wasn't prepared for was the havoc that broke loose inside of me in the next two days from the simple act of sitting in a different chair. I began to see through my inner chaos that it was really about growing up. I had a sense that we were about halfway in therapy, which was a pretty amazing insight because up to that point I had felt it could go on forever. There had always seemed to be an endless backlog within me, but that was what my intuition told me. It turned out I was spot-on. I could see that in asking if I could switch chairs I was really asking if I were old enough to take charge of my life. I wondered how far I had developed. Had the child within really begun to grow? I felt as though I were an adolescent, just going into high school. I felt very grown up compared to the primary school children, but I was also being hit by the realisation that there was still quite a way to go.

There was a blackness descending over me that hadn't been there for ages. So I just kept writing in my journal. What was so terrifying? I began to see that the depression grew out of an awareness that we were on our way home. Therapy has a beginning, a middle and an end, and I felt I was right in the centre. I was also hit by the irony of therapy. There was no going back. I guess it was a bit like childhood. Once you find out there is no Santa Claus you can't keep pretending there is. In growing, you just become more conscious – it's a natural process that can't be reversed. That's where the havoc and pain came in. The push was to go forward and the pull was the fear of growing up. I saw, for the very first time, that these rites of passage meant both leaving behind an old way and entering a new stage. These new steps were reflected in the reversal of chairs. I was taking responsibility. Power and responsibility – I could see they both went hand in hand.

I also became aware that becoming conscious and responsible meant giving up dependency. That was where the terror entered; that was the inner battle. A part of me screamed 'No, I don't want to grow up. I can't make it on my own'. Then I remembered saying to my mother when I was around thirteen that I just didn't want to grow up. Looking at that time from this end of the telescope I can understand why I had felt like that. I had virtually none of the building blocks necessary to enter an adult world. It was like a part of me knew I'd just have to try to figure it out on my own, and that was scary. I also saw why I was so attached to dependency. I had never gained any sense of power, so naturally I believed it all came from 'out there', from somewhere or someone else. I'd be good and I'd be protected. I thought I wanted protection from life. I saw life as harsh, cruel and unrelenting in its punishments. I never knew it was protection from my mother that I wanted. I wanted to enter a world that knew nothing of her rules, a world that one day would be seen as welcoming, exciting and exhilarating. Amongst all this I became aware that my addiction to dependency was a prescription for victimhood. People who act hopeless and helpless and unable to cope, create a response in others that is not about equality.

There I stood in the middle of my tension bridge. But this time one end had been blocked off. Forward was the only direction. I could see that in these future steps I would have to leave most of the old me behind. I could no longer keep creating stress that threw me into depression, nor could I keep undermining myself. I knew I would begin to make money and become debt-free. I knew I would establish myself and become visible. And I was absolutely terrified.

It made me think of Cinderella. I wondered what Cinderella would have down if she had realised she didn't need to be downtrodden or bedraggled or to work ceaselessly to appease someone who didn't care about her. What if she had stopped waiting for the Fairy Godmother or Prince Charming? What if one day she had seen how simply crazy it all was? What if she had become aware that she could be whoever she wanted to be, do whatever she wanted to do, and have whatever she wanted to have? Would she have found the courage to walk out and slam the door behind her? Would she have made a life of her own, based on her own talents? Would she have claimed the cake shop and all the cakes?

Dependency – the hardest thing for me to relinquish. I sorted out my external stressors. I negotiated with my bank manager and others to make payments based on my earnings. I couldn't create more money than I had and I couldn't keep terrorising myself. My house was on the market and I trusted that it would sell and that things would be cleared. I faced each of the people whose phone calls I dreaded and discussed the truth of my financial state. It became something I could handle, and they were happy with the new arrangements.

I had become more assertive. I started doing some body therapy. Every time I went to see Karen, my body therapist, I would stand in front of a full-length mirror so we could both see how I held my body. I saw how my body reflected my relationship with life. I saw the stance of a terrified child, a victim: the collapsed chest, the hunched shoulders, the locked knees, the feet placed neatly close together. I began to learn about my body. I had always taken it for granted, as though it were something you just dragged around. Karen helped me see that the collapse of my chest and the rolling forward of my shoulders meant I couldn't breathe properly; I couldn't take in enough oxygen to feel fully alive. It was as if my whole spine could not support me. It gave me a feeling of spinelessness, like a person who has no stance in life – no internal dynamism. It all fitted. The body told the same story as the psyche.

Karen worked on the deep connective tissues of my body to get them to release these old patterns of tension resulting from trauma. As I looked in the mirror at the end of a session I couldn't believe it was the same person. I saw a woman much, much taller than she ever was. She stood straight with her chest uplifted, her arms relaxed and her eyes focused ahead instead of on the ground.

Fear had been vanquished. I felt like a million dollars. However, as with the gains in therapy, I'd sometimes lose my way and drop back to the old frightened Me. As time went by, the changes became integrated. I walked down the street differently. Instead of clinging to the side, I'd walk down the middle, swinging my arms. There was energy in my walk. The biggest breakthrough was changing my stance. Karen pointed out that in our society women tend to have a narrow stance, whereas men stand with their feet apart. In doing this, women send message to themselves and to others that they are an 'easy pushover'. As I altered my way of standing I began to feel the connectedness to the earth: it was supporting me. The qualitative outcome was that I began to feel like a woman of substance. As with my psychological therapy, I felt the old distorted Me dropping away. It was time to start letting go.

My body taught me that when I went into the old pattern of locked knees and rigid arms, I went numb and into shutdown. I didn't feel anything, I was totally in my head. Karen said that this was the position of 'the eternally powerless – the victim'. In that body position you don't fight back, you have no sense of your own rights, and you accept blame and fault for whatever has happened without question. You are frozen in fear like a rabbit in a blinding light. I knew that state well enough from the dictatorship I'd lived under. It became clear to me that the body stance of a victim signals to an abuser 'Do what you like to me, I definitely won't complain'.

I began to understand how my body had been my give-away. I knew from my studies in psychology that about ninety per cent of our communication is nonverbal. Our verbal communication is only a small expression of who we are. If there is a mismatch and the words don't convey the underlying feelings, there's no question of who wins. I saw that in all my strivings to portray myself as strong and independent, I was giving double messages. What came over were fears and lack of self-confidence. Trying so hard to cope and look independent only increased my dependency on others. I was still searching for outer acceptance instead of an inner one. A part of me still believed that to be healthy meant coping and being in control. It became clear that the split between my mind and my body was what had caused so much inner anxiety.

Karen opened up a whole new perspective regarding child abuse. She helped me see that my body contained the collection of my life's experience, all the photographs – positive and negative. My body had been present for each and every experience, not my head. When I was abused my mind had gone blank; the wall of forgetting. The body and feelings knew the truth, because they contained the secrets. The mind's job was to circumvent painful feelings, to keep things under control, to keep the person functioning. I saw the relationship between my feelings and my body. Dealing with some of the backlog in my childhood had reconnected me to myself and to my body. I knew my body was aching for attention. Body therapy enhanced the process, by encouraging my body to bring up more memories that had been locked way. I knew intuitively that I was again on the right path. To bridge the gap between my conscious mind and my unconscious was to heal the split between my heart and my head, my body and my mind. I hoped to reach a reconciliation.

This reawakening of my bodily relationship had repercussions in all aspects of my life. I particularly noticed it in the workshops I was again conducting. My presentation was more dynamic and clear. The previous year, I'd often had to sit down to quell my anxiety. Now I stood with my feet apart and I spoke directly about my ideas. I moved around a lot. I let the energy in my body have some expression instead of pushing it down and trying to hide. I also began to create more space in the workshop for silence. Before I had tried to fill every minute, giving my all and making sure everyone got more than enough. That was why I'd always been exhausted afterwards. Now I was a lot more at ease with myself, and I no longer felt the need to overcompensate. My aim was to provide enough and then to encourage others to actively participate. Sometimes there'd be awkward silences, but as I relaxed into them someone always contributed. I began to see and feel equality in relationships. The bonus was that everyone seemed to gain more, even me. I'd come home fulfilled instead of totally depleted.

Some time later, my house was finally sold and all the business finalised. I needed to go back and sort out all that it contained. What a job! It was painful to arrive at a much-loved house that I no longer owned. There were memories everywhere. The picket fence that a friend had built and that Michael and I had painted white. The roses that hung over it, which I loved so much. The big wide verandah where there'd been so many conversations with friends. I'd put so much into this home. I went into each room and just sat quietly. Walking into the living room always delighted me and so it did this day. I'd chosen a dusty pink for the walls and a shade just a bit darker for the mantel and fireplace. The furniture was cream. The couch lay under the windows, which I opened to let in the breeze through the lace curtains. I looked at my paintings on the wall and at Michael's piano in the corner. We had shared some warm times within these walls. It was such a great house for parties. There were so many nooks and crannies in which to sit and talk. But we'd usually end up here in the living room. It was a huge room – a warm, spacious and nurturing space. Sometimes it was quiet and peaceful, but it expanded for parties and became just right for dancing.

I went to my bedroom, which was painted a pale blue. I lay on the bed and thought of all that had happened since the day I'd made the decision to leave this behind. I really appreciated what a huge move it had been to go to New York; to leave my home, practice, colleagues and friends had been no minor leap of faith. It had been difficult, but it had proved to be the right decision. I just wished I hadn't lost my house. I later took a look in Michael's room and recalled many fond memories. The memories were not confined to the house, but they had happened here.

My next memories emerged from the room I had had as my study and therapy room. After having worked with Ruth for almost eight months I had decided to move my practice to home. I had an architect build a side addition onto what had been a verandah. My study opened onto it. This addition was my favourite place. I'd spent ages finding windows from demolition sites to get the effect of space and light. The windows went almost the full length of the outer wall, and French doors led onto an enclosed courtyard. During work hours this was the waiting room. In the evening I loved sitting there looking out onto all the greenery. It was also where my friends Sophie and Mathew had sat with me for many evenings helping me edit my book. Their love and caring had been such a support over all those years, and it was particularly wonderful to have them work with me on my book. There was something very special that had linked us together in that creative work, even though at times it was painful because of the issues it brought up in each of us.

I re-entered my study and sat in the chair beside my desk. It too was a cosy room. The walls were a wheat colour with a dark forest green on the doors and the fireplace. Above the mantel of the fireplace still hung the certificate for my Fellowship which was also in a green frame. I had never hung up any of my degrees, but this certificate was precious. What made it special to me was that it had been presented to a woman who had made and was continuing to make an outstanding contribution to the welfare of women and children. I began to weep. I wept for the child within me. I knew that in my work as a psychologist I had taken what I had learnt of abuse and neglect in my own childhood and had created something positive to help others. In that instant I realised that the legacy of abuse in my family had stopped with me. The bond to my Auntie and my commitment to therapy had never allowed the abuse I'd experienced to be acted out on Michael. The only abuse was to myself. The weeping was the sadness I felt in seeing I had not yet learnt how to protect my own inner child. So much of my time, money and creative energy had gone into this house, but because I had never been able to stand up for myself, the child in me had to go through grief yet again. I felt a deep love and respect for this child and I allowed her space to mourn what had been. I resolved to take this task a step at a time to allow the grieving to be experienced in the present, not pushed away as I'd done as a child. I needed to say goodbye respectfully.

It took me four days to sort everything out. Each room was permeated with fond memories. I loved those rooms. Even the old kitchen, with its sloping pine floor that made you feel like a sea captain, each morning going to retrieve a cup from the cupboard then staggering up to the kettle by the sink. It had a fireplace like every other room in the house except the bathroom. But in this one was an old wooden stove. I had always found it charming. I'd cleaned it up and put a basket of dried flowers on it. I spent time wandering through the garden, reintroducing myself to all the trees and plants I'd planted. Most of the gardening I'd done had been around the pool because it seemed to beckon soft greenery. As I sat there looking into the water, all the summer memories floated to the surface. Beach balls, laughter, Michael's splashful jumps, his friends, my friends – playful, fun moments. I collected them all and went inside.

There was so much still to be done; at times the task seemed too great, but I was getting there one room at a time. I decided to send virtually all of the furniture to auction. It seemed the right thing to do since that was where most of it had come from. I loved old furniture and it suited the house, which was built around 1900. First I had the movers come in and pack what I wanted, so that things wouldn't get mixed up. There wasn't a lot. I took just my books and paintings, plus some dishes and small objects that held positive memories. On the third day when the men from the auction rooms arrived, everything else had gone. When they'd finished loading everything onto the van, one of the men came back and asked if that was it. I stood in my study surrounded by vases filled with dried flowers. There were about twenty-two. I was astounded by the number of flower arrangements I had made over the time here. I had loved making them; I had spent hours creating them. What was I to do? I couldn't take them back, and even if I removed the flowers I couldn't use all those vases. My dilemma was magnified when the man said he could take the vases but he couldn't take the flowers. He went outside for a coffee and I sat, anxiously. The prospect of taking them out seemed unbearable. It was as though the vase and the flowers had become inseparable. But reality demanded something be done. I took them out. The pain was as bad as I'd guessed. It was done. He left with the vases, and I was left with a room full of dried flowers and two vases that I'd decided to keep. I gave one vase to a friend who was delighted to have it. The other one I wrapped carefully so the flowers wouldn't get crushed, and put it in a bag to take back with me.

It was finished. I stayed for a while to say goodbye. I went into each room and thanked it for its memories and for what it had given me. I then closed the door gently and walked away. As I got to the corner I looked back. She was truly a grand old lady. I felt at peace inside. We were friends, we'd both given a lot to each other. Everything was complete. Turning the corner wasn't the wrenching experience I'd expected. It was more like just turning a corner.

It took a while in therapy to process all I'd felt about leaving the house. What became clear was that I'd created an environment very similar to that of my grandparents' home. I had tried to create externally what I'd been longing to bring to consciousness internally. In dismantling that outer reflection, an elastic band snapped and what was outer became inner. It would take quite a while to make all of that conscious, but I felt the strength and beauty of the loving I'd received from my Auntie and my grandfather at a much greater depth. It seemed that in leaving my external home I had claimed the true psychological home within me. Yet something was missing. As we talked more about my home, I realised I had attempted to create an ideal environment. Everything was soft and delicate; it was a picture of painless pastels. I'd painted only the beautiful. There were no contrasts. Where was the black?

I then began to think of all the vases. What were they about? They'd had such power. As I explored their meaning, what seemed most striking was that they had all contained dried flowers – dead flowers. That was the key. My hopes and dreams of my childhood. Just like the theme of my book – the death of a baby. Those dead flowers were the parts of me that had never had the chance to grow, even though I had had an awareness of them; they had lived in a big old home a generation before my parents. How many there were! I had a sense they were not only mine but my parents, as well. Dreams unborn, lives unlived.

It took me ages to talk about the vase that I had kept. It was a black vase – not a glossy black, but a flat, dull black. I didn't like the feel of it either. It had a strange texture, almost like a blackboard. When I picked it up and held it, I'd get an eerie sensation as though someone were scratching their nails on a blackboard. I couldn't get it out of my head. I knew that whatever it represented, it was awful. I had the same feelings about it as I had had years back when I felt the blackness following me. I didn't want to talk about whatever it was, but it would not leave me alone. The longer I left it the more I felt the 'nothing' caving in on me. By the time I had the courage to take it into my therapy, I was beside myself with anxiety. I put it on the table in the centre of the room. It looked innocent enough, sitting there holding the tiny pink dried flowers, but it felt like a hydrogen bomb. I had had a few glimpses as to what it symbolised, but I couldn't put words to it and whenever pictures came I turned away. I knew, but I couldn't allow it into consciousness. It had become my most terrifying experience in therapy.

I couldn't express the sheer horror I knew I was about to experience. It felt like death and madness; my death and my mother's madness. I moved around the room trying to say what was happening inside. It was now like a volcano. I couldn't stop. My body was shaking incessantly. I grabbed for words, any words, to try to save my sanity. There weren't many: 'She tried to kill me, she tried to kill me' – that's all I remember. Suddenly, I felt compelled to break the vase. I picked it up and threw it with a force I never knew I possessed. As it smashed against the far wall I heard the most bloodcurdling scream come from deep within me. Then there was nothing. I lay in a heap on the floor. The only sensation I was aware of was a hand on my shoulder, and on my back. I have no idea how long it was before I got up. When I was finally able to stand, I could hardly walk. I was disorientated; I didn't know who I was or what had just happened. It was quite a while before I was able to go home. Then I curled up in my bed, and over the next three days I mainly slept. When I awoke, it felt like there was nothing there. But it was different from every other 'nothing'. This time it wasn't that I was filled with nothing, it was that there was nothing in my head. No battle, no rules, no dictator.

When I next went to therapy, I had a vague memory of what the room was like when I had left. I recalled bits of broken black glass everywhere intermingled with pieces of pink flowers. I said to Neil that I felt I had made quite a mess and that it must have taken him ages to clean it up. I was sorry to have done that to his room. He assured me that the mess was not mine to clean up – it never had been. With his simple words, a further healing began. I didn't have to clean up my mother's chaos anymore. I was also acutely aware that I had not gone through it alone. My thanking him seemed tiny in comparison to the gratitude I felt.

It would take a long time to come to terms with what had happened. Maybe 'come to terms' isn't the right expression, because what had happened came through my body. It felt before words, beyond words. The healing was not something I was conscious of, but when I stand on top of the mountain and look over the terrain, I know that day changed my life totally. The 'nothing' would make some desperate attempts to reconstitute itself, but it never took over again. Now I knew it intimately, from the inside out. All my life I'd been running scared from my fear of death. The vase shattered the illusion. It was not death that haunted me, it was the terror of madness and of losing contact with human warmth. I felt freed from the trap of my mother's mind, my mother's madness. In releasing myself from the grip of the blackness I knew for the first time what freedom felt like. Perhaps those who have freedom as a birthright don't appreciate its value. I knew I would never take it for granted. I cherished it like a priceless jewel.

Connected to freedom was a feeling of home. It reminded me of a dream I'd had where I was visiting a family in their home:

I was the architect who designed the house. I went to the daughter's room which was enormous and very colourful. She had many toys and beautifully decorated dolls' houses. When I left the house and looked at it from a distance, I saw it was several storeys high. I was surprised I'd built anything so big and stately.

So even though I had lost my outer house, I felt that there was a home being built inside. It was modern and substantial, a home where a child had plenty of space and freedom to play – a sanctuary that would not be bought or sold.

CHAPTER 20

Hopes and dreams

The memory of the dead flowers in the vases stayed with me for months. By removing them from their containers and throwing them away, my inner space had become free. In the shattering of the black vase, I could feel the presence of my own, intact pink vase. The pressure of the black vase had kept the pink one in pieces. My anger bursting through gave me the power to say 'No' to the blackness and 'No' to the mother who had abused me. Only then did I start to feel my lifeblood. The Me who had been aching to come out all these long years finally took a stand. Some bonds are like chains that need to be broken.

Of course, the sense of freedom was still new and scary. I thought of what I'd said in a recent talk to bereaved mothers. Maternal grief was about dreams – a woman's hopes and dreams to be a mother. When those dreams are shattered, her self is shattered. What reinstates new dreams and a stronger sense of self? Grief. Grief is the bridge that links us back to our inner self. Then we are naturally linked to others and to the outside world. It is the most natural healing process available to us. Yet it seems we are brought up in a society that has its limelight on perfection, a society that has made the left brain all–powerful. Logical, rational, concrete knowledge is seen as the key to a successful life. There is a growing belief that we should also be able to control death, particularly the death of a baby. But somehow in denying death, the richness of life has become lost. Perhaps when we took grief and death out of life, we removed the vitality. In going through the grieving process, bereaved women seem always to find the same secret – that life is precious. Recognising that death could come so quickly, so unannounced, seems to instill a deep respect for life. They find that life can not be controlled; it is to be lived. They seem more appreciative of what they have and develop new values of living. Nothing is taken for granted. Somehow in facing the death that took their baby, they become free of their fears, not just of death but of living life fully.

I sat there immersed in what I'd said to other women. Could I claim it for myself? With each relationship I had formed in my work with bereaved mothers, a part of my own grief had reached some healing. Then I thought of my therapy. I could see that no matter how I looked at it, it too was a journey of grief. When a childhood memory had surfaced, I had felt the accompanying emotions. They moved through me, clearing a space. I came to see that grief is like a rainbow – it contains every colour of emotion, but the central colour is always love. To express all our natural emotions about any aspect of our life that is over, is to enter grief and then to re-enter life, for to move ahead and grow naturally means to leave something or someone behind. It's always a circle – a beginning, a middle and an end, but the outcome is always love. Grief is the bridge home.

The image of the black vase appeared before me. I had a sense that it symbolised all the grief I'd felt about my mother. I had been doing therapy for almost two years when I found the courage to break the blackness. I would say that the majority of that time had been filled with memories of my mother and of her abuse, intermingled with the pink aspects that were my Auntie and my grandfather. As each of these surfaced, I went through a period of grieving. I saw and felt what had really happened, and I grieved for what I'd longed for as a child and what I'd lost. Breaking the vase was the most courageous psychological step I'd ever taken.

I can't imagine how much time I had spent in therapy shaking in fear. Sometimes it would happen if something was mentioned that hit an inner wound; other times I'd sit down and it would start. It always preceded a breaking through to my consciousness of forbidden, forgotten times, or of 'not me'. But the lead-up could take weeks. The force of my mind to keep buried experiences from surfacing was powerful, and it seemed that the battle of my mind and emotions got played out right there in my body.

It wasn't only in therapy either. Sometimes when I'd go for a walk I'd begin to shake as though I were experiencing mini-convulsions. My head and arms would twist and turn involuntarily. After a while, Michael and I would laugh about it, but a lot of the time it was distressing. I never understood these shock waves running through me until after I broke the vase. Then they stopped completely. I'd had two forces within me – one trying to finally have a voice, and the other trying to silence it. It was the injunction my mother had planted so well in me: that if I ever told anyone what she'd done, she'd kill me. Even though I was grown up and my mother had been dead for many years, it had remained a strong part of me. The force that had tried to keep me quiet and not remember and not speak had been the part that had saved my life as a child, but as an adult it was killing me; it kept me from knowing my history and myself. It kept me running scared and being quiet. I could never just relax and be me, for then the anxiety would surface and the prison warden would re-enter. The battle had been going on for years. Now it was gone. The day I shattered the black vase was the day I shattered the voice of my mother. There were no more 'secret' memories that had that power to break me into pieces.

Around this time I wrote in my journal:

People are not perfect.
Life is not perfect.

If either were true, life would be empty
    as would people.

Life is all colours.
It has the terrible as well as the beautiful.
It is rich.

Would we ever appreciate love if we hadn't
    experienced separation and loss?
Would we appreciate the sunshine if we
    never had the nightfall, or spring without winter?

Can we appreciate life without understanding and
    respecting the importance of death and grief?

Appreciation seemed to be entering my life and all the colours attracted me. I wasn't fighting the black or trying to be all good and perfectly white; I was more even. The pushing and striving to do more or to be more for others dissipated. I seemed to be more content being who I was.

Having a clearer inner space inspired me to continue the sorting out process in my outer life. I needed to face unfinished business. There were five drawers in the cabinet beside my desk, plus two desk drawers. They were all full of things marked 'To do'. There was a lot going on. I was organising about ten workshops in different cities, doing work related to the video production, and giving seminars and lectures. In leaving details unfinished, I ended up feeling overwhelmed and overburdened. It wasn't a new experience; it was a reflection of my childhood. At home I was always trying to clean up messes that never seemed to end. I didn't want to keep doing this to myself. I could see too that it wasn't just about feeling overwhelmed, it was about continually living in the past. When I had stacks of old business facing me each day, I caved in. It kept me from being in the present.

When something came in, it became a burden instead of a fresh challenge or an interesting idea. I had talked about the clearing of space in my therapy and through that I began to see that just as each therapy session – and indeed therapy itself – had a beginning, a middle and an end, so too did each day. I guess it was a simple insight, but it brought a whole new way of being into my life. I got yet more pieces of paper and wrote 'Beginning', 'Middle', 'End', 'Each day', 'Completion'. I put one in my bedroom and one next to my desk. They really helped me to focus on my day and to choose what I could realistically accomplish before putting the rest away. It wasn't just my work. I also became conscious of the messes I made in the evenings, like not doing the dishes or leaving my clothes in a pile or starting some new project and leaving the papers spread all over the room. It was all a throwback to the chaotic evenings of my childhood. It was hard at first, but I just kept focusing on the idea of beginning, middle and end. The evening was a time to have things put away so I could relax and not have to wake up to chaos. Gradually it formed an even pattern.

The other step forward was the realisation that I could do only one thing at a time. I'd often get out one set of files for a particular workshop and then think of something else I needed to do. Soon I'd have four or five projects laid out. I saw it was an old mind-game to keep me confused and overwhelmed. I sorted out my filing cabinet and resolved to take one thing out only and not go on to something else until I put the first back. It didn't need to be finished completely. My desk became simple.

There were two people outside my life who had quite an impact on my search for simplicity. The first was a psychologist I went to hear one evening who spoke about freedom, an issue that obviously grabbed my attention immediately. The most important thing he said was 'Whatever weighs on your mind, sort it out!' He went on to explain that if our minds are continually burdened with issues we haven't yet resolved or things we haven't yet done, we are at their mercy. To have a sense of freedom and to allow natural creativity to flow, the mind needs to be free of worries and of lists of things to do. 'What's pulling you down right now?' he asked the audience. 'What hasn't been done or said or dealt with that your mind goes on and on about?' The idea was either sort it out, or drop it if it no longer was of any value to your life. That talk remained crystal-clear to me and was a guiding light. It just rang true for what my next steps in growth were to be. I needed to give up fear and worry, which entailed reducing things to worry about. I wanted peace of mind.

The other person who really inspired me was the host on a television program. I had been on his show and also had several contacts with him on issues related to maternal grief. What surprised me was that he dealt with all incoming business each day. I asked his secretary how he did it. She said he just found that leaving things ended up creating more work than responding to them as they arose. So he set aside time each day to deal with what came in, so the next day always started afresh. I resolved to deal with my mail and my phone calls each day. It became easy. I used to believe that all these awarenesses came only in therapy, but I'd begun to see that when you're open to new ideas, the teaching and learning experiences are all around you.

There was still the issue of the empty pink vase. What flowers were to emerge? The more space I cleaned the bigger the vase got, but still it wasn't clear to me what my new hopes and dreams were. Amongst my wanderings I read a book that was eventually to lead me to the flowers. The book was *The Power of One* by Bryce Courtenay. I was inspired by the impact one person can have on the whole future of a child. It meant so much to me to read a story where it is clear that the main bond for a child does not need to be with the mother. It gave me hope that the loving connection to my Auntie would be strong enough to pull me through. What touched me, too, was the powerful effect of being believed in, how a person blossoms and claims their own power which has a ripple effect on all those they meet. Everyone gains from the power within. Being believed in creates a belief in one's own self.

Soon after I saw an ad in the paper for a luncheon with Bryce Courtenay I rang up and bought a ticket. I must have been the first because I sat at the table just next to him. He was as gifted a speaker as a writer. When I got home I wrote pages and pages about what he'd said from the notes I'd scribbled on my napkin.

He began by saying that we have lost our way as a society. We have forgotten the need to tell stories – real stories. In this fast-paced world we've put words ahead of the story. 'I'd like to be known as a storyteller,' he said. My heart leapt. Yes. That's what I'd felt for years. In all my workshops, it seemed that my main role was storyteller. I knew intuitively that left-brain information went nowhere, while a story about a real person entered the heart and had a lasting impact.

He went on to say that the business of writing books is about taking your clothes off and mingling with the crowd. He said that too often books are distant and don't touch the heart. We need to be in the business of telling stories, of speaking the naked truth. We all need to tell our story from our roots. 'Yes!' a voice inside me yelled. If nobody tells their story how do we know the truth of people's lives. Do we stay in fiction and illusion, pretending there's no pain, no struggle, no bumps in life? How do we share and learn from our humanity?

Then he talked about dreams. 'We all have a dream,' he said. 'The trouble with the sleeping dream is that you die. You need to live your dream.' I was absolutely beside myself with the excitement. Oh yes – I want to live my dreams. No more deaths of dreams. I wanted to have real-live dreams. 'It's so easy to play it safe,' he went on. 'Safe and secure. You have a roller-door. We've been attached to a myth of what we've been told life is and we don't believe we have any say. Find out what your dream is!' He also said that before he wrote *The Power of One*, he wanted to be a writer so much he could taste it. Oh, my heart wouldn't stop singing. I knew at that moment that more than anything I wanted to write my book. I also knew I needed to tell my story. There were other dreams surfacing, but not as powerful as my writing.

I went away from that lunch filled with more enthusiasm than I'd ever had in my whole life. Yes, I did live dreams and I was going to bring them to life. I wanted the cakes and the cake shop too. I knew I needed to complete the projects I'd started and also to have enough money to allow myself a quiet space, for one day in the not-too-distant future *Fire and Irises* would become a reality.

The dream that seemed to be most prominent for me right then was to complete my video. The grant I'd received from the government was for $13 000. It wasn't until I entered this new field of endeavour that I realised how expensive it was to make a decent video. Although I'd done the filming, the scripting and editing was much more expensive and I had only $5000 remaining. That would allow me to do a ten-minute video, at most. Yet it was very important for me to include all the main issues of my work. I wanted to do my book and my ideas justice. I realised that if I had the money I would have just paid for it myself. But money was a real scarcity. So with my briefcase packed with new enthusiasm about living my dreams combined with the belief that anything is possible, I went fundraising. I approached the corporate sector, since that seemed to be where the money was. In the end I raised an additional $25 000. My hope of doing an hour-long video was within my reach.

I learnt quite a bit in the fundraising process as well. It was another validation of the importance of asking for what you want. What I began to see was that in the past my hopes and dreams often turned to fantasies that remained as such. I saw that it mainly had to do with believing in myself. I'd get ideas like wanting to do the hour-long video and all that it would contain. I'd see it in my imagination. However, to take action on behalf of my creative ideas was such a big step. This was the case in all areas of my life. Real action meant standing up and valuing my talents, valuing me. It was my anger that gave me the impetus to act. Looking back in my journal I saw the entry just before I embarked on the fundraising. I saw how I gave myself yet another kick in the pants. I wrote:

> I'm fed up with prison. I'm tired of feeling not good enough. I'm tired of sitting in the basement fantasising about life. Life is out there, not in my fantasy. I've decided I'm going to come out and show myself and all my colours – including red – instead of just sitting and letting things happen to me. Fear is totally useless. I'm tired of feeling powerless, helpless and hopeless. I am not powerless. I am certainly not hopeless. And I have heaps of hopes, talent, energy and creative ideas. I am going to use them. I matter. My dreams matter.

The next dream that asked to be given birth was an article I had written for Mother's Day. What had initially inspired it was my contact with bereaved women. I began to see over the years that Mother's Day was often the most painful day in the year for them. Somehow there was an overriding belief in our society that the day was to be one of flowers and chocolates and pleasant memories. No black was permitted. These women just went along with the charade and kept smiling. No one mentioned their baby who had died or the hoped-for baby who never came into existence. It seemed crazy. Most of the women in our society suffer some form of maternal grief, yet they all had to play out some myth of happy families and grieve silently. It angered me to see so much pain was being hidden by so many just because there was a belief it had to be a happy day. The more this went unspoken the more individual women would never know they were not alone, and I knew that loneliness and isolation were not the places for grief to speak. I had learnt through my therapy the destructiveness of silence.

I had written the article over a year ago and had sent it to women's magazines. The replies were unanimous – in essence it wasn't a nice article. It was too depressing, too negative. I decided to revamp it into the style of a newspaper article; another new experience in writing. I headed it 'News Release' and paid Associated Press to fax it to the major newspaper in each capital city. It was taken up by several of the big newspapers, and then it filtered down to the smaller ones. It also had a ripple effect, for I got several invitations to speak on radio on the topic just before Mother's Day. The fulfilment I felt in knowing my words had some influence in breaking the deafening silence was far, far greater than the monetary cost of the endeavour. I felt a new freedom in finding different vehicles to express myself.

Another live flower had grown out of the inner vase.

Over these months, most of my new-found energy went into the production of the video. I remembered what Bryce Courtenay had said in his talk about dreams – 'Get involved!' It had hit a core inside. I knew that in making the video I had to be involved in all aspects – every single one. I had always thought that expertise lay on the outside, yet I was beginning to learn that that was only in the minds of those who stood and watched. Like a child looking longingly in a cake-shop window, I now wanted to go in and find out how to make the cakes myself. It also had to do with taking responsibility for my creations. When I had first sought quotes from various producers I had no idea what the breakdown of the money actually meant. Like most specialised areas, this too had a language of its own. If this was to be my creation and not someone else's, then I needed to gain entry into this foreign country. I was extremely lucky to find a co-producer, who was happy to teach me the tools of the trade. Soon scripting, editing, voice-overs, montages and fade-ins all became commonplace words and experiences.

As well as my technical involvement, I also appeared on camera linking together the different interviews with bereaved mothers. It was a tribute to my therapy that I could tolerate the visibility of the experience. Seeing myself on tape was a shock. I was not as unattractive as I'd imagined myself to be. I had always thought that if I looked okay in photos it was due to good photography. But somehow the video gave a three-dimensional Me. I liked the woman I saw.

We had been in the studio for most of the day and it was fairly late in the evening when the time came to integrate all the parts and bring the video to completion. I was tired – tired of the work, tired of the video; just tired. Then I watched as all the parts merged: the introductory voice-over with footage of mothers with healthy newborn babies, the music, mothers with their babies in intensive care, the paediatrician and I talking, the bereaved mothers and their stories. I was awed by the creative process. It just flowed. It was beautiful. It reached out and touched me. I felt the joy, the pain, the sorrow and the struggle of life and death.

I stood in the centre of the room immersed in the images before me, tears streaming down my face. I didn't try to stop them. I felt I was standing there with no barrier between myself and what I had created, and for one brief second we met. It was exquisite. Life and I were in alignment. I'd only had that experience twice before: once when I first held my son, and again at my book launch.

I saw the full length of the creative process abbreviated, like pushing an accordion together. I saw the beginning – the initial dream – then the frustrations, the ups and downs. I saw the plain hard work of trying to bring the dream to life, and the labour pains of letting go and wondering if it were all worth it. I saw the time of facing the real dream. It was then that I felt embraced by life, as though I were washed in waves of all the energy that had gone into it. In saying 'Yes' to life, life mirrored 'Yes' back, filling me with a deep sense of satisfaction. I felt proud of myself and proud of the video.

Then the video came to the end, to the dedication I'd written: 'This video is dedicated to all women who have grieved over the death of a baby or the loss of a hoped-for baby, and to the memory of those children'. Right then I knew something healed in my heart. I felt deeply touched by the pain of being human and about the sorrow women go through silently.

I then recalled how adamant I'd been that this dedication be in those exact words and that it appear before any of the credits. It wasn't until the moment I saw it that I knew it was my way of acknowledging my personal grief for the presence–absence of a daughter. I thought later: 'It's like realising I can't undo what has been done in the past, yet not knowing if I would have done it differently. But I can learn and create something out of the experience that is a contribution – a tribute'. I realised then that much of the energy, motivation, love, and caring that I'd put into this project was related to somehow paying tribute to or acknowledging a daughter that might have been. The dedication was also to the child within me who had died, and to a mother I never knew because she was lost in her own unknown grief.

And of course to a great-aunt who gave me the hopes and dreams to bring me back to life.

CHAPTER 21

Blessings

My cousin rang me in the middle of the night to say my father had suffered a heart attack. Although he was now out of immediate danger, the doctors were not optimistic about his recovery. At that moment I knew I loved my father. All the cold wars between us, the distance, and my anger at his not protecting me vanished, and I felt the strength of the bond. I had to go. I postponed my work commitments for two weeks and packed. Michael and I left the next day.

I'll never forget the moment Michael and I walked around the corner into his hospital room. When he saw me his face simply glowed. This time it was he who opened his arms and gave us a warm hug. We sat on each side of his bed and as he held my hand I felt his love. For the first time I felt I belonged to a family. I could also sense his relief that we were there. He still tried to be brave and strong, saying that it hadn't been necessary for us to come, and that he'd be back on his feet soon, and that my cousin shouldn't have phoned. But I knew he didn't mean it. We stayed a couple of hours and then went to the house.

I took time to write in my diary. The first images that came to mind were of the airport – baggage everyone carries and the rush people are in. I'd got such a shock at the possibility of Dad's death that it made me aware of how short life is; yet we fill it with outer things, as though they're the answer. I'd known that I had been running away from my inner self most of my life, but it seemed that everyone else was running. Don't people take time to go inside where the real wealth is? Don't they stop and cherish the peace and quiet? What about relationships? How do we relate at any depth when there's so much rushing and outer activity?

I realised that what I wanted most in my time with my father was a real relationship. I wanted to get to know him and I hoped he'd see me for who I was. I knew there would be a lot of things to do, for my cousin had told me my dad had wanted to get things sorted out. The house was to be sold and everything dealt with. I knew it was important for me to do it – there was no question of that. There had been so much pain in that house, it was essential to clear it as I had done with my own house. Yet I wanted the balance. I needed time with my father, time to say goodbye.

Each day we visited him in the afternoon and again in the evening. In between was the sorting out of the house. I couldn't believe how much there was. It looked neat externally, but the drawers, closets and cupboards were jam-packed. Even my mother's clothes were still there. And the china; my mother had collected enough china to fill a shop. There were nine dinner sets; one of them had one hundred and twenty pieces. What were her dreams? They never had anyone come to dinner, that I can remember. There were also seventy or eighty china teacups, some of them exquisitely delicate and beautiful. Most of them had been there when I was a child. I then came across a picture of my mother and father. She was sitting holding a cup of tea and he was standing behind her. Why, I wondered, are women so often portrayed in a sitting position? Sipping tea – it was nice, but it was hardly a powerful activity. This lack of power stayed in my mind until the night my father talked to me about the things he wanted to leave people. He had a list of those things he treasured most. He said he wanted his Lodge medals to go to Michael, and some other significant Lodge objects to go to my cousin. When I got home, I felt sad. While most of the money from the house was to come to me, there was no special object he had thought of leaving me. It was related to the issue of power in the family. The men received symbols of power. Where was the valuing of the feminine? I was to be kept safe, but not powerful. I decided to ask him for something. That evening, I talked about the symbols and how I felt about not being given one. I explained that the symbol was connected to the memory. I wanted something to remember him by, something he valued personally. He seemed to understand, but then he said there were some watches from my grandparents in a safety deposit box. No – that wasn't it. They weren't connections to him. I found my courage and asked him if he would leave me his signet ring. It was black, with three connecting gold links on it. I'd always remembered him wearing it. I also liked what he'd said the links stood for – friendship, love and truth, the three things I valued most in my life. Initially he said 'No, it could only go to a man', but eventually he said I could have it. Something happened inside. I felt solid and lighter.

The following weeks were busy despite my resolution to go slow. The house had been sold and we had only three more weeks before the new owners moved in. There was so much to sort through. I became overwhelmed. I could feel the blackness nearby. What was I to do with everything? What should I throw out, give away, sell, keep? I realised it was important for me to keep only those things that brought me pleasant memories or that I particularly liked. I also recalled something I'd learned in therapy – to travel lightly, in all ways. I have no idea why that made such a difference inside and outside of me, but the shift was huge. It became easy to sort things out. There was very little I needed to keep. I stopped worrying and went with my feelings.

It was important to me to sort out the disheartening chaos and handle each of these objects with respect. I needed to clear the space myself; I couldn't just pretend it wasn't there and have someone else come in and take it all away. This was my history. Even though it was painful, I knew it needed to be done for my psychological health – my inner sorting out.

The whole experience of being there also had much to do with relationship and responsibility. For the first time in my life my father had given me responsibilities and had trusted me. I was being his hands and his eyes. I would check with him which objects had meaning for him, and which ones didn't. I had organised to have whatever possessions he wanted transferred to my cousin's house, for although the doctors wouldn't say much about his condition, he believed he'd be able to go to a nursing home when he got better.

Most days I'd bring in some small objects or photos and ask him about them. That's when the stories began. Michael and I heard many stories about my dad's youth. It was a surprise to me that he was such a wonderful storyteller. His memory was outstanding. On many occasions the laughter brought the nurses to the door, wondering what was going on.

Then one night while I was sorting out some things in the basement, I saw an old box up on the rafters. I pulled it down, brushed off the cobwebs, and opened it. Inside was a musical instrument. I had never seen it before. It was simply beautiful. It was handmade in wood; it invited you to touch it. I took it upstairs and showed Michael. We sat on the front porch as he tried to figure out how to play it. Soon he got the feel for it and the sound that emanated from the instrument was like a combination of a violin and a harp. The delicacy of the music drifted through the stillness of that hot summer night and enveloped my heart. I'd organised for my cousin and his wife, a friend of my father's, and Michael and I to meet in my father's room later that week. My dad had clearly stated who he wished to leave his gifts to after he died. I had talked to him about how important I felt it was to have a ritual of giving while he was still alive, so we could appreciate the symbolism of the gifts he'd chosen. It turned out to be a deeply moving time for us all. We learnt more about my father, and about the meaning behind his gifts, and he in turn felt the love and appreciation from each of us. The last one he saved for me, saying he was proud to give it to his only child.

I then pulled out the musical instrument I'd hidden under his bed. I put it on his lap and asked him to tell us about it. Once again his face beamed as he told the story of how everyone in his family had played a musical instrument. This autoharp had been his as a child. I asked him to play us something. He began slowly, but soon he was playing complete songs and was singing the words. We all joined in and the music seemed to bring us closer together.

I was surprised to learn that my father was at all musical. He played with such ease and his voice was a delight. All these talents hidden away in basements. Not long after that I found a portfolio of watercolours from 1922 painted by my father. My father painted! The one that I liked most was a painting of a single yellow iris with a green leaf on either side of it. I asked if I could have that one in particular. He seemed pleased I wanted it and asked if I'd like them all.

During this time with my father, I faced some challenges related to growing up and taking responsibility. I acknowledged to myself that my father was no longer the strong person he had always tried to be. In fact I saw him doing what had been my greatest weakness – just fitting in and making no demands. It became clear to me that his needs, even though unspoken, were not being met. I noticed that although he had his own pyjamas, he was always in those awful hospital gowns and I could sense his embarrassment. I asked him why he wasn't dressed in his pyjamas. The nursing staff said they didn't have time to help him and the gowns were easier to manage I then entered into a discussion of quality of care of patients and their rights to dignity and respect. It wasn't well received, but I never saw my father in a hospital gown again.

The other issue was the realisation of just how fragile my father was. Being in the first bed by the door in a large ward was distressing to him. He got little uninterrupted rest as the noise bothered him a lot. I went to the head nurse and asked if he could be transferred to a private or semi-private room. She said it simply wasn't possible. I pointed out to her that there were two empty rooms, both of which looked out onto gardens. My father always found the garden to be a nurturing place. I felt it would do him the world of good just to see some trees. 'Absolutely not. The rooms are to be kept for emergencies.' 'But couldn't he have one until they are needed? 'I asked. 'No! He is fine where he is.' Over the weeks I had found this 'heart ward' more and more heartless. The nurses seemed to be mainly computer technicians, sitting in front of a row of display units of beeps and flashes, and writing reports. They seemed to have little awareness of the psychological needs of the patients. But my therapy had taught me that mountains were only mountains if you stood in front of them and looked up instead of going around. I went to the director of the hospital; he seemed to have an appreciation of individual needs. As a result, the next day my father was transferred to a private room in a quiet corner overlooking the garden. He seemed contented.

My father had been glassy-eyed and distant since our arrival. He was also getting amounts of money mixed up, which wasn't like him. Then I noticed how many pills he was being given each day. I asked what they were for and he didn't know. One of the friendly nurses told me he'd been put on antidepressants. I became very angry. I managed that day to see his doctor and asked what was going on. He said my father seemed a bit negative and depressed. Depressed? My father was obviously dying even if no one would say it out loud. He'd just sold his house, and most of his belongings were going to auction. Didn't he have a right to feel down – to *grieve*? The doctor dismissed my concerns, saying that as my father's doctor, he would make the decisions. We had to sort this out. This doctor was a surgeon caring for my father's physical condition – he was not in charge of his mental health. I spoke to my dad about it and he said he didn't want his mind like that. I empathised. I wrote the doctor a note saying that as next of kin I would not agree to my father being given any further psychotropic medicines. They stopped. My dad seemed much clearer and less confused.

We were now close to the end of sorting out the house. There were two treasures I found in the final process. One was a necklace my Auntie had given me. I found it in a drawer full of meaningless junk. Going through everything piece by piece had been worth it. The necklace contained a round crystal with a mustard seed in the centre. It symbolised the love my Auntie had given me to contain and protect my inner self until the day I found the right soil in which to grow. I knew the soil was my therapy. I knew I could never have kept myself safe, even through a secret, without her presence in my life. All my adult searching had been to find a place of safety and trust for that seed to blossom.

My other find was in the basement – also in the rafters. It was the fishing rod my grandfather had given me with my name engraved on the reel. It brought back so many fond memories of sitting on the steps at the bottom of the ravine at my Uncle George and Aunt Ruby's place. There was a little creek hidden away there, and he would sit quietly for hours on end, fishing rod in hand. I used to love sitting beside him. It was another time we used to talk. I had totally forgotten those memories until I picked up the rod and reel. I was beginning to see the importance of keeping only those things that take you to pleasant times.

More memories came from other members of the family. Michael and I had dinner at my cousin's house and my Aunt Ellen was there. We were sitting in the living room after our meal and I noticed her staring at me intently. 'You know, you look exactly like Auntie did at your age,' she said. 'I just can't get over it.' I was astounded. I had only known my Auntie as an old woman. The knowledge deepened the bond, and fuelled my desire to know more about her.

That afternoon stories of Auntie were abundant. I was enthralled, lapping up each one. These stories seemed vital to my journey. By painting the pictures and giving names to her character and to her talents, my need to know and understand her was fulfilled. I was amazed at the array of her talents and at what she'd done in her life. By being made conscious of the depth and breadth of the person I'd loved so dearly, I felt an inner expansiveness in myself. The bridge was being reinforced in new concrete.

Aunt Ellen also spoke of my father in his younger days, yet not once was my mother's name or existence even alluded to. I asked about Auntie living at my parents' place and caring for me as a baby. Aunt Ellen remembered that well. She spoke of how close we always were. I guess our love was always obvious, no matter how I later tried to hide it. I knew this had a lot to do with my mother's rage. I said I'd understood that Auntie had stayed until I was about four years old, and that when she and my mother had had a fight, Auntie was sent away. Aunt Ellen was shocked. After a few minutes she said 'fight' like it was the first time she'd spoken the word. No, no fight in our family! Pain, grief and anger were silent, taboo subjects. She took a breath and changed the subject. I later realised the similarity in both my mother's and my father's family. All conflicts, all pain – all the black aspects of human life – lived under carpets. My mother's pain must have been too great to keep under cover. Feelings must have an expression. If they don't, they erupt onto the most defenceless person.

Although I still didn't understand the reasons behind my mother's craziness or her rages, it seemed that she must have been trying to carry some unbearable cross to have become the way she was. But what I felt was going to be a rather casual and almost perfunctory breakfast with a friend of my mother's actually helped open more secret doors ...

When Joan rang from the country saying she'd like to come up for the day to visit my dad and wondered if we could have some time together, I wasn't very receptive. Joan was my mother's only friend in the last ten or fifteen years of her life. She was younger than my mother, but her family lived near my grandparents so they had known each other for a long time. I'd been seeing so many different visitors at the hospital, I was tired of not having enough space for myself. However, breakfast seemed like an easy, quick arrangement.

Over coffee she started talking with a great intent and urgency about my mother. She said that she'd always known there was something terribly wrong with the relationship between my mother and me. It had concerned her a lot. She never could figure out why it was that my mother disliked me so much. 'Right from the beginning she just wasn't like a mother; it was like you were something she just had to put up with,' Joan said. I was speechless. Here we were in this bright busy yellow clanky clangy diner filled with truckies and people dashing to work. I thought we would probably talk about my dad's health or how her farm was going. But she didn't mince words. She was here on a mission.

'I haven't seen you in almost twenty-five years,' she went on. 'But I've thought of you often. I always hoped life would work out for you, that you'd find a peace and happiness you didn't have at home.' Here was someone who had some idea what it was like for me and who also realised how it could affect my whole life. She had even taken time to remember me and to wish me well in my absence. She then told me that a couple of years ago she'd borrowed the book I'd written from my father. It had helped her to deal with her grief. She had always wanted children but had been unable to have any. I was pleased she'd found it valuable. She said that she wasn't sure whether what she had to say would help me understand why my mother hadn't loved me, but something had occurred to her when she'd read the chapter on twins in my book. She asked if I knew that my grandmother's first pregnancy was with twins. I didn't. 'Well it was your Uncle George and his twin was a girl. She died soon after birth. Your mother was born next. They named her after the baby that died.'

My mind went swirling back to the conference, when I stressed the idea of a replacement child to doctors and nurses. I explained that if the grief isn't resolved with the baby that has died and the mother quickly becomes pregnant again, the new baby will suffer, for that child will always be held up against the ideal baby that died. I pointed out that one of the signals that the new baby isn't being recognised as a separate individual, is when it is given the same name as the deceased baby. Is that what had happened? Did my mother never have a chance to have an identity? Was she always living in someone else's shadow? I didn't know the answers there in the diner, but it felt like someone was putting together a huge puzzle inside that had lain untouched for a lifetime.

That was what she'd wanted to tell me. She thought it might help, even though she wasn't sure if it all made sense; she'd just had this strong urge to come up and see me and tell me what she knew. She felt I might be still trying to understand why my mother didn't love me, and that maybe it was a key. I was so grateful and so touched by her actions and her caring, that I reached across and kissed her. Understanding helps – to be understood and to have a deeper understanding of yourself and your history. I was so grateful she had taken the time to find me. I knew by the way she had spoken that her main aim in this trip was this talk. To think I'd tried to avoid it.

Joan also told me of my mother in the last years of her life. She said she had been just a shell; there was no one there at all. She visited her a few times but my mother didn't recognise her. My father dressed her and fed her and she sat in a chair in the living room, staring into space. When Joan spoke to her, my mother would get very anxious and would reach for the tissue box she kept beside her. She'd pull out tissues, one after another, and rip them up and throw them on the floor. She never spoke. My father never told me that. Secrets, damn secrets! He cared for her all on his own. He never asked for help, nor did she get any. Two sides to the coin. The madness remained hidden from the outside world.

There was one other part of the puzzle she gave me just at the very end. Joan told me that it was actually my mother who'd arranged to buy the house we had. My father wasn't interested in owning one. He just wanted to rent. My mother had worked for a real estate agent, Eric, who put a good price on the house and my mother convinced my father to buy it. My father had always appeared to be the overly responsible, security-orientated person, and my mother the scatterbrain. But there was yet another dimension. Joan said that Eric had given my mother a block of land in northern Ontario that one day she could live on, perhaps with him. That block was precious to her – it was a guarantee of escape, but somehow over the years she didn't have the money to keep up the taxes on it. She lost it just after I left home. Joan thought that was when my mother had totally given up hope. That really shook all my perceptions. I could see a reason behind why my mother had taken the money from my education account, why she had stolen money from my purse when I worked in the evenings and school holidays at the chemist, why she had sold all these things in our house and blamed me for it.

She was desperately trying to hold onto one space, one piece of property that was hers. I would never have understood how she could have done these things if I hadn't gone through losing my house just a few months back. In the process before it sold I was beside myself trying to work out ways to retain it and the security that went with it. I was beginning to understand some of my mother's behaviours.

Life seemed unreal when I walked out of the diner. The inner puzzle composer was working at a rate of knots. I went and sat on a bench by the water and wept, not knowing exactly for who. Was it because of the baby with the same name as my mother and myself who died over eighty years ago? Is that why my grandmother was so hard, so severe, such a tyrant? Is that why no one liked her? Surely my grandfather wouldn't have married someone like that? Was it the death of her first daughter that disconnected her from her heart and her self? Was she lost in her own grief over a baby and unable to connect to the next daughter? Was it the waste of my mother's life? She obviously was a bright, talented young woman. Right from the beginning did she ever have a chance to be who she was? Did anyone ever help her see her true self or did she just try to be someone she wasn't? Did she ever become conscious of the abuse to her daughter? Yet my mother's sister, Aunt Ellen, seemed so 'together' even in her late seventies. Ah, but she wasn't cursed with the name of a dead ideal baby. More than that, she'd told me that since my grandmother couldn't cope with even the first two children very well, Auntie had pretty well raised the youngest. Different mothering! It made all the difference.

For days afterwards I felt emotionally exhausted. It seemed like the insights, links and knowledge I'd gained in my talk with Joan equalled about a year of therapy. It would take quite some time to integrate it all, yet the pieces were coming together to reveal the whole picture. Before, there had been too many missing pieces for the child inside to have any real hope of understanding herself and her history. I wrote it all in my journal, knowing I'd find time to process it later.

It was three weeks since we had arrived. All I knew was that I needed to stay until everything was completed, and I didn't know when that would be. The external sorting out was approaching completion, but I knew there was still so much to be said between my father and me. I felt that if there could be a sense of completion between us, then something would heal within each of us and in the family.

My growth in therapy gave me strength to deal with my daily visits to the hospital. On some days my father would look paper-thin and be gasping for air, unable to talk. It seemed as though he wouldn't live through the day. The next day he would be on the road to recovery. Such swings – I couldn't really make sense of them. On the days he seemed close to death he actually seemed most alive emotionally; he would speak from his heart. Yet when his energy returned, he often reverted to his intellect and was critical and harsh and authoritarian.

The most painful experience was seeing him after the auction. My father had told me that whatever money came from the auction was mine, since the contents were mine anyway. I felt so relieved, because money still remained a major issue in my life. Although I'd sold my house, it was for less than I'd hoped for. I still owed $25 000 on it, which I was paying off, but it left me without any cash in hand. All my income was dependent on workshops, and I had postponed six of them in order to come home. I had even had to borrow the airfare to come. The money from the sale of the house would provide enough to pay back the airfares and cover the rent for the month.

After the success of the auction I visited Dad, feeling proud of myself and Michael for all we'd done. I was also feeling fairly exhausted, as it really had been a phenomenal task. Then everything went backwards. There wasn't a 'Well done' or a 'Thank you'. He simply said 'Put it in my bank account tomorrow'. I almost fainted. But my anger caught me. 'First you tell me I can have the money and I do all the work, then you turn around and retract your offer.' I think Michael's presence helped, for he looked shocked as well. He'd been there when my father had first made the promise. My father looked away. I walked out. Once again it had thrown me. It was a familiar trap – promise-excitement-smash. I wondered if deep inside he saw me as his illegitimate child.

Later on I met a friend of my father's. He told me how proud my dad was of me, how much he appreciated all the work I'd done on the house, and how concerned he was about me because I'd looked so tired. How could he say that to a friend and not to me? It was another secret way of communicating. On my next visit I went in briefly and conveyed that I'd transferred the money to my account that it was completed.

There were more bumpy times between us. I told him I was very tired and that it had taken a lot out of me so I was going to rest a couple of days. His response was to say that he was more worried about my cousin, because he'd done so much. That really floored me, because Michael and I had done everything. I explained that to my father. 'Oh yes,' he said, tapping his index finger on the side of his forehead. 'But he did all the brain work.' There we were, back to the uselessness of women and the power of men. Now I could see why my mother had lost her mind.

My hopes of our reaching a relationship were fading. I did what I needed: I rested, got some of my energy back, and some of my anger out. I was not going under again. Having a break away from my father was essential.

When I went back to see him something had shifted. I can't say how or in what way, but the war was over. We began to talk honestly and at a depth I'd always hoped for. There was something else. (It's strange how things just hit you suddenly. It's not something you work out logically; it's more like clouds clearing and your seeing what was there all the time.) When I walked in and saw my father, I knew without a doubt he was my real father. There were just so many features about him that were a reflection of me. I'd never seen the blue of his eyes except when I'd looked in the mirror. There were other similarities too, like the wave in his hair, and his long arms and legs that were disproportionate to his body length. It may have been these characteristics registering all at once, or it also may have been that something changed within my father during the time I hadn't been to visit him. Whatever the ingredients were, we began a relationship that day. I told him I felt he really was my father. He smiled. I think he was happy.

Death and grief were issues that had been with me all my life and about which I'd written and spoken widely. But to be with my father and to acknowledge to myself that he was dying was wrenching. One of the things that had been so obvious over my time with him was that no one talked about his death, not even his doctor. Whenever I asked his doctor about his prognosis, he would say that my father would recover and live in a nursing home for years. It made me wonder if we were talking about the same person. I could see my father losing his life energy. I turned to the friendly nurse and asked her to look up the doctor's report. It said that my father wasn't expected to leave hospital, and that his prognosis was two to three months. I thought a lot about what I'd learnt in therapy and from my own experiences and from my family. I could no longer follow a system of silence and secret carpet-sweeping with painful issues. So our talks changed. Intermingled with more stories of his life I brought up the topic of death, much to the consternation of some of my relatives, but to the relief of my father. We talked for hours and hours, sharing our ideas, and over the next week or so I saw his terror diminish. We were finally speaking the unspeakable.

I told him stories of people I'd worked with in therapy who were dying and what insights they'd given me, plus what I'd learnt from bereaved parents. It seemed important to have no unfinished business. So we went along that path until everything external was in its place. I then brought up the idea of things left unsaid to people and we talked about those that mattered most to him. Was there anything he hadn't said that he would like to? Yes – but he found it so hard to express himself. I understood, but I said I felt it would make a big difference to him and to them. For a week I asked that he have no visitors except those on a list we'd drawn up. This time he was getting quite weak and each visit took energy. My dad had time on his own with each person. I don't know what he said to them, but sometimes I'd be coming in just as they left, and I could see by their faces and his that he had spoken from his heart.

During that week I finished clearing the house. I did the main part first and then the basement. I got the hose from outside and washed it completely. Since the day I arrived I'd put on all the basement lights, and they'd stayed on all this time. It felt important symbolically. I then put on some meaningful and up lifting music on my tape recorder, and lit two candles – one in the closet in the hall, the other on the basement step. I sat in each place quietly, allowing the past to leave me internally and externally. I felt it was now my history. When I'd finished I went down to the basement again. As I stood in the centre where the furnace used to be, I brought to mind my dream. Then I raced up the steps leaving the basement door open, and walked through the house, which was so light and clear. Finally I went out to the front porch where Michael was waiting with the suitcases. Completion. I felt it.

Although I'd made and remade flight bookings for our return, I was now clear we'd leave in three days. I had spoken to my father's family doctor about how long he felt I should stay or how long my father would live. He said it could be days or a couple of months. He also said that he felt my father would try to hang on as long as I was there, and that I shouldn't be surprised if he died soon after I left. It was such a dilemma. I wanted to stay but I had also twice rescheduled workshops and they were now fast approaching. Plus Michael was anxious to get back. Having talked it over with my father, we chose the date.

Those three days before leaving I spent mainly at the hospital. I wanted to talk to him about how hurt I felt that he had never spoken about what I'd done in my life or that he'd never seemed proud of me. Despite my resistance to saying anything that might hurt his feelings or receive a non-response, I remembered that when love is present all feelings are safe. So I said it. He told me that he wasn't a very good communicator, but that he wanted me to know he was very proud of where I'd gone in my life and what I'd done, and of the great job I'd done bringing up Michael to be such a fine young man. I was a tribute to him, he said. I cried and cried in his arms. The black mark seemed to be washing away. He then told me that even though there'd been some tough times between us, he had always loved me. He had never said those words before. It felt like I'd waited a lifetime to hear them. They went straight to the central place within, and I cherished them. I was loved. What touched me further was that he apologised for not being a better father. He was sorry for what I'd gone through as a child. The healing continued inside. The path between us now seemed clear and open.

When I went back later that day it seemed there was only one thing to talk about. My mother. As I mentioned her I could see he was already withdrawing. It was too painful. But this time it was different. I began to tell him of my therapy, and of how much I'd learnt and that I'd come to some inner understanding of why she treated me as she did. I also explained that in clearing the house, something happened within that gave me a deep sense of peace. It felt like the past was over and the wound of my mother was healing. That seemed to open doors and he was able to talk more about the pain he felt in the marriage. Initially he focused on how he felt things like this should be swept under the carpet. I told him of my experiences and of how this only intensifies old feelings and doesn't release them. He began to blame my mother for their unhappy marriage, but as time went on he acknowledged he just wasn't able to communicate with her at all. Maybe that's what she had been searching for. I tried to convey that there probably weren't any clear answers. Perhaps we'd all lost out in one way or another. We talked a bit more. My mother's memory had some presence and understanding there in that room, that afternoon. As I was about to leave, my dad held my hands in his and thanked me. He said the thing he admired most about me was my honesty. It hadn't always been comfortable, but now he saw I was always honest with him. We'd both come a long way. It meant so much to me for him to say that. Secrecy had been the family coat of arms, but now it seemed it had changed. While it had been very hard at times to keep bringing up painful issues, my therapy had shown me there was no other way to a real relationship – with yourself or with anyone else.

In the evening Michael and I went in after visiting hours. There was a fireworks display, one my father had always loved. He had taken me to it each year as a child. We rolled his bed to the window and sat beside him and watched. He seemed bright and full of energy. We talked about some of the fun memories of my childhood – the way I loved to ride on his shoulders coming back from the fair at the nearby park … The day he made me an icerink in the backyard … The time I convinced him to come skating with me in the big rink at the park and how he went sprawling across the ice … My first bike and his teaching me how to ride … The days he spent teaching me how to play baseball. More and more memories just tumbled out – light ones to carry home. I left that night with unexpected gifts. With each positive memory he mentioned, others later came to mind. The space inside that had been filled with grief was now empty and would allow the other colours to emerge.

I stayed up most of the night writing. I needed to process what was there and to make sure there was nothing I'd left unsaid. I went to the hospital at 6 a.m. so we could have some quiet time. I told him how much it had meant to come back home and that for the first time I felt we had been able to talk. Yes, he agreed it had been very good. I told him I loved him and would never forget him. I thanked him for being my father. That was all I needed to say. Then we sat quietly. Words were no longer needed. I left before breakfast. Michael and I were coming back in a few hours to say a last goodbye before we went to the airport.

It was the hardest thing I'd ever done, to go that one last time knowing I would never see him again. In the weeks we'd been there, so much had happened between us. In one sense I had taken his role as head of the family with all the responsibilities and the decision-making that went with it. Even though it was not always easy, he'd handed power over to me. That was something I hadn't ever experienced in my family. As Michael and I walked to the hospital it felt right to hand back that power in some way, for now he truly felt like the father I'd always longed for. I respected him.

When we got there he was sitting in a chair in the corner with his dark blue pyjamas on and a blanket over his knees. He looked so well groomed and dignified. Michael stood at one side and I sat at his feet. We talked for a few minutes and then an image came to mind. I recalled that my father had told me his role as head of the Lodge was to bestow honours on members. I asked him if he would give Michael and me his blessings. I knelt in front of his chair, Michael on the side. He put his hands on our heads and made the most heartfelt blessing for each of us that I could have hoped for. At the end I told him I loved him, and Michael did as well. Then a kiss and a smile and we left. He had asked me not to look back as I left the room. I didn't. It was a painful doorway to pass through.

CHAPTER 22

Fire

*I*t felt good to be on the plane. For the first time going back to New York felt like going home. We had been gone over four weeks. After only a week or so into our visit, I realised I wouldn't make it back in time to give two papers at a conference on grief and loss. My dilemma was what to do about it, since the programs were already set. I rang a friend, who said she'd be happy to present them if I faxed them to her. I got out my drafts and began. It was such a stifling hot night, I went onto the front porch and sat on the floor and wrote them. They took me most of the night, but by daybreak I felt a deep sense of satisfaction. I had expanded my ideas and felt more creative in my writing.

One paper was on the effects of the loss of a baby on the whole family. This time I included the grief of the father as well as of the extended family. The other paper was on children's grief. Children's grief remained a high priority, deserving a paper on its own. It seemed very important symbolically to have written them on the front porch of my childhood home. Sitting there with the two papers in front of me, the dream of fire and irises came back to me as vividly as when I'd first had it. The dream seemed to take the child I had been and merge her with the Me writing these papers on the porch. I recalled the words of the man in black leather: 'You must understand the darkness, you must understand the black hole, you need to know the gravedigger's book'. Then I ran after him up the stairs to the front porch, where he disappeared. Right then I knew that what I'd written came from the wisdom of the child who knew about the blackness of the inner and outer basement. I saw that all the work I'd done in the area of grief could not have been possible without the basement. The basement and the porch were now inseparable. The journey had been to join those two disparate parts of the house. I knew I'd never forget the pain of bringing the unconscious 'not me' to consciousness.

It had all started so simply with the introduction to self psychology. Once I was linked to self psychology and later to Neil, I began to see who and what was inside me. It was that bond that enabled me to write my book *Loss of a Baby,* and that book helped me to discover my own story in its pages. I'd written my story without knowing it. There was so much to learn about myself, the blackness, and the black hole. The black leather chairs provided the safety and protection to find the words to speak what had been forbidden. The gravedigger's book was not about the grim reaper or even about death itself – it was the fear in my mind of death. They had no connection. Their connection was severed that day in Neil's office with the shattered pieces of black glass. My fear was of losing contact with human love.

My therapy had led me back to explore my personal blackness and the gaping black hole. Yet that early morning, I had a sense that the blackness and I were no longer at odds. I had an image of a coalmine. In fully entering the depth of the blackness I came up each time – not with coal, as I'd always thought, but with diamonds. I recall my mother saying to me at Christmas time that Santa Claus would probably just leave coal in my stocking. Yet every Christmas that I can remember was spent with my grandparents and my Auntie, and my stocking was filled with everything but coal. That's how therapy felt for me. In entering my therapy I really was terrified we'd find an indelible black mark or nothingness that meant I was of no value and had no hope. What I found instead was more and more understanding, which grew into an appreciation of myself. So much of my old self had burned away. It felt that what was left was what mattered. The childhood house was gone internally and externally. It had never been home.

I could see how the healing allowed me to have on the outside what I'd always longed for – a relationship with my father. The irony was that it was the blackness that had bonded us. We had spoken of the issues that had been forbidden, probably for generations. To speak of death in any form – psychological or physical – was taboo. No one had dared mention the word to my father – not our family, or his doctor, or the nurses, or his Lodge friends, or even the minister at the church he belonged to. When he and I had talked about it, it felt like a leaden weight had been lifted. When words were spoken death lost its power. We didn't come to any profound conclusions or answers, but in sharing the hidden feelings we were transformed.

My subconscious then led me to a dream I had had about a week previously. Although it was about Neil, I knew it was also really about my father and my relationships with men.

> *I was walking with Neil down a narrow street in southern England, heading towards the ocean. We sat by the water and I was talking to him about some problem I was trying to sort out. I asked him if he knew the answer and he said he didn't. Then I realised he was no different from me, he wasn't an authority on everything. Somehow it all just seemed to be ordinary between us.*

Throughout my childhood I'd idealised my father. Later I put every authority figure on the same pedestal on which I'd put my father. I had viewed men as all-powerful, knowledgeable and in control. This inequality had been present in my marriage. What a shock to see it all so clearly. I saw how difficult it must have been for Neil, for I had been so dependent in that first year, hanging on his every word, not recognising my own contribution or fully acknowledging that it was my own words that mainly filled the space. The answers and understanding had evolved within me. It was I who had told my own story in a contained space. The dream I'd had was about coming to maturity, about treating others as equals and expecting the same for myself. Pedestals might be an essential ingredient in childhood and initially in therapy, but they eventually become self-defeating. It had been important to hand myself over to therapy, to stop trying to keep myself in control. Through the process of letting go, more and more parts of myself could be reclaimed. By the time I needed to be with my father and take on my re-sponsibilities, there had been enough inner changes to enable me to be there as an adult entitled to be treated respectfully, an adult who could insist on respectful treatment for her father. I had learnt about rights and human dignity. The combinations of these experiences allowed the idealisation of others to begin to dissolve. This dream made me feel as though I were taking charge of my life in an ordinary way. Not as an expert, not as a helpless victim, but as an ordinary human being. It was probably the most liberating dream I'd ever had.

I also knew that there was an important inner connection to the outer reality of my letting go of two homes within a few months. It felt that the childhood home was about saying 'No' to abuse and about refusing to idealise men or authority figures. Selling my home in California seemed to be about saying goodbye to another form of ideal – the times with my Auntie that I had kept trying to recapture. The ideal I had had of her kept me from being who I was. But somehow as I'd been able to grieve over her loss, she became more ordinary, more earthy. My Aunt Ellen's stories made me see her as a woman with many dimensions. She wasn't a character in a fairy tale. She was a person who had had her ups and downs, but who had used her talents. That was clear and that was the legacy I wished to claim from her.

Back home. Oh, it was so good to be in my own space. I had indeed travelled lightly. My necklace, the fishing rod, my dad's paintings, the autoharp, some photos. One additional object I carried back was a Ming-like vase – blue and white. What had attracted me to it was that it had a lid. It was self-contained, an image that seemed important. I had never seen it in the house before, so I don't know if it had been my mother's. It seemed feminine, and strong and contained. That was the symbol I wished for myself.

The following week I felt mentally, physically and emotionally depleted. That exhaustion, combined with my dream of equality, allowed me to take a risk in therapy that I'd always shied away from. I actually lay down on the couch. I knew it had always been an option, but it had felt too much like really letting go. More than that (although I hadn't been aware of it), I had been trying to read Neil's nonverbal responses to see if I were 'doing it right', and to see if he was accepting what I was saying. I had still needed his reassurance. It was a huge step for me. Initially it arose when I spoke of exhaustion. The couch seemed inviting, but I approached it with great caution.

First I sat on the edge, talking to Neil. Then eventually I lay down. The release was amazing. Everything became quiet inside. I felt such peace. I was ready to let go of control, ready to let go of seeing Neil as the expert. Now it seemed to be just me, with someone there so I could speak. Another change of perspective and a way of being. My mind slowed down, I spoke at ease. Perhaps most importantly I just talked about whatever arose. My agendas of things to be talked about were left outside. I also noticed new things like all the birds in the trees outside the window. I'd never heard them or seen them before. This sanctuary was to become vital over the next few months. I had about fifteen workshops coming up in fairly quick succession: five at local hospitals and the rest away in other cities. I wasn't sure how I'd get my energy levels back to normal, but this seemed to be a start. My batteries felt recharged with each session. This was to be my quiet, protected haven for the child to continue her journey.

My first workshop was scheduled to taken place ten days after we got back. It was for the staff of one of the maternity hospitals. I was looking forward to it, because it had been a big step to convince a number of hospitals to hire me to train staff in their workplace. That way staff did not have to travel from different places to attend, and all I had to do was turn up. The administrative work was done by them. This was another beginning, but the day was not as I had envisaged. Early that morning I received a call that my father had died. I had no idea what to do. I felt bereft. How could I conduct a grief workshop? I rang Sophie and talked it through with her. Life seemed too much at times. I'd already postponed this workshop twice. Sophie said that I could always take my grief with me. So I did. Once everyone was seated I told them about my father and about how much pain I felt, but decided it would be all right if I talked about it. Then to my amazement I began to talk about my father and what he meant to me. One of the nurses came over and sat beside me and held my hand. That was what I needed. I had felt so alone. When I finished, people in the group began responding and I felt I was in a caring community, even though I had only met a few of them before. Somehow the process took over the day. I think everyone shared their experiences of death and loss in their families and how they dealt with it. It helped me realise that everyone has pain in their lives and we all go through a similar blackness. Grief is not something one should keep to oneself. I just didn't know how generous strangers could be.

I had to decide whether to return for his funeral. I was still exhausted and trying to recover for the upcoming workshops, yet I wanted to go so much. Every detail of the funeral had been organised and my cousin and his wife had said they would take charge of everything else. I felt torn apart. Then I got a feeling that all goodbyes had been said and that everything was complete. I knew it wasn't necessary for me to attend the funeral. Once I'd made the decision I wrote a eulogy to my father and sent it to my cousin to be read at the funeral. I then organised a small service with a few friends to be held at the same time as the funeral. That little ritual made me feel as though I were there. It was also good to have my friends with me.

The next week I conducted workshops on the other side of the country. On the plane coming home, I'd fallen into a deep sleep and had had a nightmare that I had killed my mother. I woke up distressed and disorientated. What was this all about? After all these years, all this therapy, where did this come from? Then I thought 'How can I tell Neil this?' I felt bad again. At my next session I talked about it. I couldn't believe there was still anger beneath the surface. Once we began to look at it I could understand the connection to my father's death. Even though he had never been able to really protect me from my mother's abuse, she had never hurt me when he was there. His death had brought back the intense feelings of vulnerability and of being under threat. I was feeling what the little girl must have felt many times: absolute rage at my mother for trying to destroy me. Thank God Neil understood and his room was robust enough to contain my anger. I hit the walls, kicked the door, grabbed a box of tissues and smashed it mercilessly against the table. I screamed and yelled words I wouldn't have dreamt I'd utter. Neil's acceptance and understanding were there throughout. It all seemed okay. He treated my outburst as if it were an ordinary thing to do, which reassured me that it had to come out sometime. Any child who was threatened with their life would feel the same. Children have no power of expression when they're abused.

As I was leaving, I said something like 'How will I ever get my mother out of me'? He suggested that if one of us had to die, maybe it could be her and not me. That was it. 'It isn't the baby who has to die!' I rejoiced. 'That's right,' he said. 'The baby can live.' This day as I walked home my step was lighter than it had ever been. The inner mother who hated me was dead. The baby was free to live and grow.

From the dream of murdering the mother who had wanted me dead, I understood that it was now time for me to take responsibility for caring for and nurturing my inner child. I finally understood that until you love yourself as you are, you can't give love freely. I'd had it backwards all my life. I'd learnt to put the other first, whether it was wanted or not. That wasn't love, it was a desperation to be loved. No one benefited. One need provided for the reciprocation of another. The time with my father had brought me to a full awareness of the meaning of love.

From the time I visited my father I had known it wasn't as a dutiful, nice daughter. I was there because the bond had pulled me there. The change in my relationship with him was a result of my therapy. I could no longer not be true to myself. When he tried to play power games I countered them, when he tried to put me down I refused to accept it. Once when he accused me of some mistake and in so doing used my mother's full name, I tersely told him to stop confusing me with my mother. The blur in our family of females was disturbing. My name went back on my mother's and father's side for generations, like we were all nondescript. It was only the times my father hurt me that I showed my sparks. The other sparks were when I felt he wasn't being treated well. Anger had built me a self to stand on, to protect myself and those I loved. In the remainder of our time together I knew that I had treated my dad with respect, compassion and honesty. This was how I'd been treated in my therapy; it had had a ripple effect. Even though it was foreign to my father initially, speaking the truth and saying what we felt eventually gave us a common language. I could see that I would not have been able to freely love my father if I hadn't found some keys to self-love.

I had also learnt a great deal from my father relating to the idea of self-love. When he talked of his life it was often interspersed with regrets. There were so many things he wished he'd done, risks he wished he'd taken, places he wished he'd seen. And of course there was his marriage. He spoke to me of them and gave them credence. We saw what might have been. His hopes and dreams. I felt his excitement as he entered into them. Those stories hit a cord deep within. I wanted to get to know the child in me and know what she would love to do. If I nurtured her and followed her, I knew my life would open up. I did not want to look back in my eighties and think of all the things I could have done, or would have liked to have done or become, or of the talents I had left untouched. Regrets, like empty dreams, are lifeless.

So I put a big piece of paper on the wall and listed all the things I'd really like to do. Just for me. Just for fun. More joy was in order.

My first priority was to return to my running. Every morning, my dog Buffy and I left at 5.00 a.m. and met my new running partner, Graham, at the corner. Initially, it was a little discouraging as Graham was very fit and a fast runner. I stopped trying to keep up and developed a pace of my own. It worked well. We ran to a park where we did exercises and Buffy had a play. Over the next six months I was eventually able to keep pace with Graham without trying.

Starting to feel my body come to life inspired me more. I joined a gym. Physically and psychologically it was the most beneficial step I could have made. It wasn't until I really got stuck into it that more of my repressed anger surfaced. It felt good to take it out on the Stairmaster rather than let it linger inside. I began to feel the buzz of fitness. My workshops took less out of me. I was more resilient. I also slept better and needed less sleep. So much energy was wasted on fear and worry.

The other fun thing I began to do was sailing. I saw a course advertised for beginners and I thought 'Why not?' I had always loved watching sailing ships and once had been on board, but I had never dreamt I could learn to sail. Those first few weeks were very demanding. I was learning all the knots, as well as a whole new language. What I appreciated about my teacher was the way he dealt with my anxiety. Initially I was again trying hard to 'get it all right'! He asked me to try not to think so much, and simply to get a feel for it. The more I trusted that inner sense and stopped worrying, the easier it became and the more fun I had. Sometimes we'd stop and drop anchor and watch the sunset. I don't think I'd ever felt so peaceful. It felt like being in a bubble, just rocking back and forth to the natural rhythm of the water. On the last day I sailed the whole course myself which took about two hours. It was one of the most satisfying and rewarding experiences of my life. Perhaps it was the outer reflection of what I was increasingly feeling on the inside. The aim of sailing was really to go where you wanted to go, regardless of which way the wind was blowing; to navigate through life from one's own centre of initiative.

The experience of sailing made me conscious that I had never learnt to swim. So I began swimming lessons. I learnt how deep-seated my fear of suffocation was. It took the teacher ages to convince me to put my face in the water. It all seemed to revolve around safety and trust. What I discovered was that my fears knew nothing of the real world. Life and water were supportive and relaxing.

Then came another special treat. For years Sophie, Mathew and I had spoken about going to the self psychology conference in Chicago together. That year we made it a reality. Those days of the conference were very special. I was with my closest friends, talking about the papers and presentations. It had been almost ten years since self psychology had entered my life and led me to places inside and out, and it was reassuring to be amongst so many therapists who had adopted this new way of viewing their clients. I hoped this 'therapy with a heart' would keep on spreading through old ranks and clever new models. I was renewed and rejuvenated after the four days. Leaving Sophie and Mathew was also okay. Separations didn't jar as much anymore. The child inside was trusting in the ebb and flow of life. She knew now that real bonds of love and friendship are indestructible.

I'm not sure what happened at the conference to catapult me into a new awareness. On the plane coming back I had a strange experience. As I got up to walk about and stretch my legs, I could see a string of negative thoughts flying towards me. They came at a pace slow enough for me to catch them. I imagined that each was a piece of wood and I would break them in two and throw them out the plane window. I began to laugh to myself. It seemed quite good fun. As I sat down I had another image of a whole pile of these pieces of wood. Were these all the woulds, shoulds, musts and have to's that had made up my house of fear?

It seemed that the foundation of that old house had four main cornerstones – fear, guilt, shame and abuse. After I had been with friends and had felt that I was valued and was doing something positive for myself, the old worry machine began cranking away again. All these worrying thoughts were injunctions and threats about being alive. I could see that none of these thoughts had any substance. An ancient tape, repeating the same scare tactics. They were not real. Life was not like that. The space I'd entered unsuspectingly was 'not home'! I named it and felt exhilarated that I had found ways to challenge these outmoded trains of thought. Just to see them, catch them, break them up and throw them out. They were not worth attending to. I could consider these thoughts of doom and gloom as merely a signal in the 'not home' space in my head. I just had to move out of it. What a difference from feeling that I had to sit and listen to it all. Now I had a useful signal that told me to reconnect to my heart and my body. What was left of my demolished old home was only good for firewood.

I remembered that in my dream, 'Fire and Irises', a circle of men were gathered around this pile of firewood, including my father. They were chanting – not giving orders or being authoritarian; they were just singing a musical chant. It felt like the masculine parts of me were softening, becoming more gentle, more connected to the feminine. And it was a circle they formed, a symbol of connectiveness and the feminine. I was making all these links, and while I wasn't sure exactly what they meant, I had a sense that the old authoritarian dictatorship of endless rules that I'd lived under for so long was finally being burnt in the fire of love and understanding. I felt the power of the dream and how it seemed to signal my way home. I also had a sense that this pile of wood waiting to be burnt was not only all the bits of 'not home', but also of the false outer Me. It seemed to be a fire of truth. In telling my own story, my own truth, it seemed to ignite the deadened parts of my past that I no longer needed.

One night I awoke with another awful, nightmarish, terrifying feeling. Surely there wasn't more to remember? Why did there have to be more? But the feeling refused to go away. By the time I got to my next therapy session I was in tatters. I hated being like this. Another black hole. The shaking started again. The refusal to speak was fighting the need for the truth.

I remembered my father crying. The only time I ever remember seeing tears in his eyes was the day we left the hospital. But this memory was different. He was bent over a chair with his head in his hands, sobbing. I don't know how old I was, maybe four or five. I recalled my mother trying to comfort him. I was confused. Nothing seemed to have happened. Eventually he went to bed and I asked my mother what was wrong. She was reluctant to tell me but finally did. It was about something that had happened long ago, before I was born. At the time my father used to drive those big transport trucks. One day a child ran out in front of him. He couldn't stop in time. I cannot recall what she said had happened to the child. I knew from the pain I saw in my father that the child had been either killed or severely handicapped. I had a sense that the child had died. After that he never drove trucks, he only fixed them. My mother said that on this day every year, my father had cried.

I was totally washed out by the end of the session. Where did the grief in my family start? Were both my parents totally grief-stricken? I cried night after night; it felt never-ending. I wasn't sure who all the tears were for. The child who was hit. My father's pain and grief and guilt, even though, as my mother told me, it wasn't his fault. He was always so meticulous about his driving, about everything; he was so in control. I have no idea how he lived with it, especially since it seemed he never spoke to anyone about it. I remember my mother saying I must never mention it to anyone, not to my father or to anyone in the family. Another secret.

I wondered if that was the time when my father shut down forever. If he had had no one to help him, I don't see what other option he'd have had. Is that when he ceased relating to my mother and just became tough and cold and started drinking? Is that when his softer side died, his love of music and painting disappeared? Is that when my mother turned away for the things none of us can live without – love and understanding?

Then there was my birth. A child is all feelings. My parents couldn't tolerate feeling. To them, the risk of exploring all that underlying pain and grief would have been horrendous. I thought of my book. How many deaths, how much grief had I encompassed in my writing that I was totally unaware of? When I was writing it I had an image of being surrounded by a spiral river of tears. That's how it felt now. Everyone was in so much pain. Everyone had died emotionally and had given up on their hopes, their dreams, their selves. My career had been focused on trying to help others understand grief and how to resolve it. Now I saw it was me trying to understand this deep well of sadness and despair that was embedded both in myself and in my family.

Everything seemed to change rapidly after I became conscious of that memory and its meaning. The greatest change was a certainty that it was all over. I had never had this before with any of the terrifying memories that demanded to break into my consciousness. I had always hoped each one was the last and would often say to myself: How much more can there be? How much more pain can I handle? This was like finding the last piece of a puzzle, putting it in place, and then putting the puzzle away intact. I felt a sense of completion about my childhood. In the months that followed I was surprised when I began to recall positive memories of my mother. Since the story of grief was completed, my psyche could allow me to recall times when she was not destructive, times of warmth and caring. There weren't a lot of them, but there were far more than I expected. I knew very little of this woman, but she was there once in a while. I wished there had been more of the real her.

This point marked a real understanding that there was indeed a beginning, a middle and an end to my journey to the past. This seemed to be reflected in my body, which had developed strength, stamina and tone. Aliveness. I now loved going to the gym. The tape in my head was being replaced by a new one. I kept telling myself a new story. It went something like this: 'I know who I am. I know where I'm going. I know how to get there. I know what I want. I know how to get it. I know what love is. I know I am loved. I know I am loving. I know I am lovable'. Over and over and over – step after step after step. I saw old rules from the old tape drop away day by day.

There was another big impact on the mind tapes. Music. I started running with earphones. I made up a tape of songs that particularly inspired me. Music entered many aspects of my life. I used it when I was writing lectures to keep in touch with myself. I danced to it. I also used certain songs about love and children in my workshops that seemed to convey more than I could in words.

Over my years of therapy I had brought in many photographs of myself and my family. It was as though I were trying to put together the pieces of the puzzle that was my life. One day I brought in only two photographs, the first taken before I was eighteen months old and the other when I was eight or nine. In the baby picture I saw the gleam in my eyes. The spark was definitely there. But I saw it in no other photo. Why did I bring in the photograph of myself when I was eight? I looked like a frightened, bewildered waif. By the time I was eight years old, that spark had withdrawn to an inner sanctum. It was clear I truly had lost trust in the world; I feared outer authorities. But it was crucial for me to see and know that it had been there and to know it was kindled by the love of an old woman. This is what I had searched for all my life and what therapy gave me back: the sparkle in my eyes. I was alive again.

CHAPTER 23

Irises

'Completion.' That's what I wrote in my journal at the beginning of the new year. The sense of completion in my relationship to my father provided a solidity to all my other relationships. The sorting out I'd been going through for the year also seemed to have reached an end, as did my last therapy session before Christmas. We had worked through the beginning and the middle, and we were now near the end. There weren't any other burning issues I needed to talk about in my therapy. The space was clear, both outside and inside. There was no longer anything inside me forcing itself to the surface. That pre-Christmas session was the first time I had experienced a lack of urgency.

I woke up feeling excited knowing that this was the day of my last session. I looked out the window to a dazzling, bright spring day, vibrant with colour. I felt so alive. My dreams that week had brought me gifts that seemed to say everything was fine on the inside. The first dream I had was of resigning from working in a hospital. I walked outside and got on a private monorail that turned out to be a roller-coaster. But it was a roller-coaster with less intense highs and lows. It was a pleasant, smooth ride. It went through darkness and then light. Finally it went straight through a waterfall. I felt such joy, like I was being splashed with fun and laughter. So the roller-coaster had its final appearance in my dreams. But this time I had let go, and the joy was all around me. I had wondered how I'd feel during my last session. It felt like a new beginning, not an ending. My life was mine.

I walked to the session feeling at ease. No rush, no journals, no dream books. Just me, filled with gratitude for my therapy. This time I had a clear appreciation of Neil as a therapist, not as some idealistic version of who he was. As I entered the room, it felt in some ways like the first time I'd really seen him. He was ordinary, like his room. He was no longer the God, the Guru, the Wizard of Oz. I wanted to thank him for having travelled these stormy seas with me, for having taken the risk and gone far out into the ocean to try to understand the world through my eyes. He had helped me see that the shore was a safe place to be and that land under my feet provided a sense of firmness and connectedness with life.

This inner shore was the bridge between my unconscious and conscious mind. I was now able to feel the presence of my true self, a self that was no longer at the mercy of my unconscious dragging me to dark depths of memories I had had no awareness of. Nor was this self under the command of a mind filled with rules about how not to be. There had been a total shift in gravity from my head to the centre of my self and I now knew who I was. I sensed the freedom of living on the shore where I could walk quietly at my own pace, conscious of both land and sea. If I wished I could go into the ocean, but this time in a ship. I could also travel to the city of my mind. Now that many of the rules and injunctions had been excavated and burnt, I discovered that my mind was a valuable aspect of me – it turned my dreams into reality. What inspired me from my unconscious was what mattered in my life now, but in order to make those dreams come alive I needed the uncluttered clarity of my conscious mind. I could see how utterly lost I had been when I first came to therapy, safe in neither my conscious nor my unconscious mind. They were both overflowing with the unknown past and with other people's views of who I was.

I took the time during that session to talk about what I'd seen in my journey. It was important to say anything I needed to say that hadn't been said. Part of it was about never wanting to have an internal backlog of unexpressed feelings. So often in my life I had not said what I felt because I wasn't sure if it were the 'right' thing to say, or because I'd worried about how it would be taken. That was how I missed out on life – all those unsaid words, unexpressed feelings, unlived moments. It was only when I gained this more clearly defined sense of self that I could express my gratitude to Neil. Before, his voice had seemed to be a part of my own inner dialogue. I hadn't been able to really separate him from my own self. In that session I knew there were two distinct people in the room. I felt the boundaries. That enabled me to see and acknowledge his contribution in my journey.

When I left that day I knew I'd said all I had hoped to say. It was the end of therapy, as far as going back into the past was concerned (although it took several months of different forms of goodbyes, letting go and growing up before I had truly finished). I walked away with a sense of completion that provided me with a new clarity of direction in my life.

In the new year I was certain I needed to leave the area of grief. It was very difficult at first to contemplate the move, because that's what my whole professional standing was based on. What would I do if I 'left' maternal grief? I didn't know, but I did know that there had been enough grief in my life; I couldn't keep standing in the middle of it. I also needed a sense of completion in that part of my life. It took several months to reach an end. With the production of four more videos on the subject, I was able to convey the wider issues of maternal grief and the affects on children and the family. So although I personally couldn't work in the area any longer, I had made a further contribution.

The proposal on health care for bereaved women, which I had submitted to the Government some time before, was one area of my work in grief that I had left unresolved. It seemed to have reached a dead end. But one day I got a call from a female politician who was an adviser on women's health, asking if she could come and talk to me about the recommendations I'd made.

It seemed that by letting go and not trying so hard, things just happened. It was ironic that just when I'd made a decision to give up my work in the area, more interest arose. Meeting with this politician tested my resolve. She said her party wanted to develop a policy along the lines of my proposal and she hoped I would assist. I explained that I was no longer going to work in that area, but that I would be happy to discuss any ideas. I handed over all my relevant papers to her, emptying a whole drawer of my filing cabinet into a box. It felt wonderful.

Now that I was my own centre of initiative, I had to decided what my next step would be. That decision, which in one sense I had been making over the past couple of months, was connected to money. My inheritance had come through and I had to look at how I wished to spend it. Both my parents had used money to hold onto outer security, but never to follow their dreams. I knew that I didn't have enough to buy a place of my own outright, and the thought of going back into a demanding mortgage was not what freedom felt like. Because my first video had been well received, I was offered a contract for the international distribution of four more videos, which I subsequently made. It was then that I decided it was important to back my dreams and my talents, and I chose to use some of my money to produce the videos.

Then I faced my most important dream. Could I use my inheritance to give myself a year off to write my story? Every part of me said 'Yes'. I needed time to be quiet and to rest. I was feeling the impact of the journey and I knew I couldn't push myself any more, especially while I was writing my book.

My decision was not made without support. Earlier in the year I had gone to a conference called 'A Journey into Wholeness' which focused on understanding dreams and the unconscious. In those four days of the conference, I gained a deeper appreciation of my own travels. With this came an even greater respect for listening to the inner voice, the voice of the unconscious. Several aspects of the conference were to stay with me. One speaker talked about the relationship of 'holes' to 'wholeness'. He said that to gain a sense of wholeness, one needed to explore the inner 'holes'. Those black holes, which were the unknown, foreign parts of the self, had to be brought to consciousness. As more and more were brought into our personalities, we became who we really are. What hit home was hearing him say that wholeness wasn't about perfection, it was about being conscious of one's own strengths and weaknesses, the dark and the light. The real me had mainly lived in the darkness of a basement. It was my pain that pushed me onwards and coaxed my darkness to the surface. With each journey I'd brought a bit more of myself into being. I understood what he meant about the light and the dark. The parts of me I'd claimed were neither good nor bad – they were just me. Ordinary. I could see that the journey wasn't about trying to be better or happier, or to cope better, it was to be oneself. It sounded so simple. Two years ago I wouldn't have been able to appreciate the meaning of what he said. Now it all clicked into place. It strengthened my commitment to take time to write my story because I could see that what mattered was the inner house. I sensed that in writing about the inner, the outer would be consolidated.

While at the conference, I was captivated by a painting at the back of the hall of purple irises with streaks of gold darting around them. It transported me to the bouquet of irises that emerged from the fire in my dream. That painting helped me realise that the irises were all aspects of my own self. They represented the parts I had disowned, all the 'not me's' and the talents I'd kept hidden. Self psychology had ignited the fire almost ten years ago.

The painting took me to a memory that had arisen in the first year of therapy and that had given me hope and strength. It told me there was a way out of the basement. I had discovered this as a child, but it had become lost behind the wall of forgetting. The memory came back as most others did through a linking symbol. In fact I came to realise that all memories are available, not through the conscious mind, but through the unconscious, either through a symbol of the time or through the sensual awareness of the body. That is where the story will be found.

This memory returned, unexpectedly, through a sensual experience. I was walking home from therapy one summer's day and stopped at a corner store and bought a cherry cream soda pop. I don't usually drink fizzy drinks and I didn't recall having had a cherry cream soda before. Again my unconscious was leading me, tapping, trying to tell me more. As soon as I tasted the drink, I thought of my father. I was about ten years old and in the car with my dad coming back from shopping. We were turning a corner a few blocks from home, when Dad had a heart attack. He slumped over, clutching his chest. I don't know how I did it, but I managed to turn the wheel so we got around the corner. I put my foot on the brake. The car stopped – half on the grass and half in the driveway of the vet where I used to take our dog. I raced to his office, at the back of his house. Thank God he was there. I was in such a panic, I could hardly say a word, but I must have conveyed what I needed to, for it wasn't long before an ambulance was there. I remember going back into the car and holding my dad's head up and talking to him.

When the ambulance left, I ran the two blocks home to tell my mother what had happened. Then all hell broke loose. She immediately accused me of causing it, saying 'What did you say to him?' 'How did you upset him?' I was beside myself. Instead of getting the support and understanding and praise I needed, I got abuse. I remember shaking and crying. My dad was sick, and now it was supposed to be my fault.

It wasn't long before two young policemen came to the door. They came to see if I was okay and to get some details. They told my mother what had happened and where my father was. After what my mother had said, I was terrified that they might say I'd done something terrible and that it really had been my fault. My mother was so pleasant to them; she was a different person. Then the door closed and she yelled at me more about how hopeless I was. I went to lie down and fell asleep.

Later, when I was walking through the house, I heard my mother on the front porch talking to someone. I turned around and there was our next-door neighbour, Roy, walking through the front door. He was a detective at the police department. He grabbed me and threw me up in the air and caught me. He said all sorts of nice things about me. He had been at the police department when two officers came in and told him about a little girl who drove her dad's car to safety. He soon worked out who they were talking about. So, after checking my father's condition at the hospital, he had decided to come over and tell me how proud he was of me. 'I think I should take you out for a drink,' he said. There I was sitting in the front of a police car, with the two young officers in the back. We drove to the corner shop and Roy got us some cold drinks. We stood around out front having our soft drinks. I had a cherry cream soda – it tasted like heaven. Standing there with these big, strong, handsome policemen, I felt happy, proud of myself and secure.

Roy took me home. My mother was enraged. I recall endless verbal abuse about how awful I was, and how I'd caused my father to have a heart attack, and who did I think I was, going out with Roy. I was a very bad girl. Eventually she stormed out, after putting me in the basement. I sat on the top step in the corner, as usual. As soon as I passed that basement door I began to disappear and become numb. It was the only way I could handle the fear. This time it was different. This time the fear began to leave. It was as if those powerful policemen were sitting beside me on the step. I could feel the warmth in my heart. I felt worthwhile. It was almost as if the feeling of being loved and valued by my Auntie and my grandfather had been brought here, to this house, to this basement, instead of it being kept in a separate place, a separate part of me, out of my home territory. I was alive. I lifted my head from my lap, which had become an automatic position for me to disappear into, and I looked. I actually looked and I could see some light in the darkness of the basement coming through a window which must have been left open.

I began to put together all I knew about the basement. In a sense there were two basements. Two totally different experiences. There was the basement that I was pushed into in a rage that felt like death. Then there was the basement I used to go down to with my father to his workbench to do things. That's right, I began to bring those into my awareness. He'd give me wood and nails so I could make something while he worked. Maybe that's the clue to the beginning of my dream about the man hammering nails in wood. I certainly had thought the world of my father. Like most young kids I thought my dad was the best – big, strong and powerful. So I had some clear pictures in my mind as to what exactly was in the basement. It was a map of sorts, a map of competence perhaps. Whatever it was, the combination gave me the courage to come out of my terror and slowly, gradually, go down the steps into the basement.

I remember the great feeling of stepping onto the basement floor, so much more solid than sitting on the steps. I could feel I had inner energy; there was a voice inside believing in me. I went to my father's workbench and turned on the light. I saw that the window at the side path had the storm window up. I took a chair and climbed up and unlatched the screen, just as I'd seen my dad do before. It opened – I was free! I climbed out and the first thing I saw were irises. Hundreds and hundreds of irises. They went from the footpath to the back of the property. My father loved irises and planted them around the three perimeters. As I climbed out the window, I saw them in a whole new way. They beckoned me out, welcoming me, overwhelming me with their beauty. Once I was out and standing up I saw Roy out on his front lawn. I jumped over the irises and ran to him. I remember feeling such energy in my legs as I ran to him. I jumped into his arms and cried and cried.

Roy took me inside. He and his wife were lovely. She got me something to eat and drink and Roy asked what had happened. He knew something was very wrong; I could tell by the look on his face as he watched me climb out of the basement. He asked where my mother was. 'I don't know,' I said. 'You were in the basement?' I nodded. 'She's done that before?' 'Yes.' That's about all I recall. They got me a blanket and I lay on their couch and was told not to worry, everything would be okay. I do remember waking a few times and seeing Roy in the chair opposite. He would say something reassuring and I'd go back to sleep.

I don't know what happened between Roy and my mother. He went to see her when she got home. No doubt she would have been shocked to see I wasn't there. I stayed with them until morning and Roy told me he had spoken to my mother and sorted some things out with her. He wanted me to know that she would never lock me in the basement again and if she ever did I was to do exactly the same thing and come straight to him. Looking back I'm sure Roy also later talked to my father, for I do remember that not long after Dad put in a light switch that I could reach just inside the basement door. He also hung a key to the door, on the wall. This experience didn't alter my mother's abuse in other ways, but it was definitely the end of the basement. I could see now why irises were so powerful in my dream: they symbolised freedom and a way out of the blackness …

As I approached the idea of writing my book I had an intuitive feeling that in order to really feel free to write my story, I needed to affirm my own identity. For too long I had lived under a name that wasn't me, a name that harked back to abuse, shame, silence and grief. In fact, my three Christian names were a conglomeration of 'not me': my mother's name, my Aunt Ellen's name, and a boy's name.

I took my courage in hand and went to the government office to legally change my name. I paid the money and filled in the form. It was so simple. I took only one first name and got rid of the three others. Michael and a friend of mine had come along to have a bit of a celebration. Afterwards I stood in the courtyard and made a little speech to them before we went to lunch: 'I am not my mother, nor am I my father's mother, or my Auntie's or grandmother's mother. I am definitely not a dead baby. I am also not my mother's sister. I am certainly not a boy. I am myself. I am proud to be a woman and my name is Iris'.

It is only from this perspective that I can see how many of my images, dreams and memories were connected to fire. The flame almost went out in me many times, probably more than I can recall. There is a deep understanding within that the icy winds of my childhood came very close to extinguishing it. The rules, the harshness, the absence of love and understanding almost destroyed the child I was.

That tiny spark has now turned into a fire. It is a fire that awakens me early each morning to write this book. I feel the strength of my passion throughout my body. I cannot not write my story. I feel as though I'm standing on an island looking through a telescope far out to sea. I feel the push and pull of my inner tides. The push is to write. No matter what is happening in my outer life, I feel the passion to return to writing my story. It never leaves me and I have a deep knowing that it won't until I've written the last word. Perhaps the most important thing I've learnt is not to doubt or question my unconscious, the ocean. It has truly been my guide and delivered me safely over a most treacherous and stormy sea.

Whenever I have listened to that still, quiet inner voice or the messages from my dreams, I have been on the right path. It has been only when my head has led the way that I have found myself in deep water. There is no doubt what my inner self has to say: she says to stop my other work and write this book. I hear her clearly, reassuring me that the book is already written and not to worry, simply clear the space and put pen to paper. So I've cleared the space and have no work commitments for a while. I even physically cleared my living room. I needed to remove objects so that when I awoke the empty space simply allowed whatever there was inside to emerge.

Yet to deny the pull would not be the truth. For the past few weeks I've been taking brief glimpses into the telescope and then quickly retreating to the present. It's not surprising. On one level I feel like a new baby enjoying her sense of aliveness, and yet aware of her vulnerability. I can appreciate my reluctance to approach the telescope and can only reassure myself that there is no rush and that I can take it a step at a time. I know that what is pulling me back is an awareness of re-entering the pain. I realise that if I had known of the degree of pain I would need to go through, I probably could never have found the courage to embark on this deeper journey. It does seem ironic that the only resolution to a traumatic childhood is a return to those experiences. It is not a natural thing to head towards that which hurts. Therapy seems full of opposites and contradictions.

The hardest thing in writing my book is knowing it can't be an intellectual task. In order for me to tell my story, it is essential to immerse myself in the emotional waters of the past and to leave my island temporarily. I have taken all my journals and dream books out of the trunk that's beside my desk. Here I sit on the floor in the middle of my living room. I can hardly believe how much I've written. There are ten journals and seven dream books.

I put them in order, one on top of each other, and pick them up. It's like I'm holding my own self; they contain me. I then get out my journals from 1985 to 1989 and place them side by side. There are four small notebooks – exercise books like the ones you use in primary school – plus one dream book. All five of them put together wouldn't equal half of one of my later journals. The early journals are brief notes; bits and pieces of assorted thoughts. But from the time I decided to commence therapy the change is dramatic. The writing flows uninterrupted and uncensored. I feel the sense of inner expansion. I see how, like my journals and dreams, I have grown over these years. It is a substantial baby. The idea of going back to the beginning of therapy is daunting, yet what happened in the space is now a part of me and not a separate entity. In a sense I'm asking myself to break up those parts and view them individually. To me, this form of therapy is like having a second chance, a second childhood. But just as a child can't explain how they grew up without telling the story of their childhood, I cannot convey this journey from a distance. I know that my emotional re-entry to earlier times is essential to paint the pictures.

Perhaps it will be healing to go to and from my island. It's a bit like painting, you do need the contrasts in colours – even the black is essential. To put into words where I've been and what I've seen on my travels is another form of therapy. I have such a mixture of feelings: the sorrow, despair and depletion of going back into the times of the 'nothing' plus the joys of finding a form of expression through words. To immerse myself in writing, just as in painting, is to be the child. To play with words, ideas and the emotional colours that accompany them flows into a creative space where I feel a deep sense of intimacy with myself, and a quiet calm and inner fulfilment that transcends any other activity. It is then that the contrasts heighten the experience. The joy of writing and exploring the inner terrain is balanced with the pain of recalling the lost child who leads the way. Once it's written and re-read there is a sense of a full circle being made. What happened is a part of the stepping stones that brought me here. Those stepping stones need to be honoured as much as the island. The child in me finally has a voice and she needs to speak her own truth.

Retrospective: Why self psychology?

Now that I've finished my book, I can return to my island. Each chapter has felt like an aspect of myself. The idea of therapy as a process of re-member-ing has always intrigued me. That's how I felt as the book neared completion. There was an immense feeling of groundedness beneath me and a feeling of solidness within.

For the past ten months I've been aware of the pieces but not of the whole. I had to take myself apart in order to put myself together again. It has been a painful process but one also of creation and discovery. Initially I thought I was writing about my experiences in therapy, but I've learnt so much more about myself through writing. This book is really the story of my life and the inner journey that reconnected me to myself. The greatest gift in life is to know who you are and in order to know this, you need to know where you came from. That's what my therapy gave me. Just as I gave myself my own name, I feel that in writing my story I have claimed authorship over my own life.

Having completed the book, it seemed essential to allow some time to pass, a time for separation and integration. I knew that I could not write about my experiences in therapy while I was still immersed in it. I also knew that to provide a broader perspective of what I'd learnt, I needed to look at my story from a distance. In this retrospective, I'd like to walk up my inner mountain, wearing my psychologist's shoes. I wish to draw together the many threads woven throughout my story and present them in a more objective way, so that the main issues will meet in a cohesive circle of understanding.

CHILD ABUSE

I read an article in a psychology journal about a Canadian study entitled 'Suffering of the Unwanted Child'. It claimed that when a woman is denied an abortion, the child is likely to grow up always feeling unwanted and unloved, and is also likely to suffer severe psychological problems. A link between abortion denial and child abuse was suggested. For years I'd been talking in my workshops about the importance of listening to women's dreams of having children. I'd given examples of families with unwanted children and spoken about the huge cost to the lives of those children. It never occurred to me that I was talking about myself. Several times in therapy I despaired of ever finding a way out of the blackness and the depression, and I wished that my mother had actually killed me or succeeded in the abortion. It seemed that to live in constant anxiety and in the absence of love was a living death.

In those years before this therapy, terror and emptiness were ever-present. That is the legacy of child abuse. To be abused as a child means to go into a constant state of fear and anxiety. Terror disconnects you from your body, your feelings, your life energy and the inner voice that is there to guide you. It is the 'nothing' of being out of touch with yourself. Death is not the opposite of life – fear is. Life is experienced only through the maze of the mind, not through the safety of the heart. It is a treacherous and tortuous path when you live in your mind. Fear is the only voice.

When you live in your heart, trust and love guide the way. Children who are loved trust themselves, others and life. When fear dominates you, you feel alienated from others, fragmented, and alone. Fear is the ice that immobilises every aspect of your life. The saddest part is that the longing to be loved remains deep inside, yet it is an unattainable hope until fear is vanquished. Relationships always stem from an inner need to be accepted. It appears to others that you're desperate or clinging or demanding. It's hard for others to understand that you're just trying to establish what they had right from the beginning – love and acceptance. It's a gnawing addiction, an endless search for love that cannot be found in an adult relationship. Love and acceptance have to be found within and I know of no other path that leads there except the therapy that heals the inner child.

When children are abused by their parents, particularly by their mother, they cannot speak of their feelings because they feel under threat and the wall of forgetting becomes their only protection. They are caught in an untenable bind. To speak against their main care-giver is to threaten their own survival. Children know intuitively that they are totally dependent on their parents. The inner conflict splits them in two. They are a self divided. The true self desperately wants to speak the truth and be free to grow, but the mind acts as a protector and keeps the voice silent. It is not only the loss of freedom to speak that is the cost, but also the ability to think clearly. The child's mind is tied in knots of 'nots' – sanctions, injunctions and rules that make no sense, but that have to be obeyed in order to survive. Thus the child's mind cannot focus clearly or evenly; it has no room for play and creativity.

When that child grows into adulthood the picture is not much different. Words are difficult because of the need to fit in with others; words cannot simply be an expression of their own self. Work too becomes a struggle, for there's a sense of never doing enough to please the inner tyrannical parent represented in outer authorities.

Anxiety makes decisions and the ability to understand information difficult at times, for the mind is racing so fast it isn't available for ordinary interactions. Conflict sends the person into shutdown, and makes them an easy target for use and abuse. Such people only know 'Yes'. Agreement and appeasement have been their survival tools. 'No' is a foreign word. Abusive relationships are inevitable. People who have been abused as children do not know how to stand up for themselves. They haven't attained a sense of self-worth. Perhaps the worst aspect is their dependency on others, as if their very existence is reliant on another's opinion. Their sense of self shifts with each movement of external mirrors. In never developing any inner authority, only outer authorities are served.

Unwanted children are only part of the spectrum of child abuse. We still do not know the extent of it, nor do we know the extent to which it damages a child. The frequency of abuse has been markedly underestimated. It is only overt abuse, which can be objectively verified, that receives attention or intervention. The hidden emotional abuse is often not looked for.

Child abuse is even more pervasive than we could measure in definable terms. From my experiences as a therapist and in ordinary life I feel that no one has escaped child abuse in some form. Most of us have been brought up in a patriarchal system of ceaseless rules about how we should act, what we should do, what we should learn, and who we should be. Our schools and churches are mainly socialising agents of a system that demands control and compliant learners instead of free-thinking, independent individuals. Rarely are we taught that the greatest knowledge, wisdom and wealth are within. The authority is always exterior to the self, which is often reflected in our own parenting, for we are all products of generations of patriarchal rule. People rarely have the opportunity to find their own selves and to know what they want to be and do in life. Dreams of the night and of the day are often considered childish and irrelevant. People have forgotten to tell their stories and to follow their hopes and dreams. We are like robots, working hard to get what we were told matters: an education, a job, a car, a house, marriage, children, travel. But it comes from belief in the myth that in the end we will be happy. Emotions, relatedness, time to reflect, time to dream, time to act on our dreams, all recede in importance.

Time is used in 'getting there' instead of 'being there'. We forget the call of the child within.

The tragedy of child abuse is that as an adult, one is disconnected from one's emotions, dreams, inner voice and natural instincts. Thus the abuse is replayed throughout life. As the years pass, the distance from the original true self becomes vast. The inability to remember childhood trauma makes it impossible to claim one's history. In addition, the abused person tends to believe that she or he had an ordinary childhood and ideal parents.

SELF PSYCHOLOGY

The most crucial outcome of therapy for those who have suffered child abuse is their reconnecting to their feelings. I believe that self psychology, with its focus on the underlying emotional life of the person, is the most effective form of therapy to heal inner wounds. There are many significant aspects that, to me, set self psychology apart from other therapies, the foremost of which is the focus on empathy.

Psychiatric models do not understand the inner pain of the wounded child. They focus only on the mind where judgments and lists of pathologies are found. Far too often drugs are used to quell turmoil instead of the pain being a guide to the source of the heartache.

Heinz Kohut, the founder of self psychology, became disheartened with traditional psychoanalysis because he felt his patients' complaints of not being understood were justified. He cited one particular woman who kept saying that his interpretations were interfering with her own analysis. When he began to empathise with her, he saw positive changes occur. Thus his theoretical perspectives grew out of his attempts ot understand the mental life of his patients from the vantage point of their experiences.

The development of self psychology marked a revolution in thinking in psychotherapy. Self psychology offered something no other form of traditional therapy provided, by honouring the child within. It is the self that is the psychologist, not so much the outer therapist. The therapist is there to provide, a safe, trusting, nurturing environment in which the child can speak freely and tell his or her story. It is not a place of cleverness or grand interpretations. Self psychology differs from other forms of therapy by acknowledging that all the answers and all the keys of understanding are within the client, not the therapist. When the therapist listens empathically and tries to understand, that's where the transformation occurs. The inner child, the self, needs to be heard, needs to be validated.

The professions of psychiatry and psychology place much emphasis on models of the mind. These models are based on the intellect and directed at the intellect of the client. The therapist always knows more and is the one who is in charge and leads the way. This feels like 'home' to people who have been abused as children, because it keeps them in their head, which had always felt a safe place. It can perpetuate the abuse. These people become more adept at analysing and interpreting their behaviour and their childhood, and more and more detached from the true wealth of their own self. The inner self or child needs to speak by reconnecting the feelings and symbols of the unconscious. For the child within to feel safety and trust in order to speak, the space must not be an intellectual one. To be caught in the trap of a model of the mind can destroy the last chance to find freedom. These clients will tend to believe in the power and authority of the therapist, accept the interpretations, assessments and guidance, and give up on themselves again.

The greatest irony is that psychiatry and psychology have become a science. Human beings cannot be quantified or reduced to nice, neat categories. Living with grief or depression is not like having your arm broken. There are no obvious remedies. By labelling, categorising and analysing a person, the hurt is compounded. In this process individuals are depersonalised and dehumanised; they become objects of scientific investigation, rather than ordinary human beings just like the therapist. By focusing on the mastery of therapy as a science we've lost touch with the inner mystery.

These two most accepted types of therapy in our society rely heavily on models of the mind. Kohut rejected traditional psychoanalysis because of its mechanistic theories where the therapist 'objectively' analysed the patient's intrapsychic conflicts, drives and defences. The therapist in self psychology is not a neutral, blank screen but an active participant trying to understand the patient's experience. The sense of an equal relationship is further enhanced in that interpretations or explanations grow out of the client's own process. This is different from the old psychoanalytic approach where the 'distorted' reality of the patient was seen to be in need of correction by the analyst's view of 'reality'. Self psychology does not depend on a particular personality theory, developmental model or clinical theory of what transpires in the therapeutic space. Self psychology is a humanistic form of psychoanalysis that puts the self at the centre of the inquiry.

Kohut assumed that humans have a tendency towards growth and fulfilment and it is only when these are blocked that damage occurs. Unlike earlier models based on theoretical perspectives of conflict, self psychology looks at where people have been thwarted in development and provides the means to regain their lost natural potential. In the broadest sense self psychology is a model-less model. The understanding and development of clients is viewed from their own background experiences.

This empathic perspective has several profound consequences. There is no more exquisite feeling than to be understood. The healing effect of having one's feelings, thoughts and experiences validated strengthens and enlivens the self within. Empathic attunement also provides an ambience of acceptance and understanding which encourages regression to early childhood. For people who have been abused and who cannot gain entry to earlier memories, this therapy enables the making of a potent link to a forgotten childhood. Painful as that may be, in the end it is empowering. The process allows the strengthening of the bond with positive figures and an opportunity to re-experience traumas that hindered the growth of the child. For me it allowed the relationship with my Auntie, my grandfather and other loving people in my life to be brought from behind the 'not me' wall of forgetting to strengthen my sense of self. Conversely it enabled the painful relationship with my mother to be re-experienced. With each experience the trauma was gradually repaired through the understanding and responsiveness of my therapist.

Prior to the development of self psychology, people like myself virtually had no hope of living without depression. Although self psychology is now used for the full range of psychological issues, it was originally developed for those people who had experienced childhood traumas suffered before the age of three or four. Traumas in this early stage of development, which resulted in empty depression and other debilitating symptoms, were generally not considered treatable by traditional forms of therapy. If it weren't for self psychology, my life would have been one of maintenance on medication, a depleted existence.

In many ways we live in a society that has banned the telling of stories and the sharing of emotions and truth. Everyone has a story of pain, mainly kept secret. If we all began to say what hurts and talk about our grief, there would be a sense of connectedness amongst us. We all have a right to more freedom and a responsibility to listen to and protect our own inner child.

CHILD DEVELOPMENT: AN ANALOGY

The experiences that negatively affect the development of a child are not dissimilar to experiences often reported as unhelpful or damaging in some forms of therapy. These include: lack of empathy with the child's needs; invalidating their reality; using power to control and force the child into accepting parental views; denying or suppressing feelings; authoritarian discipline and rigid rules; mental, physical and emotional intrusiveness; the disregard of boundaries that provide protection; and lack of emotional involvement. A child with these experiences loses his or her sense of self and wellbeing and perceives power and knowledge to be outside of themselves. If these are later repeated in therapy, so also is the abuse. However, the person may remain totally unaware of this, since there is no other frame of reference or set of guidelines. In a sense this forces the child/adult client back into the conscious mind, away from feelings, body sensations and a sense of self.

Just as providing an egalitarian environment in a child's upbringing promotes natural growth and potential, so too does self psychology in the therapeutic relationship. It allows the person to link the present to the past and to gain an understanding of childhood that enables the repair of early traumas. It also helps clients reconnect to their bodies. Thus the conscious/unconscious, mind/body splits may be healed. The other significant bridge is that the understanding of issues in adult therapy is enhanced by studies of infants and children. It is a therapy that makes intuitive sense, because it grows out of understanding ordinary people and normal child development.

THE RESTRAINT OF MODELS

In the workshops I've conducted, people often want me to give them a model on which they can base their therapy with bereaved women. That question always takes me back to my time before self psychology. My only guidelines were formed from a model of grieving and a stage theory of grief. I remember looking at a diagram showing each stage necessary for healthy grief resolution and the time span involved. You could find out how long a person had been suffering grief and refer to this map in your mind to determine whether they were on course or off the tracks. Your role was to help them through these stages. Luckily, it wasn't long before I entered the self psychology training and could throw the map away. For I knew as I went along, it actually told me nothing about each individual woman, her grief, or her path to recovery. I have also seen many negative effects on women who have been treated within a rigid model. They are often left feeling worse, for it has been conveyed to them that they haven't gone through a particular stage. Yet I do understand the comfort and reassurance models provide. They help us think we know the answers and the direction needed. Models are important in research, in academia, and in intellectual debate, but their place is not in the therapeutic setting. They rob people of their own truth, their own inner wisdom, and the natural unfolding of their path of healing.

FOR THOSE ENTERING THERAPY

A powerful reason for telling the story of my own experience in
therapy is my wish to open more doors of understanding for
those embarking on similar journeys. Exactly what the different
forms of therapy have to offer is often obscured by elitist language
and complex intellectual explanations. Frequently people enter
therapy with no knowledge of what to expect, or of how to
determine whether the treatment being received is appropriate.
Therapy can change a person's life and the hands you place
yourself in must be competent.

I believe the therapeutic space needs to have the same
ingredients as a loving home – safety, security, trust, respect,
empathy, emotional openness, freedom to speak without fear of
judgment – plus a sense of equality between therapist and client. It
seems to me that therapists have the most privileged role in our
society, to be entrusted with the inner life of another person and to
witness the birth of the self. The rights of the child within the client
must be held sacrosanct, just as they would be in a healthy family.

Since your mental health is a precious possession, your
decision regarding therapy needs to be an informed choice. It is
crucial to find a therapy that suits your own needs. You must be
an active seeker, not a passive consumer, in the area of therapy.
The therapist's response and how comfortable it feels being there,
are critical factors. Try to be aware of how dialogue unfolds. If the
therapist takes an authoritarian stance and is not able to explain
the approach to therapy, or does so in a language that defies
ordinary comprehension, be wary of returning. Therapy from a
self psychological perspective is not about fitting in or being
'normal', or simply alleviating symptoms. To enter the depths of
yourself and to reclaim your hidden, disowned parts brings a
fullness to your life. It's about finding the spark that opens you to
your unique creativity, and it links you to a joyful, interesting life.

SPEAKING OUT

Child abuse, like maternal grief, is an issue that needs to be
brought out into the open in our society. As with any unspoken

topic, if it is given words and more people tell their stories, something will begin to change.

Therapy taught me that to speak out and tell my story can make a difference. For me it is imperative. My intention is not to redistribute the pain, but to speak of the monster of child abuse. It destroys everyone affected, be they victim or perpetrator. My hope is that this book will contribute to the understanding of the impact of child abuse and to the future wellbeing of children and their families. My dilemma has been how much to speak. Thus my decision is to publish this book under another name and to alter the names and places of relevance. For it is not a book about blame. It is one of understanding and hope. May it inspire others to find the dreams of their inner child and to follow them. Hopes and dreams take us home.

If you would like to contact the author, write to:

The Australian Psychological Society
P.O. Box 126
Carlton South, Victoria, 3053

Or phone 1 800 333 497

Undercurrents

Martha Manning

The thoughts of death and nothingness are like a fever I can't shake. What is the distance between the thought and the act?

Undercurrents is the story of Martha Manning, psychotherapist and patient, and her journey through severe clinical depression. Her illness starts with almost imperceptible changes in her behaviour - her house is increasingly untidy, she is unable to sleep, and important deadlines pass while she feels unable to do the work. The depression spirals until one day Martha realises that she would score the maximum number of points on a test designed to diagnose a major depressive episode.

Nothing relieves the onslaught of her depression; not the love of her family, the support of her therapist, nor the comprehensive drug regime she must endure. Finally, Martha agrees to electroconvulsive therapy. Despite the debate over its safety and efficacy, ECT represents Martha's final hope.

Written in the form of a diary, *Undercurrents* is a frank and eloquent work that traces one woman's descent into the depths of human despair and her emergence into hope and enlightenment.

ISBN: 006 251184 X

HarperCollins*Publishers*

Surfing the Blues

Catherine Rzecki

In the late 1980s, Catherine Rzecki's daily life came to include anxiety attacks, inexplicable mood swings, exhilarating highs and desperate lows. She kept a journal throughout her battles with the debilitating effects of her symptoms.

Why is everything fading away? Why do people look distorted? My God, what if I look as bad as I feel! I can't let people know I'm out of control. I've got to stand up, pretend nothing's wrong.

Surfing the Blues weaves Catherine's intense experiences with information and professional advice, providing a guide to understanding the nature of mood disorders, panic attacks, and manic-depressive illness.

Catherine Rzecki has lived with the devastating effects of panic attack and manic-depression for eight years. She still has to survive the 'bad' days, but she enjoys a general feeling of stability, and has since become a professional counsellor.

ISBN: 0 207 18866 1

 Angus & Robertson, an imprint of HarperCollins*Publishers*